REMEDIES

for a NEW WEST

REMEDIES
for a NEW WEST
HEALING LANDSCAPES, HISTORIES, AND CULTURES

Edited by
**Patricia Nelson Limerick,
Andrew Cowell,
and Sharon K. Collinge**

The University of Arizona Press   Tucson

The University of Arizona Press
© 2009 The Arizona Board of Regents

www.uapress.arizona.edu

Library of Congress Cataloging-in-Publication Data

Remedies for a new West : healing landscapes, histories, and cultures /
edited by Patricia Nelson Limerick, Andrew Cowell, and Sharon K. Collinge.
    p.   cm.
   Includes bibliographical references and index.
   ISBN 978-0-8165-2599-7
   1. West (U.S.)—Civilization—21st century. 2. West (U.S.)—Environmental
conditions. 3. Landscape—West (U.S.) 4. Landscape protection—West (U.S.)
I. Limerick, Patricia Nelson, 1951- II. Cowell, Andrew, 1963- III. Collinge,
Sharon K. F591.R425 2009
   304.2′80978—dc22   2008050105

Manufactured in the United States of America on acid-free,
archival-quality paper containing a minimum of 30%
postconsumer waste and processed chlorine free.

14 13 12 11 10 09   6 5 4 3 2 1

Contents

Part 3
Lessons from Conflict

Foreword

Richard L. Byyny, M.D.

When I served as chancellor of the University of Colorado at Boulder, I had the pleasure of sponsoring a lecture series called Healing the West. At universities all around the world, natural scientists and humanists are exploring their common ground and shared goals, and the University of Colorado has embraced this welcome trend. As a physician, I know from thousands of experiences how essential it is to pay equal attention to matters of the body, the mind, and the soul—a recognition that also holds together this collection of essays.

Many Boulder residents enjoyed and profited from the Healing the West lecture series, but the audience was necessarily limited in size. Thus, it is an even greater pleasure to see this series turn into a book, accessible to the thousands of people worldwide who are in search of down-to-earth examples of citizens who are reckoning with serious troubles inherited from the past and pursuing positive and hopeful resolutions for those troubles. It is a privilege to write a foreword for this book.

The American West is a vast region from the Rocky Mountain states on the east, Canada on the north, Mexico on the south, and the Pacific Coast on the west. The region comprises mostly arid and semiarid land, where water is the limited but essential "life blood." This book describes and appraises the social, cultural, environmental, physical, biological, and ecological health of this West. It is about the land, people, creatures, and other organisms in an important region.

As a physician and a close reader of this book, I understand the term *health* as referring to a "state of complete physical, mental, and social well-being and not merely the absence of disease, injury, or infirmity."[1] By this definition, the West has many elements of ill health. Healing implies curing a disease, wound, or derangement and restoring soundness, health, or integrity. Contemplating this definition gives us a sense of the scale—*and the importance*—of the challenge carried by the goal of healing the West.

Dr. Francis W. Peabody, a legendary physician and teacher, gave a lecture titled "The Care of the Patient" to medical students at Harvard Medical School in 1925. "The secret of the care of the patient," Dr. Peabody declared, "is in caring for the patient."[2] This aphorism applies in this book. The secret of caring for the West, in coming together to enhance its well-being, is in caring—feeling loyalty to and affection and concern—for the West.

At the Center of the American West, Professor Patty Limerick has recruited an interdisciplinary group of academic experts to enlighten us about the West's problems and opportunities. They provide historical context and ideas about the region's health, interventions to deal with ill health, and approaches to prevent further deterioration. The authors make clear that the time for our attention to the West's health is *now*. They work to help us understand not just our patient's ailments, but also the qualities of resilience, charm, and vitality still unmistakable in its character.

In many ways, the approach resembles caring for a human patient. A physician begins by eliciting a history to understand what is ailing the patient. She then examines and assesses the physical manifestations of a possible ailment. Based on this information, she works to deduce the causes of the symptoms and signs to make a diagnosis. Problems can result from many causes, including trauma, infection, degeneration, cancer, mental states, and others. A primary-care physician often consults with specialists. The probable diagnosis then leads to decisions about interventions to treat the problem and, optimally, to prevent ill health in the future.

Like each of the authors in this book, the doctor draws on evidence in the literature and professional experience in making these decisions. The evidence or treatments will often be imperfect. Uncertainty is frequently present, but the doctor still has to make her best decisions to help the patient. She chooses a possible intervention and follows the patient's course carefully. Her major goals are to cure the patient, prevent ill health, improve the quality of life, and maintain good functionality. Not infrequently she may find that her chosen intervention creates adverse effects and is harming the patient in other ways. She then will change the approach based on the response to achieve the best possible outcome.

In reflecting on a life in medicine, I know that caring for patients is a privilege and a responsibility. I have found great joy in caring for people and sadness in my shortcomings. Much of the satisfaction comes from compassion combined with technical and scientific competence. For me, caring is also a combination of empathy and kindness. It involves continuity and trust. Perhaps most important are perseverance and reliability even when the patient cannot be cured. Caring means sticking with the patient over long periods of time, always with the goal of helping in times of need and illness. Many times caring means watching, waiting, and hoping: being there for the patient and those worried about the patient. It is also important to recognize that people learn the practice of medicine through experience and that experience is the foundation of expertise. We then have a responsibility to invite others into the project of acquiring experience and thus to teach them what we ourselves have learned.

These reflections are important for all of those caring for and working to heal the West. I can assure all of you who are committed to healing the West that you will find great personal and professional joy and satisfaction in helping a region in need of that help. You are in a serving profession of a new kind. To paraphrase a physician's oath attributed to Maimonidies, you have accepted appointment to watch over the West's life and health.

Cast as our patient, the American West is equally or even more complex than a human or animal organism. The "clinical approach" is yet to be defined; in truth, recognizing how much the practice known as "restoration" is still in flux and open to innovation and fresh insight is one of the values of reading this book. The authors make it clear that humans have frequently been the cause of insult, injury, damage, scarring, anguish, and stress. However, they acknowledge that humans also hold the ability to help the American West repair, regenerate, and thus heal itself. The key conviction of the authors who come together in these pages is that maintaining a healthy and balanced environment in our region has important implications for the future of humankind. This book is focused on the West, but its lessons embrace the planet.

Our knowledge about the West's health is limited, but it is expanding rapidly through the use of science, observation, and deduction, as well as the application of imagination, intuition, and creativity. We hope that modern science and technology can facilitate our ability to care for the West, just as modern medicine has aided us in dealing with human health. Our current knowledge of the therapeutic treatment for troubled human and natural communities may be more like the earlier, descriptive age of medicine than today's advanced scientific understanding of biology. But we cannot forget that even with extraordinary scientific advances in play, treating patients is still an art, and such an art will be required in healing the West as well.

This book adds significantly to our understanding of the West's health. The authors provoke us to think about the problems and issues in new ways and to imagine approaches to prevent further deterioration and to steer clear of more injury and trauma. The authors also acknowledge that clarifying and reaching agreement on what good health would mean for the American West remains an important challenge, especially in a constantly evolving, always dynamic environment.

I am encouraged by what I have observed about the increased caring for the West, but still remain concerned about the prognosis. Advances in science, technology, the study of history, and other rigorous methodologies are providing us with an understanding that begins to approach wisdom. I am encouraged by the involvement of individuals, organizations, corporations, and governments in working to learn more about interventions with the power to improve the West's health. I am encouraged by the developments in technology and communications that help all of us share our hopes for the well-being of the region we consider our home.

And yet not all is encouraging. Examples of further erosion of the West's health are easy to find. Sometimes we simply do not have enough knowledge to solve the problems. There is great need for continuing investigation of the region. There is great need to spread the knowledge of western issues to academics, political representatives, the public, and the press. There is great need for increased cooperation, concerted action, and a systematic approach in dealing with the health of the American West.

The authors of this book do not try to tell the reader what to think or do, but they do offer hope and a spirit-lifting way of thinking about the West's health. Caring and healing will require perseverance. Healing will take a long time. This book is an important beginning.

REMEDIES
for a NEW WEST

Prologue

THE LESSONS AND LESIONS OF CONQUEST

Patricia Nelson Limerick

The human heart yearns to wipe away the mistakes of the past, and nowhere is that tendency stronger than in America, land of the fresh start.

—Peter Friederici, *Nature's Restoration*[1]

AN OLD MAN in Missouri had started into a steep decline, and his doctor had tried every treatment he could imagine. At last, he suggested what many physicians in the eastern United States had told desperate patients: the only hope remaining was a relocation to the arid, sunny, healing West. So the invalid packed up and moved to Santa Fe, but the effort came too late. He had barely arrived in New Mexico when his decline accelerated. Treated by an artful embalmer, he was soon on his way back to Missouri in a coffin. In his hometown at the open-casket funeral, two old friends stood over him. "Don't he look good," one of them said. "Yep," said the other, "Santa Fe done him a world of good."

The western historian and raconteur Gene Hollon told me this story in 1983, and I have found it of infinite usefulness since then. Even though I have every reason to be deeply respectful of the intense sorrow of human mortality, the story reliably sneaks past my sense of propriety. And Gene's joke does perform admirably when it comes to conveying two central patterns of western American history: the West has long been associated with the promise of healing, but the region's performance has varied considerably when it comes to delivering on that promise.

For much of the nineteenth and twentieth centuries, in the minds of many Americans the West held the power to bestow or restore health. As historian Gregg Mitman writes, "Climate, air, and sunshine were marketable health commodities, sold by railroads, civic boosters, and physicians to consumptives and asthmatics looking for relief, if not a cure. . . . Across the western landscape, health itself was transformed into a natural resource." Even though invalids have been much eclipsed in popular memory by more able-bodied westward emigrants, they composed a very sizable proportion of the westward-flowing tide of emigrants. Studying Denver, Mitman estimates that in 1890 invalids "made up almost a third of the city's population of 100,000." "By 1920, an estimated 40 percent of the city's 250,000 residents—100,000 'lungers,' as they were known—had come in search of health."[2] Drawn to Colorado, Arizona, New Mexico, California, and many other locales, believing in the healing power of the region's aridity, sunshine, and elevation, these afflicted settlers expected the West to make them well. And now, in a historical maneuver that can be labeled a "big switcheroo," we have now cast the West as the ailing entity in need of healing. Once seen as the healer, the West has surrendered the stethoscope and white coat, climbed into the hospital bed, and exchanged places with its patients.

What befell the West? Has it been injured? Fractured? Wounded? Infected? A decade ago, preparing what I planned as a speech charged with optimism, I began to type the phrase the "lessons of history" because it was the hopeful concept I wanted to accent in the speech. Instead, unconscious impulse took over my fingers, and I typed the really much more interesting phrase the "lesions of history." I evidently wasn't quite as optimistic as I'd thought.

This is how one dictionary defines the term *lesion:* "1. An injury; hurt; damage. 2. An injury or other change of an organ or tissue of the body tending to result in impairment or loss of function." Let this analogy loose, and it steps forward to offer itself as a characterization of many circumstances in the twenty-first-century American West. The chapters in this book offer diagnoses and treatment programs for many of the principal "lesions": the disturbance of ecosystems; the reduction of biodiversity; the disruption of the cultural integrity of Native peoples and long-term Hispanic residents; the constriction of minority groups' rights and opportunities.

These injuries are unquestionably "lesions of history," and (now the optimism makes its comeback!) the "lessons of history" can help in their healing. In a way that will warm historians' hearts and deepen their sense of mission, one of the recurrent themes in this collection of essays is the desire to resurrect memory and to correct amnesia. Treating very different subjects, John-Michael Rivera and Len Ackland make the restoration of memory their priority through the recovery of "lost" writings of Latinos/as and the honest facing up to the nuclear history of Rocky Flats, Colorado. In a similar way, Joseph Ryan hopes that the residents of mining towns can connect themselves to the memories of the miners who once worked where they now live.

Both philosophically and practically, before any enterprises in healing can begin, the practitioners have to ask and answer historical questions. Where did the injuries come from? Were they intentionally or inadvertently inflicted? Did a state of greater well-being precede the injuries, and can a portrait of that earlier condition provide goals for the process of recovery? Attempting to repair past damage, as Dave Egan and Evelyn Howell put it, "brings restorationists face to face with the central role of time and requires that they understand past conditions in order to re-establish the historic processes and components needed to repair damaged ecosystems."[3] Perhaps most beneficially, this historical inquiry easily leads to the recognition that most of the human beings who brought the West's troubles into being left this world some time ago, making exercises in blame of little use and setting the stage for those who are currently alive to take responsibility for finding solutions to the problems that originated before their arrival on the planet. And, of course, those still here also have to recognize and take responsibility for any troubles they may be causing now.

Indeed, one of the happiest lessons emerging from this collection of essays is that the treatment program for the West's lesions comes with very desirable side effects. Engaging in the kinds of projects put forward in this book proves to be a therapeutic treatment program in itself. Projects in restoration, repair, and recovery act as high-strength antidotes to defeatism. They expand our understanding and appreciation of the passage of time and thereby help us develop and expand our powers of patience, easing us out of our addiction to instant results. They also give us the opportunity to reconsider the habit by which we allow an imagined ideal of purity to discourage us from action; restoration projects invite us to think hard about the ways in which "the perfect is the enemy of the good."[4] They counter symptoms of despair and fatalism with a repeated, concentrated dose of promise and possibility. The healing of the West sharpens our minds, unleashes our imaginations, rescues us from downward spirals of blame and contention, and gives our lives lasting meaning. And by keeping us alert to the limitations and contradictions in our power to reshape the world, projects in restoration immunize us against arrogance and overconfidence. In other words, the projects that come together in the category "healing the West" may help the region, but they also do a world of good for the practitioners. This is a prime opportunity for making the best of a bad situation: the more lesions the West has to heal, the more opportunities we have to stretch our minds and souls, develop our capacity to collaborate, and prove that we are creatures of consequence and capability.

In many westerners' judgment, there is an abundance of these opportunities. The signs of illness and trauma seem omnipresent: land and soil disrupted from mining, overgrazing, logging, and intensive farming; wildlife habitat reduced and fragmented; Native societies shaken and threatened; air quality diminished; open space taken over by cities, suburbs, and exurbs; the intrusion of roads and recreation seekers leaving few areas protected by their remoteness. And yet it is important to acknowledge that not everyone agrees with the proposition that the West needs healing. According to some articulate and audible westerners, the West was simply *settled* and *developed*, not injured or afflicted. There is no fudging the fact that over the past two centuries of western history, economic activity has generated a great deal in the way of profit and material well-being. It is entirely possible to calculate the benefits of this activity in a way that will show that the advantages outweigh the costs to landscapes and societies. Thus, to the folks inclined to draw up such a balance sheet, the very idea of healing an ailing region is a kind of projected hypochondria, a pointlessly agitating fit of alarmism and oversensitivity.

Western residents are far from consensus when it comes to the assessment of the West's state of health. This clash of opinion makes a fairly close fit to more literal situations of assessing health. People facing medical problems, along with their relatives and friends, often find it difficult to reach agreement on the seriousness of the situation. A paired set of overreactions—one going full tilt toward extreme alarm and the other headed full tilt toward unrealistic denial—can bring productive decision making to a halt.

In the hope of tempering the clash in the assessments of the West's health, I shall now make a declaration so dull and obvious that it wields a tremendous, sedating power to quiet dispute. *The West, like any other part of the planet, has undergone a great deal of change, and different people in different circumstances can characterize the very same change as improvement or decline, a sign of economic health or a symptom of ecological and cultural illness.* This wide variation in perspective is a reality that has refused many invitations to go away, and thus it is a reality with which we must make our peace. A determination to refuse agitation and alarmism, as well as a willingness to give a respectful hearing to those who see injury as a justified price to pay for economic well-being, will remain valuable equipment in the medicine bag of the West's aspiring healers.

And yet when it comes to assessing the health of both ecosystems and human communities, an observer working hard for objectivity and neutrality would have to say that the West in the past two centuries has had a rough time of it. Whether called "settlement," "conquest," or "American westward expansion," the transformation of the region in these two hundred years was a disruptive process, leaving in its wake a full set of injuries to nature and to humanity.

Nevertheless, if the West has seen better days, it has also seen unimaginably worse ones. The deep history of the earth provides a useful perspective to people feeling glum about the region's current environmental state. Sixty-five million years ago, to use a very large-scale example, an asteroid hit the Yucatán Peninsula at Chicxulub, filling the skies with dust and causing an episode of mass extinction. Had any anxious human beings been around to make the diagnosis, the North American West, like the rest of the Western Hemisphere, would have seemed far beyond healing. And yet the West recovered even from this cosmic blow. That phase of extinction proved the prelude to a peppy new era of mammalian proliferation and well-being.

As powerfully as a recovery program that extends for millions of years testifies to the earth's resilience, it cannot offer much comfort to a species in which mortality holds consciousness to the span of a century at maximum. As a somewhat winding route back to optimism, however, consider the implication of the point made by David Armstrong in this collection. Paleontologists have found five big eras of extinction in the earth's past. A sixth big era seems to be under way now. In the first five eras, the causes of extinction were geological or cosmic. This time the cause—as Armstrong puts it—is "cultural," involving people's attitudes and actions. If another large asteroid were to hit the earth, human action would carry no significance, and fatalism (if the asteroid gives us the luxury of the time to craft and express such an attitude!) would be the entirely reasonable stance. But if human activity is the cause of the mass extinction currently under way, fatalism loses its rationale. In a dramatic contrast to the previous five episodes of mass extinction, human beings produced the current problem, so human beings can do a great deal to correct it. And if you find a way to remove fatalism from the equation, then one of the planet's most abundant and renewable energies—the set of assets known as human creativity, ingenuity, and enterprise—is unleashed, and the realm of the possible expands.

This process is of great importance because in the twenty-first-century United States we are regular recipients of a steady flow of the finest, most persuasive, best-crafted invitations to fatalism. Every day there is a good chance that someone, either in person or through multiple forms of media (newspapers, radio, television, fund-raising snail mail, postings, Web sites, blogs), will feel obligated to inform us of the dreadful prospects bearing down on the planet: global warming, population explosions, terrorism, insidious health risks from industrial chemicals, nuclear weapons awaiting some sort of intelligent system of decommissioning, epidemics without cures, witless waste of natural resources, and so on. If you are able to endure more than a few minutes of this onslaught without becoming fatalistic and defeated, you are certified either as having unusual reservoirs of cheer and resilience or as needing a hearing aid and reading glasses.

Back in the early 1980s, unprotected by hearing loss, I commuted by bus from Arlington to Cambridge and chatted eagerly with my fellow riders. One morning an older gentleman took the seat next to me and gave me an uninterrupted twenty-five-minute invitation to despair. During the whole ride, he kept up a continuous commentary on the environmental dilemmas of the world: air pollution, water pollution, wildlife habitat destruction, fossil-fuel depletion, the cutting of the rain forests, the erosion and exhaustion of the soil, the invasion of weeds and exotics—you name it. When we came into Harvard Square, the older gentleman had the nerve to get up after this catalog of misery, turn to me, and say, "Have a nice day."

It was very hard to let him go in peace. Attacking him would not have been right, but *becoming* him wouldn't be right, either. Since the late 1980s, I have tried to find a way to give his thematically ill-matched farewell—"Have a nice day!"—more in the way of meaning and substance. This glum fellow was, after all, far from an unusual or anomalous example. "By constantly raising alarms," Peter Friederici has written, "environmentalists . . . have fed the idea that people can do only harm in the world. That's both a difficult way to motivate people in the long run and a notion that ideological opponents can easily parody for their own purposes."[5] As Egan and Howell put it, environmentalists "generally tell the story of some aspect of the environment that is in decline." In its different versions, this story "produces roughly the same effect—pessimism, outrage, and urgent calls for protection."[6]

Those who have followed the changing field of western American history may be somewhat surprised by my shift to a message provoking less in the way of pessimism and outrage. To many defenders of the western myth and a romanticized version of the region's history, I was the equivalent, if not worse, of the man who plagued me on that Massachusetts bus. Through much of my early career, I struggled diligently to replace the romance clinging to memories of western history with realism. I wrote in many venues and spoke to many audiences about the "legacy of conquest," trying to persuade Americans to look honestly and openly at the costs, prices, injuries, lesions, and lingering burdens accrued from the historical episode known as westward expansion.

And then, having devoted a great deal of life energy to pointing out what went wrong in the past, I found myself wanting to do something more productive with the rest of my life. By the mid-1990s, my goals and purposes were shifting in a direction that some academic observers no doubt took to be rightward. If the writing of western history started to slip back toward denial and whitewashing, I was ready to leap back into action, but in the enterprise of proclaiming the social and environmental costs of westward expansion, I had run out of strategies and techniques. My departure from the cause was of little consequence; an army had replaced me, working diligently at exposing both the social and environmental troubles packaged into the legacy of conquest and leaving me free to pursue other lines of work.

Of all the tools available to people committed to healing the West, none outranks for persuasive power the mythic image of the West as a place of opportunity, national triumph, and optimism. Putting this tool to work on behalf of remediation, restoration, and repair is undeniably very tricky. Allegiance to the happy and congratulatory version of the West's history was, after all, a powerful force driving the very process that produced the injuries and losses whose remedy now preoccupies us.

Given the many ways in which the Western Myth produced our troubles, twenty-first-century westerners might be well advised to take a "hands-off" approach to the whole package if they choose to be guided by a preference for purity. But here's the irony-steeped counterargument to that purity: the biggest challenges in gaining support for projects in healing are the discovery and activation of mechanisms of motivation, incentive, persuasion, and encouragement, as well as the building and maintaining of morale. The Western Myth is one big mechanism supplying all those features. To refuse to put it to use is to forfeit and surrender a very powerful tool with an extraordinary capacity to fight fatalism and inspire action.

Although many American pioneers and settlers in the nineteenth century were agents of colonial and imperial expansion, they nonetheless demonstrated extraordinary courage, persistence, ingenuity, and pluck. Contemplate the example of nineteenth-century farmers taking up remote homestead land, living in uncomfortable sod houses, digging wells by hand, struggling to buy seeds and equipment, and working against the forces of drought, hailstorms, grasshoppers, and uncertain crop prices. Then contrast those examples of exertion and persistence with our own easy retreats to defeatism, our own hesitation to take up projects in remedy, restoration, and remediation because they will be too expensive, too complicated, too challenging to our ingenuity, too time-consuming, too slow to deliver the desired results.

For all the problems contained in and created by the complex history of westward expansion, the abundant examples of pioneer pluck are an endowment to our times, an inheritance we would be foolish to refuse. Rather than surrendering its power, we can and should (in my judgment!) ask twenty-first-century westerners to accept this region's heritage and to try to live up to the examples of courage and persistence set by our predecessors. This rhetorical maneuver *does* require a degree of twisted logic and improbability. The pioneers displaced the Indians and disrupted the ecosystems, but now we're supposed to invoke their example in encouraging contemporary westerners to find remedies for these problems?

Well, really, why not?

We will heal the West because it is the western thing to do.

Healing Higher Education, or How This Book Came to Be

Among the many happy side effects of projects undertaken to heal the West, none means more to me than the parallel and connected restoration of health to higher education. Here I speak for myself and not necessarily for my coeditors or any of the contributors to this volume, though quite a few of the writers here make references to the negative appraisal that "applied" work can receive from convention-based systems of appraising scholarly work. Nevertheless, not everyone shares the idea that universities have been ailing. As a person whose primary home has been a university since 1968, however, I contemplate the current state of higher education with a feeling that matches the concern provoked by realizing that an old friend is not looking well and does not seem interested in getting a checkup.

In the past forty years, the world—of technology, of child raising, of authority and credentialing, of professions and occupations—has changed tremendously. The practices, customs, and habits of most professors have in contrast changed to a much more limited degree. A loyalty to narrow academic specialization is rigorously passed on to each generation of professors, and disciplines fragment into ever-narrower territories of expertise. In nearly every field, a distinction between "pure research" and "applied work" puts the latter at a disadvantage. Perhaps most troubling of all, academic practice seems stuck in the rut of addressing a tiny audience of fellow specialists. Many erstwhile reformers, concerned about these patterns, have called for a change in the reward system. Indeed, there are many good arguments in favor of a shift away from the basing of hiring, tenure, and promotion on conventional research and toward the valuing of innovative and energetic teaching and applied knowledge.

But such proposals run smack into the unmovable wall of customary practice. Anyone in need of a prime example of the meaning of the phrase "old habits die hard" should hotfoot it to the nearest university.

But the good news is that anyone in need of a prime example of the willingness and capability of some faculty to adapt nimbly to the times, to live in the twenty-first century, and to match their academic knowledge to practical needs would be well served by a visit to the University of Colorado and the professors associated with the Center of the American West. All colleges and universities have several faculty cohorts similar to this group, experimenting—with conspicuous success—in a fresher, more connected, more engaged, more satisfying form of professional life. If the existence and numbers of these lively and valuable scholars could be more widely known, public appreciation and support of higher education might well rise.

This book proves my point. In January 2002, we undertook to choose a theme for a year-long Center of the American West faculty lecture series. We considered some good candidates: fire and western wildlands; western water; transportation and the West; western energy production and consumption; and remedy, repair, restoration, and mitigation. In an e-mail message describing these choices, I annotated that last topic: "All over the West, people are trying to do more than lament injury. From the hope of restoring damaged ecosystems and wildlife habitats to the effort to revitalize Indian languages, there are many dimensions to this vision. A series on this theme, many faculty agreed, would certainly carry a positive and help-filled tone."

So we settled on the theme of restoration, remedy, and repair. Next, the lecture series acquired the title "Healing the West." Then a broad e-mail invitation to the Boulder faculty brought the happy result of an overabundance of responses, enough recruits for two years' worth of lectures. Humanities, social sciences, natural sciences, and engineering were all well represented, and the people working in these various territories shared a remarkable similarity of spirit. They convened on a couple of occasions to explore their common interests and commitments; they attended each other's lectures; and then, when it came time to turn the lectures into a book, they responded with great good will and cheerful effort.

No administrator or official had coordinated these individual professors' decisions to take up work in restoration, remedy, repair, and mitigation. They all were good citizens as well as good scholars, and when their scholarly work turned out to hold the promise of considerable benefit to society, they took this situation as an invitation and not as a burden.

A movement had coalesced out of an accumulation of individual choices. Without a slogan or a proclaimed "school" of thought, a desire to be positively involved in the world and to pursue goals beyond narrow academic careerism had touched individuals and produced the foundation for a team effort. In my judgment, the individuals who contributed to this volume share a distinctive character trait: unlike many academics who bemoan the failure of society to acknowledge, appreciate, and reward their work, these people are poor performers when it comes to the sport of complaint and lamentation. They are pleasant to be around. Their engagement with these projects in healing has given them a sense of being valued and a recognition that applied work requires just as much intellectual exertion and is just as rigorous and strenuous as the more insular scholarly activity that preoccupies convention-bound faculty. Many of the professors participating in the lecture series had involved undergraduates and graduate students in their applied work, giving those students a deepened sense of the meaning of their education. Moreover, on a campus fragmented by turf wars between and among the natural sciences, engineering, social sciences, and humanities, the "Healing the West" series revived—or created—a partnership among faculty from the humanities, the social sciences, the natural sciences, and engineering. Perhaps most satisfying, it demonstrated that some professors, rather than yielding to ivory-tower isolation, are simultaneously playing leading roles in the growth of enthusiasm for restoration and repair, one of the most important trends in the region, *and* applying that trend to their own territory of higher education.

Thus, it is striking to see how well the chapters' common themes, emerging from reflections on projects directed toward healing the West, also carry hope and promise for healing higher education. Many of the authors here want to cure amnesia and restore memory so that westerners will be able to reflect and act intelligently, recognizing how their conduct today connects to the history of their region; the same exercise would surely deepen and enrich our thinking about the adaptations higher education has and has not made to changing times. Quite a few of the writers accent the value of diversity, both biological and cultural, not simply because diversity is intrinsically edifying and worthy of contemplation, but because diversity makes it possible to keep a range of choices open for the future. Rather than imposing standardized measures and requirements of achievement on faculty, the same lesson of the value of diversity and the preservation of choice may add a new vitality to a world now often governed by habit and convention.

The West's universities and colleges are extraordinary resources. In the early twenty-first century, they are dramatically underutilized resources, and by virtue of being underutilized, they are also undervalued. As faculty and students become more and more engaged with the world around them, higher education itself gains in health and energy. This book exemplifies the best of what university communities can be.

Introduction

HEALING THE WEST

Andrew Cowell, Sharon K. Collinge, and Patricia Nelson Limerick

THE TITLE OF this volume is both a call for action and a provocation to thought. Action is simultaneously the easier and the trickier part of this pair. As Patty Limerick forcefully argues in both the prologue and the epilogue, there is much to be done. There are many problems in the American West (as in the rest of the world, obviously) that our generation can and indeed must address, and the immediate imperative is to get up and get to work. Work always benefits from guidelines, expertise, and experience, however, and the chapters in this book are intended in part to serve just that purpose. William Lewis's chapter on water use in the Klamath basin of Oregon is a good example: when a scarce resource such as water must be allocated between farmers' irrigation needs and endangered fish species, what likely legal and scientific issues will arise? What cautionary tales can those on the front lines of the conflicts share with us? What advice can they give us for doing better next time? And even more important, how far can the experiences and lessons learned be generalized to seemingly very different conflicts and solutions?

We have assembled here what we believe is an extremely diverse set of essays, addressing everything from disappearing Native American languages to urban sprawl and air quality to ecological restoration in the grasslands of California. These chapters testify to the great diversity of the West's human and natural landscapes, and each one looks in detail at one particular issue or problem. As the chapters show, each moment of conflict is unique in some way, as is each potential solution. Not only is it difficult to generalize immediately from the issue of preserving native languages to the issue of preserving endangered species, but it is quite dangerous to attempt to generalize even within the field of Native American language preservation itself. There are easily more than one hundred native languages spoken in the West by tribes ranging from the pueblo-dwelling, agriculture-oriented Hopi and Zuni to the formerly nomadic, bison-hunting Cheyenne and Arapaho, who still to this day live on their reservations in widely dispersed clusters of houses often organized around extended family groups, reflecting the older structure of their nomadic bands.

Yet we want to insist that it is important for westerners not to get lost in the details and particularities. Important as it is to confront every situation partially anew, it is also true that wallowing in too many details can be as bad as wallowing in self-pity. There are in fact some very useful generalizations that can be made about saving Native American languages: single-language immersion programs almost always produce better results than bilingual education programs, for example. Each chapter in this book seeks to draw those generalizable lessons for its field from its particular case study, but each also attempts to reach out across disciplines, regions, and issues to offer suggestions and parallels that tie together the West's problems and their solutions. It turns out that fragmentation of land ownership and resultant land use is a problem both for the continued health of many animal species, as Hannah Gosnell points out, and for the continued exercise of tribal sovereignty by the Navajo on their reservation, as Sarah Krakoff shows. Both Krakoff's chapter on the Navajo and Gosnell's on the Southern Rockies Ecosystem Project are finally about working out ways to live together in diverse landscapes without diminishing the human or natural richness that is present.

Perhaps the theme that ties these chapters together most closely is that of people. Behind every problem in this book—whether in the area of hydrology or ecology or ceremonial dance or civic engineering or linguistics—there are people. But every solution is also finally a "people solution." A number of chapters point to even the experts' uncertainty about how ecosystems and cultures function. Restoring vernal pools in California with all their intricate timing of winter rains, water-holding clay soils, spring blossoming of different species of ephemeral flowers in sequence, and gradual drying as summer approaches is incredibly complicated. A single puddle—at least when it is a naturally functioning vernal pool—can sometimes defy our efforts to restore or reproduce it. But answers to how these cycles function are becoming clearer thanks to the research of scholars such as Sharon Collinge. The bigger problem ironically often arises once the "solution" is relatively clear. As Joseph Ryan's contribution shows, it's not a mystery why mountain water is polluted near Jamestown, Colorado, or where the pollution comes from or even what effects this pollution has on those living things who rely on this water. Achieving a social consensus to act on the problem is a much bigger challenge, however. Many people have to come together to face the challenge, and politics comes into play.

The ultimate problem for vernal pools is that too many of them now have houses built on top of them. The vernal-pool problem originated as a land-use problem—that is to say, a political problem—and it remains to a large extent a political problem today, as development continues apace in California's Central Valley. Joseph Ryan likewise shows that the problem of acid mine drainage in the West is a problem that can be dealt with technically, but the politics and economics of the issue are quite another story.

In the past, many in the academic community have taken the attitude that politics is someone else's problem. Scholars, the story goes, should provide their technical insight to those concerned, then step back and allow the fray to begin from there. This tale is a caricature of the relationship between academic researchers and the broader public, but a caricature with a great deal of truth to it. This attitude has never been unchallenged, though, and is increasingly questioned today. Many atmospheric scientists studying global warming feel compelled to engage not only scientifically, but politically with the problem. More and more linguists are not just documenting endangered languages in scholarly publications but also advising tribes how to maintain the languages and even helping to write textbooks and train teachers. This volume is fundamentally committed to the idea that the narrowly defined "experts" in a given field can also participate in the larger social and political process involved—the "people process"—in addressing the problems in question. Almost every chapter thus includes not just a "scholarly" perspective on a problem, but a personal, human perspective as well. Brenda M. Romero's account of her ethnomusicology work in New Mexico tells how she not only learned about and documented a particular musical genre, but also ended up sharing her knowledge of that genre with members of the Pueblo once a key practitioner had passed way, thus allowing them to revive the music as a living cultural practice. Although other writers' experiences may not match this level of interpersonal involvement, all of the contributors attest to the fact that the dividing line between formal expertise (in hydrology, for example, or biodiversity) and the more general problems at hand (addressing acid mine drainage, for example, or nonprofit conservation projects in rural western landscapes) simply cannot be neatly drawn.

Up to this point in the introduction, we have not used the word *healing* or defined the term *the West*. We have so far simply been talking about taking action and addressing problems that happen to be in the West. Yet we opened this introduction by saying that the volume is not only a call to action, but also a provocation to thought. In the spirit of not wallowing in excessive analysis before getting down to action, we have restrained our deeply ingrained academic tendencies to leap immediately into too much thoughtfulness. The time has now come, though, to confront the provocations of the words *healing* and *the West*. We believe that both concepts have much to contribute to a better understanding of how to address the various problems that confront all regions of the globe, but the West in particular as a specific region with its own specific problems and solutions.

"Healing" is a widely used metaphor in talking about the West. The users can range from creative writers such as Terry Tempest Williams, whose book *Refuge* meditates on the connections between healing the land and healing the soul, to hard-core scientists: the lead article in a recent issue of the *Journal of Wildlife Management* laments that "the stabilization and increase of grassland bird populations will require healing of sick landscapes. There is no question that vast areas . . . are suffering from a chronic ecological malaise. A diagnostic epidemiological symptom of the landscape-scale illness is the widespread decline of grassland birds."[1] Nor is the metaphor limited to Euro-American culture: the Northern Arapaho tribe conducts the Sand Creek Spiritual Healing Run every summer from Sand Creek, Colorado, to either Denver or all the way to the Wind River Reservation in Wyoming, with participants running the entire distance in relay shifts. In the tribe's case, the effort serves to heal its own young people, both physically and spiritually, as they exercise their bodies and learn more about their heritage. At the same time, bonds between the young and the elderly (who share their stories as the run progresses) as well as between the Indian runners and the non-Indians who open up their homes to the runners for meals and a place to spend the night are also healed.

But as soon as we begin talking about healing, we of course have to talk about what it is that is being healed. The word *healing* requires us to identify a "patient," and as the Arapaho examples illustrate, the patients can be variable and complex. When the word is used literally, the patient is typically an individual human body, and this identification poses relatively few problems. But once we use the word metaphorically, the identification becomes much less clear. We might talk about "healing the Yellowstone ecosystem," but we must admit that the idea of an eco-system is a human creation whose boundaries are always arbitrary. The wolf that wandered from Yellowstone to Colorado, as described in Han-nah Gosnell's chapter, clearly did not feel limited by the concept of the Yellowstone ecosystem. Similar questions arise in the case of languages and how to define them. What is a language? Is it the grammar and vocabulary? If we have a good enough dictionary and a good enough grammar, have we "saved" the language? Or is it really constituted by the daily interactions by means of and uses of the language, with all of the cultural idiosyncrasies and intimate knowledge required to speak a language correctly?

Of course, every problem must be defined and delimited in these partially subjective, human terms, but the word *healing* can force us to confront fully the reality that it is we who identify the patient—that the patient is not given to us automatically. This awareness can bring a renewed sense of insight and potential, and can even lead us to define the patient more productively. Likewise, the word also demands that we squarely confront our expectations and assumptions as we address a given problem or issue. Healing is something more than "dealing with" or "solving" or "resolving." It involves the idea of addressing underlying causes, not just symptoms, and doing so on a permanent basis. Aspirin does not heal an infection, though it may reduce the pain for a while or at least until the infection becomes too severe. Unfortunately, social and natural problems are often simply given an "aspirin." The underlying causes of the problem are thus not addressed or may be misidentified. If we truly take the notion of healing to heart, we must confront our "patients" on the most fundamental and general level. When we do, we may come to realize that saving the DNA of a fish species, housed in a few living fish, even though the natural forces that led to the evolution of that particular DNA are no longer active, is not a true "healing." Likewise, linguists must face the fact that a language is the expression of a deeper culture. The loss of the language is often a symptom of cultural changes, and if the underlying problems of poverty, racism, and ideological oppression are not addressed, the language can never be saved as a living vehicle of culture. Len Ackland's chapter on the long history of the Rocky Flats nuclear weapons plant and the conflict surrounding it suggests that both the physical and the psychic wounds of the Cold War are being bandaged by bulldozed earth rather than being truly exposed and healed.

The word *healing* raises the issues not only of the nature of the patient and the underlying causes of the problem, but also of the nature of "health." Uncritically used, the word may lead us to assume that the ideal health of an ecosystem, a species, a community, or a culture can be easily determined. In fact, this is often what happens when the word is *not* used. Problems, their causes, *and* their solutions tend to be taken for granted, and the participants then immediately plunge into the worst kind of political power struggles to see who can successfully impose "their" solution. If we use the concept of healing in its most productive sense, however, we will recognize that it demands that we confront openly our initial underlying assumptions about what we are really trying to achieve in addressing the problem in question. The most productive uses of the term force us to clarify goals.

William Cronon has written at length about the concept of wilderness. Using the language of healing as developed here, he would argue first that the patient is a humanly defined concept and that there is no such thing as untouched "wilderness" in nature. He would also argue that the ideal state of "health" assumed in the concept of wilderness is likewise illusory or unproductive. In focusing on wilderness preservation, environmentalists may be defining a "patient" that is not really the right one to treat and may be focusing on a form of "health" that is actually secondary to real concerns. Perhaps the continuation of evolutionary processes—including natural disturbances such as fire, flooding, and grazing—throughout ecosystems would be a better goal than roadlessness or lack of logging in certain parts of ecosystems. Cronon in fact does argue that we are mistargeting our efforts in devoting so much attention to preserving wilderness while neglecting our own neighborhoods, so to speak.[2]

We do not want to try to resolve the question of wilderness here, but simply to point out that Cronon's arguments about wilderness are inspired by a viewpoint similar to our perspective on healing. Cronon basically argues that environmentalists have implicitly been using a metaphor of healing all along, but that they have been doing so uncritically. In this uncritical usage, the patient and its ideal state of health are simply taken for granted as givens, and certain symptoms are confused with underlying causes and root problems. For us, consciously and explicitly applying the metaphor of healing—in full awareness of its metaphorical quality—to a given issue or problem is a way of systematically confronting in a very open fashion the facts and assumptions *behind* the issue and of moving toward more productive definitions of and solutions to these problems, recognizing that all problems are finally human problems.

Once we begin to recognize that the technical issue at hand is often inseparable from the social processes of addressing that problem, a funny thing begins to happen to the concept of "healing." As often as not, what gets healed is human society, along with or even in place of the more narrowly defined problem at hand. As Andrew Cowell's chapter on work with native-language communities suggests, a full healing of the direct issue at hand may sometimes be unlikely or even impossible. But constructive engagement between different groups whose relationship has been historically rocky—Native Americans, local residents of Wyoming, academic researchers, interested residents of Boulder, Colorado— can begin to build new bridges and overcome historical "wounds" that reach far deeper than the injury of language loss. Joseph Ryan's chapter emphasizes the ways in which remediation of abandoned mines can bring whole communities together. Similarly, Brenda M. Romero's experiences with reviving New Mexican dance rituals develop new appreciation of a community's multicultural heritage.

In talking about healing, we have so far tried to stress that the metaphor calls for us to search below the surface level to look at a second layer of deeper, underlying causes of specific social or environmental issues, but many chapters in this book point to the need to go to even a third layer. And there we find that problem after problem is really a problem of relationships between groups—relationships fraught with long histories of conflict and misunderstanding. For many Native Americans, language loss is a symptom of cultural insecurity or feelings of inferiority. Those deeper problems, however, are themselves symptoms of the unequal relationship between Native Americans and Euro-Americans in which the latter has sought to impose its will on the former. As long as this relationship remains as it is, new problems will always continue to arise. If the process of trying to solve the immediate problem of language loss and maintenance can lead to deeper understandings across cultures, perhaps these deep wounds in human relationship can be moved closer toward healing. John-Michael Rivera's chapter on recovering the memory of Mexican cultural history in the United States attempts to repair misunderstandings and misconceptions between the present and the past. And David Armstrong's account of the events in the Yampa River valley likewise focuses on the way in which trying to solve a biodiversity problem with a nonhuman focus ultimately depended on restoring ties between urbanites and rural ranchers, as well as between academics and conservation organizations, thereby producing a richer human biodiversity on the political and social landscape. We must acknowledge that injured relationships have produced many of the West's problems.

But why the West? What is unique about the West that leads to specific kinds of injury and unique kinds of healing? The first answer lies in the environment: because the West is composed of arid and semiarid landscapes, the wounds or scars of past injuries are conspicuous long after the damage is done. Both soil development and plant growth are limited by rainfall, and because rainfall is so scarce in the West, recovery occurs much more slowly. For example, tracks from World War II military vehicles are still visible in the Mojave Desert, more than 60 years later.[3] The vast cavities of abandoned mine shafts in mountainous areas of the American West gaze back at us. And tracks from covered wagons along the Oregon and Santa Fe Trails are still evident in the shortgrass prairies of Kansas, Colorado, and Nebraska 150 years after the last wagon train pulled through these landscapes. Depending on the type and severity of past disturbances, recovery of these landscapes is expected to take decades to millennia.[4]

For westerners, the high visibility of past ecosystem damage heightens our awareness in a way that is less obvious in other parts of the United States. To be certain, the eastern United States is full of legacies of past human activities, including deforestation, overgrazing, and cultivation agriculture. For example, the forests surrounding Henry David Thoreau's hometown of Concord, Massachusetts, had been cleared, logged, and burned for at least 200 years prior to and during his lifetime.[5] Today, however, the deforestation of the northeastern deciduous forests that peaked in the mid–nineteenth century is now essentially invisible. The landscape looks completely forested, and to the untrained eye it appears as if it has always been that way. A closer examination reveals subtle differences, however. For example, the soils underneath what are now forests still show signs of being plowed,[6] and many of the famous New England spring flowers are more abundant in areas that escaped deforestation 150 years ago than they are in areas that were grazed or plowed.[7] So there are clearly land-use legacies in the eastern United States as well as in the American West, but they are perhaps less apparent. Conversely, in the West we are faced with them on a regular basis—they stare back at us, almost demanding some kind of response. One need only stand on a hill along the Front Range of Colorado to appreciate the magnitude of urban sprawl in a visceral way that is largely impossible in eastern treescapes: you can literally see half a million houses.

Because the West is relatively dry, a great deal of western agriculture depends on irrigation, as does ranching. The West's rural economy is about access to water in a way that the East's rural economy is not. Furthermore, western water law is highly idiosyncratic, and western water allocation and distribution (including to cities) are much more intimately tied to federal-level (U.S. Bureau of Reclamation) decisions than is the case in the East. Dryness means the interference of big government. The dryness and harshness also means that a much greater percentage of the land has remained in public ownership than in the East. So both land and water uses are closely tied to federal-level decisions.

Much of the interior West is also both geographically rugged—with many alternating sets of ranges and valley basins—and at high elevations atmospherically dry, with thinner air. Both of these factors tend to exacerbate the problems of air pollution, as in the Los Angeles basin, the Central Valley of California, the Salt Lake area of Utah, and the Front Range area of Colorado. Further exacerbating the problem is the relative lack of storms and precipitation in the lowlands, which prevents the air from being cleansed by rain and snow. The same ruggedness tends to force development into a few privileged, easy-to-build-on areas, which then become examples of what Allan Wallis and Gene Bressler call "expeditious landscapes." In these locations, the friendly, easy-to-manage geography can combine with friendly, easily extensible, tried-and-true land-use regulations and building codes to produce a perfect human storm of sprawling, monotonous, unimaginative development.

Dryness and ruggedness have paradoxically led to greater natural and human diversity. The West has retained a greater amount of its indigenous cultural diversity than the East has. Furthermore, many areas of the West (in particular California and the Southwest) were always more culturally diverse than much of the East. In many parts of the interior West, Native Americans are the largest single ethnic majority, whereas this is virtually nowhere true east of Oklahoma. Vastly more Native American languages continue to exist in the West as compared to in the East. The nearly five-hundred-year Hispanic heritage of the Southwest is also unmatched in extent or intensity by any equivalent non-Anglo heritage in the eastern United States. The West has also been historically the point of entry for most Asian Americans. Indeed, recent molecular data suggest that original migration into the Western Hemisphere occurred along the West Coast, from Alaska all the way to Mexico, and that humans then spread from these coastal refugia among the glaciers to populate the rest of the continent.[8]

The West is more diverse than the East for a number of different categories of life: plants, mammals, reptiles, and birds. It has also retained or regained significant populations of such megafauna as grizzly and black bears, mountain lions, wolves, elk, and moose, which are either much more restricted in range or entirely absent in the East. The inventory of roadless areas larger than fifty thousand acres lists only a handful of such areas in the East, but hundreds in the West.[9] Overall, the West retains many more areas that have more intact ecosystems than does the East.

And, finally, the West has a mythology attached to it that the East does not. Much of this mythology may be false or at least questionable, yet simplistic myths of the frontier—which are closely linked to the West—retain a powerful attraction in American life.

In summary, the West presents geographical, biological, and human diversity problems that are intertwined with each other in complex ways, as well as with large-scale, federal politics in unique ways. Yet most important of all, as several of these chapters show, all of these problems remain entangled in a mythology of the West—involving individualism, frontier utopian possibilities, radical social reform, and limitless ecological capacity—that can be a major constraint on confronting them. Just as the idea of "healing" can be used either effectively or ineffectively, depending on the critical perspective one adopts, the idea of "the West" can be either a way of uncritically fostering illusions, hiding realities, and avoiding a confrontation with underlying issues or a metaphor that critically provokes thought about what the West really is and is not about. Facing the "real" West is a major step toward facing the true problems that confront the region and recognizing the commonalities in the potential solutions.

Part 1
Saving What's Out There, Preventing Further Decline

1

Healing the West with Taxes

THE NAVAJO NATION AND THE ENACTMENT
OF SOVEREIGNTY

Sarah Krakoff

I ATTENDED ELEMENTARY and high school in northern New Jersey, and despite the progressive, Sesame Street–like atmosphere of my relatively racially integrated education, it offered only two basic narratives about American Indians. The first was the *Little House on the Prairie* narrative. It goes like this: American Indians are beautiful but frightening savages who had to yield to the higher purposed and better use of the land by white settlers. It is a progress narrative, with a sad nod to the necessary losses incurred. It is epitomized in a scene from the second book in the series by Laura Ingalls Wilder, the one actually entitled *Little House on the Prairie,* in which Laura and her family watch in quiet awe as a long line of Indians streams south and west past the Ingalls homestead, having been told by the federal government, once again, to move on. Even Ma, the most blatant Indian hater in the family, seems touched by the poignancy of what they have wrought.

The second narrative is similar to the *Little House* narrative, but adds another dollop of both romanticism and guilt. Although not terribly original, it makes sense to call this one the *Dances with Wolves* narrative. It goes like this: American Indians were a purer form of human being than whites, with better attitudes toward nature and a freer way of living, but we conquered them to make this country what it is and should feel very badly about that. Both narratives put a vast distance between us, the white settlers-conquerors, and them, the romantic savages. And both narratives present American Indians in the past tense. They were here. They were in the way. Now they are gone. We may feel either slightly or very sad about that, but that's the way it is.

The counternarrative is not available in popular fiction, television shows, or Hollywood films, yet it can be found by spending time within the boundaries of a modern American Indian nation, working, talking, and living with modern American Indians. They are here. Their tattered homelands have become their fonts of cultural survival. And their separate political existence, known as their tribal sovereignty, is crucial to their ability to continue to live in the present as American Indians, as separate peoples with ties to their past and hopes for their futures.

Modern tribal sovereignty is perhaps the hardest concept for non-Indians to grasp. As a law professor, I am now well versed in its very complex legal meaning and can recite its subtleties with ease. But when I take a step back from my legal academic persona and remember what it felt like simply to live and be among the Navajo, on their land, in their country, I think of it in this way: tribal sovereignty provides a protective shell around the perpetuation of tribal life and culture. Without it, many of the beautiful and striking things that I saw on the Navajo Nation simply would not be. The protective shell is not impermeable, though. To the contrary, it allows for a living, breathing, changing Navajo culture. But it is necessary to ensure that something distinctly Navajo exists, even as "Navajo" constantly evolves.

The power to tax is among the most powerful and important of sovereign governmental powers. This chapter, which presents part of a larger study of the Navajo Nation, recounts the impacts of federal law on the Navajo Nation's power to lay and collect taxes, as well as the effects of any limitations on the tribal taxing power on the nation's ability to enact core functions associated with sovereignty.[1] Those functions include providing peace and security; developing economic opportunities; allowing for the expression of social, cultural, and linguistic patterns; and creating a political system that meets the people's needs. Together, these governmental functions create the space within which modern Navajo people survive and adapt, fostering a unique and ever-changing culture that persists outside of and despite the *Little House* and *Dances with Wolves* narratives of Native extinction.

Fending off extinction, both literal and metaphorical, is a recurrent theme in this volume, and despite the diversity of disciplinary treatments of the subject, some common observations emerge. First, agency matters. Whether we are talking about the separate legal existence of an Indian nation (as here), a particular native language (as in Andrew Cowell's chapter), or a Hispanic-Pueblo dance (as in Brenda M. Romero's chapter), the people whose existence or cultural and linguistic characteristics are at stake must dictate the terms of survival. This statement is not just normative. Certainly, the Navajo *should* be permitted to dictate the terms of their survival. The statement is also descriptive, however, of a necessary component of cultural distinctiveness: if it is not the Navajo themselves (or the Arapaho or the Pueblo) who are charting their future, then it is not *their* future. Second, agencies matter. Hannah Gosnell's wolves, for example, are dependent on our federal government's panopticon qualities. Mastering the federal legal bureaucracy and putting it to a distinctly Navajo end has, as this study reveals, certainly been crucial to Navajo survival.

This surprising mixture of self-determination (agency) and overwhelming bureaucracy (agencies) is and always has been a part of the unique story of the American West; just think about the enormous federal subsidies that allowed for "free" enterprise in the form of railroads or for "free" water for irrigation. We like to tell the mythic side of these stories, about how determination and ingenuity turned an unruly land into a productive one, but we mostly suppress the side about the enabling legalistic and bureaucratic underpinnings. Yet just as it took both individuals and bureaucracies to create many of the West's cultural and ecological wounds, both must be involved in strategies of healing and restoration: the "patient" must take charge of her own cure, but she must also be a savvy user of the system.

A story about Navajo Nation taxation is not particularly romantic. It is not the stuff of little girls' fantasies of life beyond the suburbs. But it is real, and it is just one strand in the many threads weaving a counternarrative of the West, one based on healing from many things, including the misunderstandings perpetuated by stories that are only partially true.

Background and History

The Navajo Nation reaches across northern Arizona into a strip of southern Utah and bulges into western New Mexico. It is vast, consisting of 17 million acres, a land mass larger than the state of West Virginia and comparable to Ireland. The Navajo Nation is also the second most populous American Indian nation, with nearly 300,000 tribal members, 168,000 of whom live in Navajo Indian country. In some respects, the

Navajo Nation is thriving. The relatively intact land base, large number of tribal members, and active efforts by the tribal government to perpetuate Navajo language, law, and religion bode well for the continuation of this rich indigenous culture. Yet many non-Indian visitors to this stark, high-desert region are overwhelmed by the signs of third-world poverty, including roving stray dogs, roadside trash, alcoholic (and recently, methamphetamine-addled) hitchhikers, and a landscape pockmarked by mining and other forms of resource extraction. The outsider's gaze is not entirely misleading. Poverty, unemployment, and social dysfunction plague the Navajo Nation's efforts to create a viable and vibrant homeland. Less visible to the tourist's gaze, however, is the history behind this state of affairs. A word or two about the history of the Navajo Nation is required to understand the present challenges for restoration, including the vital role of the tribal governmental power to tax.

To the Navajo people, their history begins with the origin story. Navajo oral histories describe a transition from the first world to the fourth, or glittering, world, which is the site of the geographical Navajo homeland. Much of this land today composes the official Navajo Reservation. The Navajo homeland is identified by the four sacred mountains at the perimeter: Blanca Peak in Colorado in the east, Mount Taylor in New Mexico in the south, the San Francisco Peaks in Arizona in the west, and Hesperus Peak in Colorado in the north. According to the origin story, the Navajo emerged as a mature and distinct people in the fourth world, which the historical record reveals to be a time of increased contact and mixing between Athabaskan people and people of Puebloan heritage. The origin story thus identifies what it is to be distinctly Navajo at a moment of adaptation. Adaptation and distinctiveness can coexist in large part because of Navajo attachment to place: the land between the four sacred mountains tells the Navajo who they are. They are therefore free to incorporate other people and traditions without sacrificing their political and cultural identity.

The centrality of the Navajo homeland also figures prominently in what might be called the postcolonial Navajo origin story, the story of the Long Walk. In the latter half of the nineteenth century, pressure grew to expand white settlement—including homesteading, mining, and railroads—throughout the West. The Navajo, particularly after the Mexican-American War and the Treaty of Guadalupe Hidalgo in 1848, had become a "people who mattered" in the region by virtue of their size and adaptive presence.[2] Being a people who mattered also meant that they were a people perceived to stand in the way of the prevailing vision of settlement. In addition, after the Civil War, assimilationist voices influential with the new federal government began insisting that all Indians be educated into the white man's ways to ready them for the inevitable shift to an economic system based on private property and individual economic gain.

By the 1860s, the historical forces of settlement and assimilation converged to result in a policy of deliberate removal of the Navajo from their homeland. They were to be rounded up and relocated to a reservation at Fort Sumner, New Mexico, known as the Bosque Redondo, in order to "civilize" them and settle their territory. The removal campaign, led by Kit Carson, was cruel and brutal. Crops and orchards were burned, water sources were obliterated, and Navajo who were too old or weak to make the forced march of several hundred miles were exterminated.[3] The Navajo who did survive viewed their stay at the *bosque* as imprisonment. The infertile soil along that harsh stretch of the Rio Grande made for poor farming, and many more Navajo died in the effort to force them into agrarianism. The Navajo ultimately refused to give in to their relocation. In 1868, after approximately five years of failed assimilation experiments, the federal government entered into the Treaty of 1868 with the leaders of the Navajo people. The treaty provided that the Navajo could return to a portion of their homeland. Over time through a series of executive orders, the Navajo Reservation grew to include a sizeable percentage of the traditional lands between the four sacred mountains.

The Treaty of 1868 is a vital and foundational document to the modern Navajo Nation. It not only guaranteed a return to the Navajo homeland, but also promised a perpetual separate political existence. Although that existence would never be entirely free of the U.S. federal government's omnipresent power, it was guaranteed against the incursions by states as well as by other tribes. The promise of a "measured" separate political and territorial existence brought the Navajo people back to the land between the four sacred mountains, where they have been working ever since to derive a modern adaptation of tribal sovereignty to meet the economic, cultural, and spiritual needs of the Navajo people.[4]

From 1868 to the present, that modern adaptation of sovereignty has had to contend with fluctuating and at times conflicting trends in the U.S. Congress and Supreme Court. With respect to the Court, the architecture for Indian tribes' anomalous legal status derives from three cases that predate the Navajo treaty. In the first half of the nineteenth century, Justice John Marshall authored the "Marshall trilogy," which defined tribes as "domestic dependent nations" incapable of entering into foreign relations but possessed otherwise of inherent powers to govern their territory and their members.[5] Significantly for tribes, the trilogy affirmed that the individual states lacked the authority to impose their laws unilaterally within Indian territory and that only the federal government had the power to alter tribal legal and political boundaries.[6]

For more than a century after the Marshall trilogy, there was relatively little further development in the case law with regard to tribal sovereignty. A few key decisions affirmed tribes' inherent powers, recognizing their exclusive powers to prosecute crimes against tribal members that occur within tribal territory and finding that the workings of tribal government are not subject to the limitations contained in the U.S. Constitution's Bill of Rights.[7] During roughly the same time period, however, the Court, in the *Lone Wolf v. Hitchcock* (1903) decision, deferred to congressional decisions to erode tribal powers, including unilateral treaty abrogation.[8]

The Supreme Court's decision in *Lone Wolf* allowed the policy period that has come to be known as "allotment and assimilation" to occur unfettered. The allotment policies included federal statutes that authorized the breakup of Indian lands into individual parcels, with any "surplus" lands being opened for homesteading or sale to non-Indians. Assimilationist practices included rounding up Indian children and sending them to boarding schools, many of which were run by Christian groups, in order to cure the children of their tribal ways, such as language, dress, and religion. For many tribes, these policies resulted in near devastation of their separate political existence. The tribal land base shrank collectively from 138 million to 48 million acres.[9] Although the Navajo territory remained largely intact, with the exception of a significant portion in western New Mexico, the legal and educational policies affected Navajo in the same ways they affected other tribes. Generations of children grew up without their parents and were actively discouraged from learning about their languages, cultures, and religions. The development of tribal political structures was arrested during this period, displaced by the federal government's heavy assimilating hand. Navajo people were often covertly able to incorporate their own norms into the Anglo structures, but the challenges remained formidable.[10]

The federal government abandoned allotment and assimilation policies after a damning report was issued by Lewis B. Meriam finding that tribes were considerably worse off in all respects than they were at the dawn of the allotment period.[11] In 1934, Congress passed the Indian Reorganization Act (IRA), which gave tribal governments the opportunity to organize into structures that would receive direct federal support. With one brief but devastating exception during the post–World War II period, when Congress flirted with terminating the federal relationship with all Indian tribes,[12] it has generally been the case ever since passage of the IRA that Congress has supported policies of tribal self-determination. In particular, starting in the late 1960s, the executive branch's explicit policy has been to support tribal self-governance, and many federal statutes have been passed with the aim of encouraging tribes to run their own programs, ranging from courts to schools to environmental protection agencies.[13]

The Supreme Court, however, has played a much more ambiguous role in contemporary times. On the one hand, the Court has affirmed the doctrine of tribal inherent powers, including the power to tax, and has ousted state authority in Indian country in certain circumstances. On the other, it has declared that tribes lack certain categories of jurisdiction over non-Indians and has allowed increasingly onerous forms of concurrent state regulation over non-Indians within Indian country. These conflicting jurisdictional signals have complicated the evolution of tribal sovereignty in the modern era. In particular, the Court has circumscribed the tribal taxing power, a power that is necessary for tribes to meet many of the essential functions of sovereignty. Given the important role tribal governments play in protecting the existence of separate American Indian cultures and ensuring the physical and spiritual health of tribal people (a lesson learned acutely in the aftermath of the allotment period), clear information about the impacts of Supreme Court decisions on tribal powers, including the crucial power to tax, should be made available to all federal and tribal decision makers. This study of the impacts of Supreme Court decisions on the Navajo Nation's taxing authority is a first step toward understanding how and whether Indian tribes can reclaim sovereignty in the shadow of federal law.

U.S. Supreme Court Decisions and the Navajo Nation's Taxing Authority

The Supreme Court's fickle treatment of tribal sovereignty is on full display in the context of the inherent tribal power to tax. For this study, I divided the cases into three categories: first, those that affirm the tribal power to tax; second, those that recognize state concurrent taxing authority; and third, those that divest tribes of categories of taxing jurisdiction. The first category obviously favors Indian tribes, and the second and third categories present challenges for tribal authority. In some instances, the impacts on tribal revenue and consequent ability to provide government services are obvious and concrete. In others, the effects are more elusive or complicated. The picture that emerges is one of a tribal nation enacting its sovereignty in creative ways, even in the face of apparent constraints. At the same time, it is clear that some rules emanating from the Court impose nonnegotiable limits on tribal authority that in turn hamper the Navajo Nation's ability to serve the people's needs.

Affirming the Tribal Power to Tax

The Supreme Court has recognized in a number of cases that Indian tribes have inherent authority to tax nontribal members. First, in *Washington v. Confederated Tribes of Colville Indian Reservation* (1980), the Court found that the power to tax Indians and non-Indians was "a fundamental attribute of sovereignty which the tribes retain unless divested of it by federal law or necessary implication of their dependent status."[14] Second, in *Merrion v. Jicarilla Apache Tribe* (1982), the Court affirmed the taxing power, finding it to be "an essential attribute of Indian sovereignty because it is a necessary instrument of self-government and territorial management." *Merrion* upheld a tax that the Jicarilla Apache Tribe imposed on non-Indian lessees who were extracting oil and gas from tribal trust lands. The non-Indian taxpayers raised several arguments, including that the tribe's tax resulted in multiple taxation in violation of the Commerce Clause and that the tribal power to tax is only coextensive with the tribal power to exclude non-Indians from the reservation. The Court rejected each of these arguments and repeatedly stressed Indian tribes' inherent authority to tax, as well as the crucial role that taxation plays for any government to finance governmental services and activities. The tribal power to tax "derives from the tribe's general authority, as sovereign, to control economic activity within its jurisdiction, and to defray the cost of providing governmental services by requiring contributions from persons or enterprises engaged in economic activities within that jurisdiction."[15]

The trend of affirming tribal taxing powers continued in *Kerr-McGee Corp. v. Navajo Tribe of Indians* (1985), a case testing the Navajo Nation's taxes as applied to non-Indian mineral lessees. As in *Merrion*, the mineral leases were located on tribal lands. Unlike in *Merrion*, the secretary of the interior had not expressly approved the tribal taxes. The non-Indian lessees argued that without secretarial approval, the Navajo taxes were invalid. The Court rejected this argument, finding that no federal statute required secretarial approval of tribal taxes and that no such statute was necessary to authorize the taxes because the power to tax is "an essential attribute of self-government." Of particular relevance to the Navajo Nation and its perception of the strength of future arguments regarding its sovereignty, the Court concluded by stating that "the Navajo Government has been called 'probably the most elaborate' among tribes. . . . The legitimacy of the Navajo Tribal Council, the freely elected governing body of the Navajos, is beyond question. . . . [And] neither the Congress nor the Navajos have found it necessary to subject the Tribal Council's tax laws to review by the Secretary of Interior."[16]

Given the green light to pass and enforce taxes against non-Indians, the Navajo Nation has developed an elaborate and comprehensive taxation program. The Navajo Nation Tribal Council established the Navajo Nation Tax Commission in 1974. Emboldened by the new era of self-determination and committed to creating a homeland that could nurture their people in ways that the federal government had repeatedly failed to do, the Navajo Nation set out to collect revenue to fund essential programs. As the council stated in its resolution, "Various studies and surveys made by and on behalf of the Navajo Tribe have shown that taxation within a comprehensive tax program would be in the best interests of the Navajo people."[17]

In the four years following the establishment of the Navajo Nation Tax Commission, the commission continued to study the question of whether and how much to tax.[18] In 1978, the Tribal Council enacted the first Navajo taxes: a possessory interest tax (PIT), which is a type of ad valorem tax, and a business activity tax (BAT), which is a type of gross receipts tax. In enacting both of these taxes, the council again declared that "the right to tax is part of the inherent sovereignty of any nation." In addition, the economic need for the taxes was articulated: "[The] Navajo population and Navajo needs are increasing, with the increase in the need for services partly a result of increased employment and development within the Navajo Nation."[19] In these pronouncements, the direct link between sovereign authority, on the one hand, and revival and protection of the Navajo people, on the other, is evident.

Several non-Indian businesses immediately challenged the BAT and PIT, and these challenges led to the Supreme Court decision in *Kerr-McGee* affirming the tribal inherent power to tax. The Navajo Nation Tribal Council immediately declared that the date of the *Kerr-McGee* decision would be celebrated as a Navajo holiday, known as Navajo Nation Sovereignty Day. It announced with evident pride: "The Supreme Court by a vote of 8 to 0, stated that the Navajo Tribal Government as a Sovereign Nation has the inherent right to impose taxes without review and approval of the Secretary of Interior; and . . . said that the Navajo Government, 'probably the most elaborate among tribes,' is legitimate and that as a Sovereign Nation has the absolute right to Self-Government." Although recognizing and lauding the justices' decision in Washington, D.C., the Tribal Council was also clear to give credit for the instigation of sovereignty to the Navajo people themselves: "This landmark decision on behalf of the Navajo people, as well as all Indian nations, reaffirms and confirms that the Navajo Nation is a Sovereign Nation; and This [*sic*] landmark decision is also a direct result of the Navajo Nation utilizing its own in-house expertise."[20] It might be surprising, given general public hostility to taxation, to hear that the power to tax is celebrated among the Navajo in an annual holiday. The Navajo reaction indicates their perception of the strong link between their sovereign powers as a government and their continued existence as a people.

Kerr-McGee also had more concrete effects. Subsequent taxes enacted by the Navajo Nation include the oil and gas severance tax (passed in

1985), the hotel occupancy tax (1992), the tobacco products tax (1995), the fuel excise tax (1999), and the sales tax (2001).[21] The revenue from these taxes constitutes an increasingly significant percentage of the Navajo Nation budget. A certain percentage of it is earmarked for distribution to particular funds, including 5 percent to the Tax Administration Suspense Fund, 2 percent to the Land Acquisition Fund, 2 percent to the Chapter Development Fund, and 12 percent to the Permanent Trust Fund.[22] In addition, portions of particular taxes are earmarked for specific uses. For example, the net revenue from fuel taxes goes to road maintenance and construction, and the net revenue from the hotel tax goes to a tourism fund.[23]

Each of these funds, in particular the Land Acquisition Fund and the Permanent Trust Fund, plays a significant role in furthering the core aspects of sovereignty and in allowing the Navajo Nation simultaneously to heal historical wounds and to move forward creatively to a more sustainable economic future. The Land Acquisition Fund enables it to purchase non-Indian fee lands and thereby to restore the land base as well as address some of the jurisdictional problems raised by checkerboard patterns of ownership. The Permanent Trust Fund, established by former Navajo Nation president Peterson Zah in 1985, is intended to provide a replacement revenue stream for oil and gas royalties.[24] Revenue from this fund became available in 2005. The Navajo Nation needs long-term financial security for the day when income from fossil fuels ceases (or at least diminishes greatly) due to depletion of the resource. Using tax revenues in this way is a creative solution to the serious gaps in economic development opportunities in Indian country.

After the earmarked funds are subtracted from the tax revenue, the remainder goes in the Navajo Nation General Fund. This fund includes revenue from all sources, including other tribally generated revenue, such as royalties from mineral production as well as federal and state grants. From 1990 to 2002, tribal taxes went from a low of 7 percent to a high of 15 percent of the General Fund. Tax revenue thus supports a variety of programs that ensure the health, security, and long-term viability of the Navajo Nation and its people. The money goes to basic infrastructure, which is essential to further other forms of economic development, and to long-term investment in the Permanent Trust Fund. Moreover, taxes are becoming an increasingly significant aspect of the Navajo governmental budget. The Court's affirmation of the inherent power to tax has enabled the Navajo Nation to fund essential governmental programs today and to plan for a more secure economic future.

Allowing Concurrent State Taxation in Indian Country

The Supreme Court has consistently held that state taxes cannot be imposed on Indian nations or tribal members within tribal Indian country. Questions concerning state authority to tax nontribal members in Indian country are more complex, and the trend recently has been to affirm concurrent state taxation of non-tribal-member activity. The roots of the doctrine recognizing concurrent state jurisdiction in Indian country took hold after the allotment period, when significant numbers of non-Indians settled within tribal territorial boundaries as a result of the allotment and sale of so-called surplus tribal lands. (Think again of little Laura Ingalls and her family as they relied on the government's promise that they were free to stake a homestead claim on former Indian lands.) The influx of non-Indians into Indian country presented a challenge to the vision of the intact Indian nation assumed by Justice Marshall in his trilogy. Courts responded by recognizing state jurisdiction over white-on-white crimes and in some circumstances by allowing state taxation of non-Indian activity.[25]

In the modern era, the Supreme Court initially sent some conflicting messages concerning concurrent state taxation. In two cigarette tax cases decided in 1976 and 1980, the Court upheld state taxation of on-reservation cigarette sales to non-Indians.[26] Foremost in the Court's reasoning was the tribe's economic behavior. The Court disapproved of the tribe's attempt to "market a state tax exemption," notwithstanding the fact that similar market behavior often drives state decisions about tax rates. In addition, it seemed to latch on to the fact that the cigarettes were not produced on the reservation, and thus the state tax did not affect reservation-generated value.[27] During the same time period, however, it decided three cases in which state taxes were preempted.[28] Up until this point, a unique "cigarette tax doctrine" appeared to explain the Court's divergence from earlier cases.

Cotton Petroleum Corp. v. New Mexico (1989) was the first modern-era noncigarette case in which the Court upheld concurrent state taxation of non-Indians in Indian country. *Cotton* involved the state of New

Mexico's attempt to impose oil and gas severance taxes on non-Indian companies extracting oil and gas from leases on Indian trust land. The Court addressed the conflicting messages from the previous cases by stating that it was applying a "flexible pre-emption analysis sensitive to the particular facts and legislation involved."[29] As part of this analysis, the Court undertook a "particularized examination of the relevant state, federal, and tribal interests."[30] It considered the "history of tribal independence in the field at issue," as well as the broad policies that underlie the legislation. Finally, "although state interests must be given weight and courts should be careful not to make legislative decisions in the absence of congressional action, ambiguities in federal law are, as a rule, resolved in favor of tribal independence."[31]

As applied to the state taxes in *Cotton,* the Court found no preemption. The relevant legislation did not prohibit state taxation of non-Indians. The Court found that the general legislative intent to provide for the maximum profitability for Indian tribes was directed at tribal royalties, not at indirect effects on tribal taxes from concurrent state taxes. The Court also stressed that the state provided "substantial services" to both the tribe and the taxpayer, "costing the state approximately $3 million per year." The Court further relied on findings by the district court that indicated that the tribe still had room to increase its taxes and royalties, notwithstanding the state taxes.[32]

The cases in which the Supreme Court has affirmed concurrent state taxation of non-Indians in Indian country have affected the Navajo Nation in two ways. On the one hand, it is clear that tribal revenue is less than it would be in the absence of multiple taxation. Due to the Court's rulings, tribes cannot market tax exemptions in order to lure customers into their jurisdiction, as states frequently do. The tax rate in Indian country for non-Indians will therefore always be set at a floor of the state tax rate. On the other hand, the Navajo Nation has approached state governments in order to address the problem of multiple taxation on a government-to-government level. Through tribal and state legislation, as well as through intergovernmental agreements, the Navajo Nation has been able to mitigate some of the harsher effects of the Supreme Court's multiple taxation cases.

The revenue impacts of the *Cotton* rule are apparent in the context of the Navajo Nation sales tax. The sales tax is currently set at 3 percent of the gross receipts of any sale. The range set by the statute is between 2 percent and 6 percent, but in an environment of dual taxation for non-Indian visitors to the reservation, it is not practical to set the tax any higher than 3 percent.[33] In 2003, the revenue from the sales tax exceeded $4 million.[34] If that revenue were doubled, there would (obviously) be more money and more flexibility. According to Amy Alderman, legal counsel for the Navajo Nation Tax Commission, one option would be to earmark some of a larger pool of sales tax revenues for sorely needed social programs.[35]

Within this framework of constraints, the Navajo Nation has found room to maneuver. Neither the surrounding states nor the Navajo Nation wants the multiple tax burden to inhibit non-Indian business altogether. In such circumstances, both governments lose out on the potential revenue stream. As a result, the Navajo Nation has approached New Mexico, Arizona, and Utah and achieved agreements that for the most part mitigate the harshest effects of multiple taxation on non-Indians. New Mexico in particular has proved to be an important partner in addressing multiple taxation. In 2001, the Navajo Nation Tax Commission worked with members of the New Mexico legislature to reduce the dual taxation effects on coal extracted from the New Mexico portion of the Navajo Nation.[36] The negotiations resulted in mutual legislation to address the problem. New Mexico passed laws providing for severance and gross receipts tax credits to offset the Navajo taxes and authorized entry into cooperative agreements with the Navajo Nation.[37] The Navajo Nation likewise approved amendments to the BAT.[38] The result is that businesses extracting coal from the New Mexico portion of the reservation pay a tax rate comparable to the rate paid by businesses extracting coal from non-Indian country lands in New Mexico.

Similar legislation and intergovernmental agreements have been reached regarding other taxes. An intergovernmental agreement related to tobacco tax revenue sharing and enforcement has been reached with Arizona, and Arizona has passed legislation that essentially caps the cumulative tobacco tax on the reservation at the state tax rate.[39] The Navajo Nation and Arizona have also entered into intergovernmental agreements with respect to enforcement of the Navajo Nation BAT and the hotel occupancy tax. In Utah, the Navajo Nation Tax Commission worked with state legislators to reduce the effects of concurrent state and tribal taxes in the context of hotel occupancy and fuel excise taxes. Utah passed laws mitigating the dual taxation effects, and an intergovernmental agreement was finalized.[40] Regarding fuel excise taxes, intergovernmental agreements exist with Arizona, New Mexico, Texas, and California.

This complex of Navajo legislation, state legislation, and intergovernmental agreements has in many significant respects eliminated concurrent taxation in fact. The Navajo Nation has thus been able to counteract the effects of the Supreme Court's concurrent taxation jurisprudence to the advantage of taxpayers and of tribal and state governments. By approaching other governments to achieve a taxing environment that does not discourage economic investment and development, the Navajo Nation exercises its sovereignty in a positive (and mutually beneficial) way against the backdrop of federal decisional law. Its response can only go so far, however. The Court's concurrent taxation cases have virtually eliminated the possibility that tribes can use competitive tax policies to attract non-Indian businesses onto the reservation. And new tribal taxes, such as the sales tax, are lower than they would be in the absence of dual taxation. Yet within these very real constraints imposed by the Court's legal definition of sovereignty, the Navajo Nation nonetheless is enacting sovereignty on the ground in creative and powerful ways.

Categorical Limitations on the Tribal Power to Tax

Cases in which the Supreme Court has rejected categories of tribal jurisdiction have proven more difficult for the Navajo Nation. A series of cases, beginning with a decision concerning criminal jurisdiction over non-Indians in 1980, has eroded tribal authority over non-Indian activity within reservation boundaries.[41] It appeared possible until recently that the sovereign power to tax might be treated differently than other civil powers and that Indian nations would continue to be able to impose and collect taxes on non-Indians within reservation boundaries on the same terms that states impose taxes on individuals within their territorial boundaries. A case arising from within the Navajo Nation, *Atkinson Trading Co. v. Shirley* (2001), has rejected this possibility, however, and created problems for the Navajo Nation that extend beyond the holding of the case itself.[42]

Until *Atkinson,* the Court's treatment of tribal inherent powers to tax appeared to differ from that of other tribal governmental powers. As discussed earlier, in *Merrion* the Court affirmed the tribe's power to tax non-Indians and found that the tribal power to tax was not merely an extension of the tribal power to exclude non-Indians from the reservation. *Merrion* recognized that it had long been the executive branch's understanding that tribes retained the power to tax activities on lands in which they had a significant interest, irrespective of land title.[43] That understanding was bolstered by an early circuit court opinion affirming tribal taxes on non-Indian businesses located on non-Indian lands within a reservation.[44]

The argument that the taxing power is different and should not be measured by land title is also supported by the justification for the power to tax. Governments provide services to areas within their geographical region irrespective of land title. The power to raise revenue to fund those services is a necessary and indispensable attribute of government. The governmental authority primarily responsible for police, fire, and other health and safety services determines an area's general character. In the area surrounding the tiny island of fee land on which the Atkinson Trading Company runs its hotel and trading post, that governmental authority is the Navajo Nation.[45] As the Navajo Nation noted in its briefs before the Supreme Court, it provides fire and police protection, emergency medical services, and health-inspection services to the Cameron area.[46] The Atkinson Trading Company thus benefits from the advantages of a "civilized society" that the Navajo Nation provides to the Cameron Trading Post and its customers.[47] In addition, it is quite clear that the Atkinson Trading Company draws customers to its business by advertising itself as a gateway to Indian culture. The trading post's Web site shows photographs of Navajo waitresses and walls adorned with Navajo rugs, and it includes the following marketing blurb:

Time was when it would take days, sometimes months, to travel across the reservation and trade for the fine Native American arts and curios that can be found here now. The Cameron Trading Post today is a center for local trade as well as a source for Native art representing cultures throughout the American Southwest. In traditional patterns passed down through generations, this selection of hand crafted weavings, baskets, pottery, jewelry, and carvings are mementos to be treasured, found in a variety to suit any vacation budget. A large variety of regional curio items are also available, popular among locals and visitors alike.[48]

None of these arguments were availing before the Supreme Court, however, and it held that the Navajo Nation could not impose a tax on a non-Indian on non-Indian fee land within the Navajo Nation's boundaries.

Atkinson has clear, if not deep, revenue effects on the Navajo Nation. In addition, the Court's recent decisions limiting tribal powers create in the minds of non-Indians doing business on the Navajo Nation a presumption against tribal authority in many circumstances. These decisions are more difficult to negotiate around than the concurrent state taxation cases in that they put the Navajo Nation at a distinct disadvantage in bargaining.

First, with respect to direct revenue effects from *Atkinson,* the Navajo Nation Tribal Council passed the hotel occupancy tax in 1992.[49] Prior to the *Atkinson* decision, the tax was imposed on non-Indian guests at fourteen hotels located within Navajo Nation boundaries and at a small number of bed-and-breakfast establishments. Since *Atkinson,* however, the Navajo Nation has ceased collecting the tax from two hotels on non-Indian fee land, the Cameron Trading Post (the Atkinson hotel) and Goulding's at Monument Valley. The Navajo Nation has also stopped collecting the nation's sales tax for any transactions between non-Indians on non-Indian fee land.[50]

Atkinson's revenue impacts are clear in the context of the hotel occupancy tax. In the three years preceding the *Atkinson* decision (when both the Cameron Trading Post and Goulding's were collecting this tax from non-Indian customers), revenue from this tax ranged from a low of $1,167,353 to a high of $1,169,686.[51] In 2001, the year *Atkinson* was decided, the revenue from the hotel occupancy tax dipped to $881,533. In 2002, this tax revenue totaled $948,291, and the total projected revenue for 2003 was $624,000.[52] The amount of revenue lost is not enormous. Although the Cameron Trading Post and Goulding's are significant tourist establishments on the Navajo Nation, they still constitute only two out of fourteen hotels within reservation boundaries, but the lost revenue is also not likely to be recouped. Some Navajo Nation

officials have suggested creative ways to induce a consensual agreement
with the non-Indian hotel owners. For example, Navajo Nation District
Court judge Allan Sloan speculates whether the Navajo Nation's with-
drawal of the provision of police and other emergency services from the
Cameron area will cause Atkinson's to consent to the tax in exchange
for these services being restored.[53] But the Navajo Nation so far has not
and likely will not adopt this somewhat confrontational strategy. Furthermore, whether the owner of Atkinson's, for whom resistance to the Navajo
hotel occupancy tax was presumably ideological (considering that the tax
was passed on to transient, nonrepeating customers and therefore not a
factor in hotel profits),[54] would consent even under such circumstances is
highly speculative. The tax revenue that is lost due to the direct effects of
the *Atkinson* decision is therefore likely lost for good. The Navajo hotel
occupancy tax funds tourism-related services that the Navajo Nation government provides. The loss of this income therefore hurts the nation's
ability to engage further in this relatively nonexploitative form of economic development.[55] Extrapolating from the Navajo experience, we can
see that it is likely that this fairly nonnegotiable outcome has far greater
revenue impacts on other tribes, almost all of whom have far more non-
Indian fee land within their boundaries than does the Navajo Nation.

Another effect from *Atkinson* in the taxing context is the altered
negotiation posture that the Navajo Nation must now take with respect
to consent to rights of way and other limited interests in land across
Navajo Indian country. *Strate v. A-1 Contractors,* a case decided prior to
Atkinson, held that for the purposes of tribal civil jurisdiction, non-Indian
rights of way across tribal trust land are the equivalent of non-Indian fee
land.[56] Therefore, to preserve the authority to tax the use of such rights
of way and similar interests in land, the Navajo Nation Department of
Justice now includes consent-to-taxation clauses in all of its right-of-way
agreements.[57] Although this solution appears to be responsive, there is
some question as to whether it creates barriers to negotiating with non-
Indian businesses that did not exist prior to *Strate* and *Atkinson.*[58]

Atkinson is a significant legal setback for the Navajo Nation. The case
presents a virtually nonnegotiable barrier to the ability to collect income
from non-Indians doing business on non-Indian fee land within reservation boundaries—regardless of whether the Navajo Nation provides the
benefits of governmental services to the area and whether the Navajo

Nation's cultural and aesthetic benefits are the primary reasons for the non-Indian presence. The revenue effects are evident, and, although limited in amount, they are also highly unlikely to be recovered. Moreover, *Atkinson* and related cases that limit tribal civil jurisdiction of all kinds also create a climate of awkward business negotiations with non-Indians and undermine the legitimacy of tribal institutions by inviting an unending flow of challenges to tribal authority.

Conclusion

The Navajo Nation is doing what it has always done: adapting and resisting. The power to tax has been essential and well used, and it will grow in importance as extractive revenue wanes. The Navajo Nation has responded to the challenge of dual taxation in interesting ways, reaching out to the surrounding states and negotiating with them as sovereigns to achieve a mutually beneficial economic solution. With respect to the cases that divest tribes of jurisdiction over non-Indians, there is little the Navajo Nation can do other than to seek redress in Congress, which it is pursuing along with other Indian tribes. For the Navajo, the immediate economic effects are not great, but the long term impacts on the Navajo Nation's ability to negotiate on equal terms with non-Indian businesses will likely suffer. Time will tell.

Time will also tell whether the Supreme Court will continue in this vein of unilateral divestment of tribal powers. If so, it remains to be seen how well Indian nations can continue to adapt and enact sovereignty in the shadow of federal law. One working conclusion from this research is that tribes need enough legal sovereignty to ensure their continued existence as separate nations, capable of fostering growth and development of their endemic cultures. Part of this growth and development, as it turns out, has been to grapple with the federal legal doctrines that restrict sovereignty. But too much intermeddling by the Supreme Court, a body that is unaccountable and extremely difficult to override in Congress, might well be more than even the Navajo Nation, a nation formed by adaptation, can absorb. For the people of the Navajo Nation and for everyone else in the West and beyond, let us hope that the Court leaves room for continued adaptation and resistance, and therefore for the continued enactment of tribal sovereignty. That room to maneuver is crucial to the restoration of a culturally and politically rich western landscape.

The story of the Navajo power to tax probably will not be made into a screenplay anytime soon, nor will it become a book series that captures non-Indian children's imaginations. It is, however, a nuanced story about a group of Americans who have lived in the West for a long time and are hoping to heal their own wounds. By telling this story, perhaps we can heal a wound in the dominant society as well—a wound caused by the violence and colonialism at the core of our western experience, which we dress thinly in narratives imbued with guilt. The new narrative is an action tale about survival and adaptation. It may be less romantic, and in the case of taxation it may even be annoyingly bureaucratic, but it has the upside of being true.

2

Indigenous Languages of the West

A PROGNOSIS FOR THE FUTURE

Andrew Cowell

THE WESTERN UNITED STATES is a place of incredible linguistic diversity. Europe is dominated by a single large language family, Indo-European, which stretches from Iceland well beyond the borders of the continent to Iran, India, and Afghanistan. It has one other small family, which includes Hungarian, Finnish, and Estonian, as well as the Basque language, which has no known relations. Three families total. In contrast, the western half of the United States is the home of up to forty-four different unrelated language families, according to some counts (though recent research is revealing more and more potential distant relationships). There is more linguistic diversity within two hundred miles of Taos, New Mexico, than in the whole European continent. Among these language families are Siouan (Lakota, Crow, Osage), Algonquian (Arapaho, Cheyenne, Blackfeet), Athabaskan (Navajo, the Apache languages), Uto-Aztecan (Comanche, Ute, Shoshone), Caddoan (Pawnee, Wichita, Arikara), and many more. In Colorado alone in the nineteenth century, six language families were represented.[1] For the sake of illustration, imagine Colorado with English spoken in the southeast, Swahili in the eastern-central region, Turkish in the northeast, Chinese in the mountains, Arabic in the southwest, and Tahitian in the northwest. And in terms of diversity, nineteenth-century Colorado didn't remotely approach other areas, in particular the West Coast.

I chose six very different, unrelated languages to assign to Colorado on purpose. I want to stress that all these language families were highly diverse and as different from each other as Chinese is from English in their vocabularies, sound systems, and overall structure in some cases. The western United States and Canada together make up one of the world's great areas of linguistic diversity, both in terms of the overall number of native languages and in terms of the number of different language families. This fact underlines the thousands of years of divergent evolution that produced the rich and complex mosaic of cultures in the West.

But this mosaic is rapidly disintegrating. Two hundred different languages may have been spoken west of the Mississippi at one time.[2] Most are still spoken today, but many are spoken only by a few older people, and by 2100—if we're lucky—only a dozen of these languages may continue to exist. It is even possible that none of them will continue to be used as the everyday language of a Native community. In fact, most linguists argue that not a single native language of North America is unthreatened except for the Greenlandic Inuit language.

People often talk about biological extinction—endangered species of plants and animals, for example—but in comparison to the biological situation, the linguistic one is clearly far worse. We are facing a total meltdown of linguistic diversity. Some might point out that of course the diversity of languages in the West is constantly growing as new immigrants arrive from all over the world, which is clearly true. But all of those immigrant languages have a home somewhere else, too, so the overall world linguistic diversity isn't increased by their relocation in the West. In contrast, the western United States is home for Native Americans, and the loss of literally hundreds of Native American languages will dramatically change overall world linguistic diversity.

My claims may at first seem surprising or even shocking: no native-language communities by the year 2100? We often hear that Navajo has more than one hundred thousand speakers, that there are radio stations in Navajo, that kids come to school in Arizona knowing no English—so how can the Navajo language be endangered? And if 125 of the West's 200 languages are still spoken, how can they all disappear so quickly?

Before continuing, we should stop and reflect on what the disappearance of a language means. A language is not just an abstract system of sounds and speech patterns: it represents one of the most sentimental of all things human. A language includes not just words, but stories, storytelling patterns and structures, jokes, songs, puns, riddles, lullabies, and proverbs—all of which are deeply embedded in the sounds, structure, and vocabulary of the language in question, and none of which can ever really be fully translated into another language.

Stop and think about what it would be like if you and a few of your friends were the last speakers of English on the planet and that everyone around you had switched to speaking Arapaho. Think of the kinds of experiences and affections that are encapsulated in phrases such as "once upon a time" or "we hold these truths to be self-evident" or "Merry Christmas," and then think about what it would be like if people around you hardly ever said those words, and you knew that when you passed away, those words would never, ever be said again by anyone for whom they had the meaning and experience of a whole culture behind them.

Of course, the youngest people would be perfectly happy with the Arapaho equivalents, but the people of your children's generation would always remember what it was like when they were kids to hear you say "rise and shine" as you came into their rooms in the morning rather than the Arapaho equivalent *hiiθooθeyooke'*. When languages disappear, whole ranges of experience, history, and embedded culture go with them.

As the preceding remarks make clear, I'm talking about language disappearance not in terms of a lack of documentation, but in terms of the end of the use of the language as a medium of daily existence. There may always be dictionaries and collections of texts, as we have for Old English or Sumerian, and even lots of audio recordings of a language. But what interests me here is not material sitting in a library or archive, but language used by living people. In this sense, analogies can be drawn to efforts at saving native species in zoos or a single "preserve": "extinction" may be avoided through artificial ponds and holding tanks or through audio tapes and dictionaries, but once species cease to be functional members of an ever-evolving ecosystem or languages cease to be functional vehicles of ever-evolving cultures, the nature of their existence as living entities becomes highly problematic.

Today most Native American languages are not used in this way, at least by the great majority of people in their communities. Many are still known by a few elderly speakers, but are never actually used in daily conversation. There are maybe twenty-five fluent speakers of Hupa left in California, twelve of Kootenai in Montana, twelve of Makah in Washington, six of Iowa in Oklahoma, three of Wintu in California, three of Plains Apache, one of Quinault in Washington, and one of Klamath.[3] Of course, there may be others who can understand these languages somewhat or who can say a few words or sentences. But anyone who has taken French, Spanish, or German for a few years in high school or college will realize the vast difference between knowing a language in that way and growing up with it since birth. Once these fluent people die, the language largely ceases to exist except in archival records and memories. Della Prince, the last speaker of Wiyot, passed away in 1962. Martha Johnson, the last speaker of Coos in Oregon, passed away in 1972. Truman Daily, the last Otoe speaker, died in 1996.[4]

So even if 125 Native American languages are in existence today, perhaps only 75 are in use in their communities. But even in these cases, the use may be fairly restricted. Last year I was eating dinner with an Arapaho family up on the Wind River Reservation in Wyoming, and I experienced a microcosm of what Native American language communities are like around the country. The older man with whom I worked decided on this particular evening that he was not going to use any English. He went on all night in Arapaho: I listened very intently, but inevitably missed things. Nevertheless, I tried to keep up my end of the conversation in Arapaho and got by OK, if awkwardly. In contrast, his own children, in their thirties and forties, were able to understand everything he was saying—certainly better than I could—but none of them uttered more than a couple of words of Arapaho during the meal. They had grown up hearing the language, but never learned to speak it, either because they refused, knowing that their parents could also understand English, or because the parents used English with them and Arapaho only among themselves and with the older generation. At least two of the children were married to Sioux or Cheyenne people, who of course understood nothing. The grandchildren who were present basically ignored the conversation because they could understand none of it. Ironically, they did at times use a few words of Arapaho, which they had learned at school, so they actually spoke a little more Arapaho than their parents did, but understood far, far less. The older man's wife spoke Arapaho to him, English to the kids and grandkids, Arapaho when her sister called on the phone, and then English again—she felt uncomfortable speaking a language that most of those present couldn't use.

This situation is more or less what things are like in most Native American communities today where the native language is still used: only those tribal members older than a certain age—thirty, forty, fifty, sixty, depending on the community—can speak the language. Parents usually want what is best for their children, and in many Native Americans' view that was and is the ability to speak English well and get a good job because of it. There is also widespread intermarriage between tribes and with whites, which acts as a further factor in favor of English. Households also tend to be large and multigenerational, so even the older fluent speakers are forced to use English the majority of the time. Language programs exist, but they have rarely produced competent speakers.

If nothing changes, the future is clear for such communities. For the Arapaho, the cut-off age for fluency is nearing sixty. Twenty years from now, only those older than eighty will know the language and will probably use it very rarely: the language will enter the stage that Hupa and Kootenai are in now. Thirty to forty years from now, the last, lone speaker may pass away, and the language will be gone. It's very depressing to me to know that I might be around to see that. I've had lots of chances to have dinner with people like the ones I just described, hear them tell traditional stories in Arapaho, make jokes, sing songs. Even for me, a nonfluent speaker, the language already is connected with many pleasures and fond memories. I wonder what it will be like to have nothing but old audiotapes to listen to.

So even though there may be seventy-five active language communities today, there might be only twenty-five within forty to fifty years. But there are places where kids are still learning the native language at home—the old-fashioned way, so to speak—among them the Navajo, Hopi, Zuni, and Havasupai tribes, Taos Pueblo, and several others.[5] At least here, you would think the future is assured for the language, but the fact is that every year a smaller and smaller percentage of Navajo kids arrive at school knowing only Navajo—from 60 to 70 percent or more twenty to thirty years ago to just 10 to 15 percent today. More and more children are now bilingual in English and Navajo.[6] At the same time, more and more arrive in school knowing only English—from 5 percent a couple of decades ago up to 25 percent now, and rising. All we need to do is extrapolate: essentially all children will soon be bilingual, and an ever-increasing number will be monolingual in English. Even the fluent Navajo speakers will more and more feel the necessity to use English. At a certain point, Navajo may simply seem less useful than English, and virtually all parents will begin raising their children as English speakers. If that happens in, say, 2020, then Navajo will have until only around 2120 to survive and will cease to exist as a community language by 2100 at the latest. All the trends indicate that this scenario may very possibly—or will even be likely to—happen.

So within one hundred years, there may be literally only a handful of living Native American speech communities. Numbers of speakers don't matter—even the more than 100,000 speakers of Navajo. The key question is, Are children being raised with the language? A language with 250 speakers, but where all kids are raised with the language at home, is in many ways more secure than a language with 100,000 speakers in which the children are being raised primarily with English.

The shift from one language to another can occur very rapidly. Until 1945, all Arapaho kids learned the language at home or from grandparents (who were monolingual). Then that stopped—fairly quickly—between 1945 and 1955. The speech community then slowly eroded beginning in 1945, and by 1995—fifty years later—English was overwhelmingly predominant, and most people in the tribe were effectively monolingual in English. It took just ten years for the state of spoken Arapaho to go from most kids knowing the language to almost none being raised with it.

The big question is of course why this shift in language preference on the part of parents occurs. Why would you decide not to use your own native, most comfortable language with your kids? I was told a story once at Wind River Reservation that suggests the reason.

Back in the 1940s and 1950s, at the height of the Western movie craze, people from the reservation would go in large numbers to see cowboys-and-Indians films. I've been told that these Arapaho audiences—especially the kids—would almost always cheer for the cowboys. They would clap when the Indians got shot. The same person told me that when they went down to the river to play cowboys and Indians, none of the Arapaho kids wanted to be the Indians; they all wanted to be the cowboys. I then asked the person telling me all this, "But what language were you kids using when you played cowboys and Indians?" He said "Arapaho, of course—that's all we knew."

That story speaks volumes about the time when language preferences changed on many reservations in the interior West—the 1930s through the 1960s. Even though the kids were using Arapaho, the seeds were already there for change. None of the kids who were engaged in that game of Arapaho-speaking cowboys—which would have been around 1945 in this case—ended up raising children fluent in Arapaho.

This situation goes back to the beginning of the reservation era in the West and more particularly to the time when people actually began to pay attention to the reservations in the 1890s and early 1900s. Government policy at that time was one of acculturation and assimilation of Native Americans to the white community. The prime means of accomplishing these goals was through the education of the young. Government- and church-sponsored boarding schools, set up both on and off the reservations, had one essential task: to take the "Indian" out of the "red man." Key means of doing so were the active encouragement of English and the very active suppression of native languages. Many people alive today have told me stories about the treatment they received for speaking Arapaho at school. One particularly poignant story I heard was about a young boy who was sitting in the classroom one day. The door was slightly ajar, and the wind was blowing hard. As he sat there, he listened to the wind whistling and murmuring through the crack in the door. The Arapaho believe that songs come to a person in dreams, visions, and inspirations. A song started to come to this boy in the shifting sounds of the wind, and he was mesmerized. He started arranging the sounds and words in his head. He got so engaged that he started to hum some words in Arapaho. And then WHACK—the nun at the school smacked a ruler down on his hand without warning and began berating him for speaking Arapaho.

More generally, the government acted in every way it could to diminish the authority of native-language-speaking elders. Traditional religion was discouraged or banned. Traditional governance was replaced by U.S.-inspired models.[7] The Bureau of Indian Affairs (BIA) took over more and more roles for the tribe. In all cases, the traditional authority of the elders was diminished and that of educated, English-speaking children was increased—the latter were now the ones with the jobs, the money, the positions on the Tribal Council, the links to the BIA, and the leadership roles on the local mission advisory boards. In more and more contexts, knowing English was worth more than knowing the native language. This policy ultimately went so far as to advocate not just the breakup of communal land ownership, but the termination of "tribes" as such—and thus the destruction over both time and space of the Native American community institutions that sustained the native languages.[8]

Ironically, many or even most individuals of many tribes successfully resisted all of this pressure for many years—up through the end of World War II in the Arapaho case, for example. For fifty years, despite all the measures used, they kept raising their children with Arapaho. But, of course, this outside assault certainly weakened the cohesiveness and strength of a specifically Arapaho identity—in particular as embodied in the language. If we can turn to the title of this volume, *Remedies for a New West,* and to the metaphor of sickness and health it implies, then we might say that the Arapaho language and culture's immune system was severely weakened by these assaults and that the "body" of the Arapaho, collectively, had a very reduced resistance to further attacks or germs.

Then came the period I have already mentioned, 1945 to 1955: Arapaho soldiers came back from World War II knowing English well, having seen the world, having made money, having discovered opportunities. At the same time, access to—or infection by, if you wish—outside, English culture became increasingly pervasive. The last of the pre-reservation, traditional elders passed away at this time (the last chief died in 1938), and radio, movies, and especially television began to make more and more inroads. The sense I get from talking to people is that the negative perspective inculcated regarding Arapaho was now complemented by the Arapaho's own suddenly increased awareness of the potential positive attributes of English. English was no longer just the language of nuns who beat you and of BIA representatives who tried to ban the Sun Dance, but of an exciting world beyond the reservation that promised new hope for the future. So virtually en masse the Arapaho decided to switch to English as the language in which their children would be raised. This switch had certainly already been occurring slowly prior to this time, but in ten years the balance tipped radically.[9]

We might say that the immune system collapsed. At the time, however, that is not at all how many Arapaho people saw things. In fact, the parents who decided to raise their kids as English speakers saw things from exactly the opposite perspective. They were essentially "healing" what ailed them. They had literally taken a physical beating because of their use of Arapaho, and they had taken a mental and spiritual beating as well. Getting rid of Arapaho was not the final illness—as we might be tempted to diagnose the situation today—but rather for them was the medicine to make things better.

Of course, the "illness" was inflicted from outside, and the medicine was in large part forced down Native Americans' throats throughout the West. People did not just decide for no reason to abandon a key part of their cultural identity—they were forced to do so. To a significant extent, the Arapaho wanted to stop the beatings, so to speak—to spare their own children the rod of authority that punished Arapaho speech. But it is important to recognize that many Native Americans at the time—and many still today—did not see themselves as simply the helpless victims of this outside assault. Indeed, as I said, they resisted it for decades in many cases, despite all that was done to them. When the shift to English occurred, they saw themselves as making an active, positive choice for their children in response not just to the localized outside pressures they had endured on the reservation for fifty or seventy years, but to the more generalized attractiveness of English in the larger world.

From 1945 to 1975 on the Wind River Reservation—and generally throughout much of the interior West—this state of affairs continued to prevail. Children were raised with English, and it was felt that they would or could always pick up the native language later if they wanted. Although this never happened, there were still plenty of native-language speakers. The grandparents were still around as well, and Arapaho and other native languages continued to be a vital part of the lives of their communities. The illusion persisted that things were somehow OK.

Two things happened to shatter this illusion. First, there were the social movements of the 1960s and 1970s and the rise of native awareness and pride in native identity. Second, partly in response to the increased focus on native identity, many tribes began to realize for the first time that not only could the children not speak the native language, but that even those of middle age could no longer do so. Around 1977, the Arapaho first recognized this situation and decided to start a language-retention effort. They invited a linguist who had worked on the reservation in the early 1950s to come back and produce a standardized writing system, which did not exist at that time.[10] They began trying to teach the language in the school system, and when they encountered resistance from the local white community, they went ahead and founded their own school district on the reservation where they could emphasize language and culture classes. They began producing curricular materials and working hard to document the language through video- and audiotaping. They set up two cultural resource centers on the reservation, where all curricular and documentation materials could be housed, and established a tribal language and culture commission, with paid positions.

The Arapaho response to language loss is typical of that of many tribes. Virtually all of these programs focused on six key areas. First, tribal resolutions were passed, and the federal government was convinced in 1990 to enact the Native American Language Act[11] in order to set up a legal basis and legitimacy for language-retention efforts and the mechanisms for funding them. Second, documentation of the languages was encouraged, both in the form of recording by local people and in collaboration with academic linguists, who were increasingly asked to contribute applied, useful knowledge to the tribe's own language programs rather than simply publishing theoretical studies in professional journals. Third, the languages were to be taught in the schools. Fourth, literacy was seen as a key component of the school-based language programs. Fifth, immersion schools—in which the only language used would be the native one—were begun or at least attempted, especially for the preschool years. And sixth, a huge bureaucratic infrastructure of associations, conferences, and institutions evolved to coordinate all of these efforts among the various tribes and to share knowledge and information.[12] Just as bloodletting, which once seemed like such a good idea, was abandoned by more modern medicine, the "cure," letting go of native languages, was now rediagnosed as a factor that exacerbated the "disease," loss of culture. The six measures just mentioned were the new "cure" that government, the tribes, and linguists proposed for what was now seen as the growing problem of language loss. New disease, new cure.

Unfortunately, as with many promising new cures, this one turned out to be largely a disappointment and even a dismal failure. Today, the Northern Arapaho tribe has yet to produce a single competent speaker of the language using the methods in question, even after more than twenty-five years of efforts. This experience is not radically different from that of other tribes. Indeed, it differs only in that the Arapaho have put more effort into the attempt than have many others.

This is not to say that there have not been some scattered successes or that at least some of the six proposed measures cannot work, at least in theory, and a number of hopeful signs can be seen in some areas.[13] The Blackfeet tribe has a successful, though small, K–8 immersion school program. The Mohawk (back east) also have a successful immersion program. Many tribes look to the model of Hawaii, where since the 1970s Native

Hawaiians have set up immersion preschools, multiple K–12 immersion schools, as well as bachelor's and master's programs at the University of Hawaii not only focusing on Hawaiian language and culture, but also conducted in Hawaiian.[14] Thousands of children are involved in these programs, and many fluent and even native speakers are being produced, as some Hawaiians have begun to go back to raising their children using Hawaiian as the first language in the home. The Hawaiian program has largely followed the six steps proposed for Native American language-retention programs, so there is no reason that they cannot succeed. In addition, a seventh technique has been developed, especially in California. The so-called master-apprentice programs pair a young person of a tribe with an older native speaker, and the two agree to live or at least to spend several hours a day together, using only the native language, with financial and other support from linguists and the tribe. These programs have produced, on an individualized basis, several fluent or near-fluent speakers of a number of near-extinct California languages.[15]

So why the failures for the most part? First, and most important, it is very difficult to become a fluent speaker of a native language without being "immersed" in situations where that language is the primary one. Whether that immersion occurs at home or in a school setting is less important than that it occur. At the University of Colorado, students who study French or Italian for several years at a very advanced level, with good teachers and good curriculum, still do not normally attain full fluency. Those who go abroad for a semester or a year, however, show much greater ability in the language. Even then, however, fluency remains elusive and rare—despite the facts that there is a long tradition of teaching these languages and that their vocabularies and structures are very similar to English, relatively speaking.

In contrast, there is little or no tradition of training teachers to teach Native American languages. Even if there were, little immediate benefit may be gained because most teachers are of necessity older individuals, long out of school, and without any formal training in educational techniques. Their primary qualification is that they are native speakers of their language. Nor is there much curriculum to use or anywhere else to go to find an immersion-like setting. And finally, Native American languages are for English speakers virtually without exception much more difficult to learn than French or Italian—perhaps five times more difficult. As a result, it is extremely difficult in the real world for language education in school to produce fluent or even competent speakers of Native American languages. Learning a language at home is far and away the easiest, cheapest, and most effective method, just as preserving native ecosystems is far easier than reconstructing them artificially, as Sharon Collinge's chapter shows, but the former option no longer exists for most tribes. Thus, immersion schools and master-apprentice programs are the second option, at least until new fluent speakers can be produced to become parents in their turn. The list of successes, especially the Hawaiian one, clearly shows that immersion methods hold the only real promise.

But immersion programs are expensive to run, hard to train people for, hard to produce curriculum for, hard to get going in the face of state educational bureaucracies, and hard to sustain over long periods of time.[16] To be fully effective, they also must begin quite early, at the age of two or three, and continue for many years, ideally to the age of sixteen. They involve significant burdens on parents because in the best examples, such as the Hawaiian one, the parents also agree to take classes in the language and to use it at home. Unfortunately, the reality of most tribal situations is that neither the money nor the expertise nor the socioeconomic setting is available to produce effective immersion programs, especially ones that would produce enough young speakers to foster an actual living language community. Although small signs of progress are visible—such as increasing amounts of money being made available for language programs on some reservations due to the construction of casinos—it remains difficult to be highly optimistic.

At this point, my prognosis should be fairly clear. First, if we want to preserve Native American languages as living vehicles of people's lives and cultures, we should do everything we can to support communities where children are still learning the language at home. Unfortunately, the reality is that such situations continue to decline. Second, immersion-type programs will be necessary to produce fluent speakers who will use the language on a regular basis. Again, unfortunately, such programs rarely have managed sustained success, though there are some hopeful signs of change.[17] Thus, based on current trends and conditions, I cannot honestly offer a very good prognosis for the future, with only a few individual tribal exceptions, though I very much hope I will turn out to have been a pessimist.

Indeed, I would say that from what I know, language-retention, revitalization, and preservation projects are almost universally under-supported and underfunded. That fact, I think, points to an underlying ambivalence about native languages and their survival in general. I would like to explore that ambivalence here in the closing portion of this chapter.

I think we can say with a fair amount of accuracy that most people support preserving native languages, just as they support habitat restoration or limiting acid drainage from mines. But the trouble starts when one asks both how to do what everyone agrees on and how much to spend on it. In other words, it's a question of priorities.

When we look at efforts to retain native languages, we quickly see that this goal is not as high a priority as some people might suggest. Let's start with my home, Academia. As much as linguists lament the loss of native languages,[18] as sources of very interesting data, for example, surprisingly few of them are working on these languages. And more important, those who are working on them tend to shy away from any kind of applied linguistics such as writing curriculum, doing teacher training, or examining ways to improve the success of retention efforts. This tendency isn't universally true (Dr. Steven Greymorning of the University of Montana has focused his efforts with the Arapaho on just this kind of applied work), but academia nevertheless has a strong bias toward theoretical research and away from applied knowledge—in the salary and promotion process, in the way grants are rewarded, and in who gets the plum jobs. In a given year, the number of articles published by linguists on English—or using English as the primary example for their theories—almost certainly exceeds the number on Native American languages combined.

Much the same can be said of the federal government. If you look at how much money is spent on saving endangered species (efforts that are also underfunded despite the large funds spent), the amount is clearly greater than the money spent to document endangered languages.[19]

If we turn to local communities and state educational organizations, there is also a clear ambivalence or even—to be honest—hostility on the part of non-Natives toward language-retention efforts. The three Rs are virtually always given precedence, and Arapaho classes are squeezed into fifteen minutes a day sometimes or often just fifteen minutes a week. Even the world's best teacher can't do much with that.

Many of the problems faced by Native educators on reservations, by the way, parallel those that Sarah Krakoff discusses in relation to political sovereignty (chapter 1). Both federal and local laws and policies (the No Child Left Behind Act) constantly erode tribes' sovereignty. One of the great ironies of the West, in fact, is the complex tension created by individuals and groups who have come to the West seeking their own realm of autonomy (homesteaders, ranchers, Mormons, for example), free from excess federal involvement, but who desire to impose strict controls and regulations on others and even invoke federal aid, money, laws, and policies to help them do so. Where Native American rights are concerned, the rhetoric of freedom so dear to many rural westerners gives way to the rhetoric of power and strong federal "protection" for (Euro-American) "rights." As John-Michael Rivera indicates in his chapter, the American public ignores the fact that imperialist and racial discourses are behind the U.S. image of inclusion and democratic egalitarianism (see also the quote from Francisco P. Ramirez in that chapter). Appeals to power in local western politics are often framed as appeals to "universality" and "egalitarianism," but such rhetoric is often both a form of amnesia about the past and an attempt to erase the results of that past (especially in relation to Native Americans) in the present. In this context, native languages are a living reminder of both History and deep, fundamental Difference.

Of course, new western historians have shown how these same frontier individualists were in fact always linked to and dependent on federal power and subsidy, as well as on international markets and finance, and that their rhetoric typically masks their own history as well. Now, in yet a further irony, many Native communities are increasingly strongly tied to the federal educational and welfare bureaucracies, especially financially, even as they fight federal laws and policies concerning language and education. Thus, in several ways, Native parents and Native communities reveal the same ironies and ambivalence one finds elsewhere in the West. Furthermore, many parents continue to fear that working on the native language will put their child behind in English. Many tribes lament language loss, but then point to 50 percent or even 75 percent unemployment and ask where they should spend their limited resources. In the face of housing shortages, poor medical care, rampant substance abuse, malnutrition, and high suicide and death rates, just how important are Arapaho language classes?

But an even bigger question can be posed, I think—one that is different from the acid drainage or habitat-restoration issues. In these two cases, everyone would agree in principle that it would be nice to fix the problems, but that the relative priorities matter. Of course, even when health and even life may be at stake (as Joseph Ryan's chapter underlines), there can be profound hesitation and ambivalence on the community's part. Unlike in these two cases, however, there is far from universal agreement that language preservation is itself a good thing, even in principal. The opportunity for ambivalence is thus all the greater.

Again, if we look to linguists, there are certainly many who think that language-preservation efforts are potentially counterproductive and that language shift and language loss are a universal, natural phenomena.[20] People use the language that suits their needs. Why should we try to counteract that?

Likewise, among the general public, many question the wisdom of retaining linguistic diversity. Although ballot initiatives against bilingual education in many western states, such as California, Arizona, and Colorado, primarily target immigrant languages, they have negative impacts on native languages as well. The Navajo raised this point repeatedly in Arizona, but they were ignored, and the measure passed.[21]

Finally, however, we need to return to the Native communities. "We"—by which I mean the largely Euro-American readers of this book and workers in government and academia—can't save any native languages. Only the communities themselves can do that, though once they decide to try and do so, we can certainly offer help. And that decision generates a great deal of ambivalence among many people who question not just the priorities, but the wisdom of even trying.

A native language can be a very divisive issue. Elders feel devalued when no one seems to care about their language anymore. Young people resent elders' implication that they're not "real Indians" if they don't speak their language, but they also feel a sense of inadequacy. The middle generation resents the elders for not passing the language on to them and feels inadequate as their own children come home from school with questions about the language that they can't answer. Elders resent their children when the children blame them for not passing on the language because they remember when those same children refused to speak the language, saying it wasn't "cool." They also know they did what they thought was right at the time. Tribal councils and Native educators get tired of fighting, tired of trying, and tired of failing.

Though it's often hard to get anyone to say it publicly, at least one segment of some Native communities simply wishes the language issue would go away and believes it causes more trouble than it's worth. I have heard leaders say, "These are modern times now, that's the past." Just as certain people in the larger world believe (wrongly in my opinion) that once the whole world or the whole country switches to English, many forms of cultural divisiveness will disappear, there is a silent minority—or even a majority on some reservations—who certainly regret the passing of elders and older ways, but who also see language preservation as a lost cause and an impediment to tribal progress. Most tribal councils' public rhetoric remains strongly pro–native language. The votes and funding decisions, however, suggest that beneath that rhetoric lies a much more complicated situation. A number of fundamentalist Christian Native American church groups also actively associate the native language with Native religious traditions, which they see as anathema.

In sum, I think that one can still reasonably ask—and some Native Americans do still ask—whether trying to preserve native languages is even a correct thing to do in principle. The people holding this view may be marginalized or considered not to be "real" Indians by either whites or Native traditionalist groups, but they certainly exist. Some of them are in fact the oldest, best native-language speakers themselves. Thus, there remains a debate about what the "disease" and what the "cure" really are in this case.

Faced with such a situation, what should "we"—and again I mean the largely non-Native audience—do? Rather than needlessly "wallowing in self-pity" (to steal a phrase from Patty Limerick), we can do several things. First, I believe that most Native people, as well as most people in general, are in favor of language-preservation efforts in principle. Those who are not always have the opportunity to opt out: outside of certain parts of the Southwest, it is a rare reservation indeed where one feels obliged to use the native language or is "oppressed" by that language. As things now stand, attempting to acquire the native language is becoming increasingly a choice in many places—that is, where it is still even possible. I think people should be given that choice for as long as possible.

Second, I believe that any documentation of the languages is worthwhile. At the least, certain songs, prayers, and key vocabulary items can be preserved. Native languages can continue to have a life in certain ceremonial contexts, for example, much like Latin in the Catholic Mass. Brenda M. Romero's chapter on the *matachines* reveals how cultural rituals and objects can undergo vast changes over time while constantly maintaining a vital function in the creation of community identity, and even small elements of linguistic performance such as songs or prayers can fulfill similar roles. Moreover, her contribution shows how the availability of these forms can be crucial for reconstructing identities over time. John-Michael Rivera's chapter likewise points to the importance of archives not just as places for preserving the past, but as resources available for the construction of alternative futures.

Schools might hope to produce competent readers of the languages and thus provide access for future generations to the large and growing amount of archival material. Provided documentation is especially good, it is even possible that someday in the future, tribes that have lost their languages entirely but whose socioeconomic conditions have changed for the better might try to revive the language the way Israel revived Hebrew. Such efforts are already tentatively under way among several groups—the Miami, the Wampanoag, the Wiyot, and the Mohegan. The increasing benefits of money from casino gambling make this option more and more a possibility in some areas. Again, we can help give the people of the future a choice. To fail to document now is to make that choice for them in the negative.

Third, efforts to foster retention of living native-speech communities still seem worthwhile to me, despite the odds. From a very subjective perspective, it seems to me that such efforts sometimes play the role of a kind of an extended funeral or "mourning" process, which allows people to come to terms with what is being lost or will be lost, to appreciate it and save as much as possible, and to better face the necessity of moving forward. In this sense, the effort itself, no matter what the result, might be seen as a healing process within Native communities. Likewise, to the extent that non-Natives are involved in these efforts, the opportunities for cross-cultural encounter, understanding, and communication are enormous. This cooperation, too, can be seen as a form of healing process. The educator or linguist or anthropologist of today, for example, fills the place of the missionary or Indian agent of the previous two centuries, in a position both radically different but also uncomfortably similar to that of his or her predecessors.

In the best of circumstances, one hopes that such an effort will not be one of mourning, but of recovery or even of retention in some cases. A few communities may be lucky enough never to need outside help; some do not want it; others welcome it: the diversity in this regard mirrors the diversity of Native communities generally. As someone who has donated many hours and a great deal of money to native-language preservation efforts and who plans to continue doing so, I believe that in a large and complex world, a diversity of cultural viewpoints and opinions is an asset to everyone as we confront the future. Although language and culture are not the same thing, the two are nevertheless intimately bound up as vehicles of diversity. But beyond this notion of the general utility of diversity (which appeals to "us" more than to many Native Americans perhaps, who resent being seen as just a potential last-ditch place for industrial culture to turn to when in need of rescuing), there is the general humanistic need to offer people choices about their own futures. Given the number of such choices that Euro-American society took away from the Native Americans in the past—and continues to take away in the present in some instances—I think we should at least try to do our part to enable them to have the maximum range of choices about the future of their own languages. To enable choice is to support life; a complete lack of choice is most powerfully represented by death.

Finally, we must turn to the idea of an ecosystem. As Hannah Gosnell notes, species are parts of ecosystems, and it is ecosystems that sustain species. In the same sense, a language is part of a cultural system, and it is the cultural system that sustains, makes use of, and gives life to a language. Linguists have too often tried to "save languages" without recognizing that language loss is typically a symptom of cultural change—just as species extinction is typically a symptom of ecosystem decline. If a language is linked to a cultural identity that also offers strong hopes for the future, good economic prospects, and a positive set of social roles where individuals can achieve meaning and fulfillment, that language will likely continue to be spoken, and that cultural identity will likely continue to be embraced. Although many Native Americans are fighting hard to ensure that this is the case for their families, communities, and cultures, the truth is that for many of the younger members of these communities, the attractions of the indigenous language and the identity attached to it are not sufficient to overcome the enticements apparently offered by an English-speaking identity, so they choose either not to pass the language on to their children or not to use it themselves. Probably the best ways to preserve native languages—or at least to enable true choices for the communities in question regarding whether they want to preserve these languages—are to end ethnic and economic discrimination against Native communities and to empower the people within those communities both economically and socially. Language loss and the obstacles to language retention seen in this chapter are not really fundamentally "illnesses," but rather symptoms of social and cultural oppression whose effects are far more pervasive than just language loss. "Treating" language loss independently of these sociocultural sicknesses will always be, at best, a limited form of healing.

3

"Oh Give Me Land, Lots of Land"

Allan Wallis and Gene Bressler

SUBURBIA! It is a form of urban growth and development that many people love and a form that many people love to hate. At its best, suburbia epitomizes our hopes for attaining—that is, living in—the idealized residential landscape with its promise of clean air, wide-open spaces, great schools, wide and easy-to-drive roads, cul-de-sacs, a car-oriented way of life, and a host of new homes with new appliances and new everything.[1] Suburbanites seek what one might call the perception of everything that's big, new, and clean . . . and of course affordable. Millions of Americans want this suburban lifestyle and will work hard to obtain it. Moreover, as countries around the world become more affluent, they, too, are becoming more suburbanized. A suburban home is the ultimate expression of American consumerism.[2] The bottom line is that people like it. We like it a lot.

So why are so many of us critical of suburbia? Well, in its weaker form, suburbia epitomizes perceptions of urban growth seemingly out of control. It's a symbol of sprawl and profligate resource consumption, particularly of water. Even worse, many believe contemporary suburbia is the root cause of congested freeways, big-box development, and the image of living in an anonymous "Anywhere, USA." Some would argue that the arduous process of finding one's way home through a morass of winding streets and dead end cul-de-sacs amidst a sea of monotonous-looking suburban homes requires the use of a geographical positioning system. It is no wonder that sales of these location devices for our cars have rocketed in the past few years.

The challenge for designers and planners who would like to offer an alternative is not to convince consumers that suburbia is the evil empire incarnate, but to offer design solutions that retain all of the desirable elements of suburbia, but in forms that are sustainable: more compact, more resource efficient, and more affordable over the lifetime of the investment and not just in terms of "getting in the door." This design

FIGURE 3.1. The Challenging Suburbia Studio at the University of Colorado brought students, faculty, and practitioners together to explore alternatives to suburban subdivisions of the "expeditious landscape."

challenge is especially significant in the Rocky Mountain West, where open space is perceptibly plentiful, but the land is often fragile, and where access to water in most places is increasingly more challenging.

A recent issue of *Urban Land,* the magazine of the Urban Land Institute, was devoted to the challenge of developing land in the American West. Con Howe, director of the institute's Center for Balanced Development in the West, states the challenge succinctly: "[The] clash of images between the West's vast natural landscape and its built environment is at the heart of the issue of balancing development in the region. How can the West accommodate demographic and economic growth while preserving its special land resources?"[3]

In this chapter, we examine two founding images about western lands—one promoting unbridled development, the other cautioning for thoughtful conservation. After briefly characterizing the rapid rate of development occurring within the region, we focus on the ubiquitous suburban subdivision design as a scale at which it is easiest and perhaps most appropriate to understand how the myths and realities of western lands collide. We then trace the development of subdivision design as it was transplanted from the Northeast and industrial Midwest to the Rocky Mountain West. We argue that this transplantation has failed and continues to fail to adjust adequately for the unique characteristics of western lands and consequently has resulted in scarring the landscape. The region needs alternative development paradigms that can simultaneously heal the West while accommodating a population that is expected to double within the next thirty to forty years. We suggest working with a combination of market mechanisms and regulatory reforms that strategically and thoughtfully direct growth in patterns that are more environmentally, socially, and economically sustainable.

Founding Images of the Region

In the period following the Civil War, as the Rocky Mountain West was being settled and transformed from territories into states, two rival images of the region informed its development. As Wallace Stegner recounts in *Beyond the Hundredth Meridian,* one of these images was offered up by William Gilpin, a highly sought after advisor on matters regarding the western territories.[4] Gilpin's book *The Central Gold Region,* published in 1860, boasted of the fertility of western soils and the land's unlimited potential for agriculture productivity supported by abundant waters from mountain streams.[5] The undeniable value of Gilpin's fanciful imagery was that it helped to foment land development, which in turn fueled the new western states' economies and established the *illusion* that settlement in the Rocky Mountain West could proceed on the same basis as it had in the East and the Midwest.

Major John Wesley Powell, twenty years Gilpin's junior, held a diametrically opposite view of the western region's landscape capacities. He observed that the Rocky Mountain West was generally arid, its soils poor, and much of it suitable for agriculture only with the aid of careful irrigation and strict conservation. Rather than inviting exploitation, Powell's description cautioned for careful stewardship of the landscape.

Development of the West over the past century and a half provides ample evidence that Powell's prescription for the future development of the region should have been supported rather than Gilpin's. But the lure of Gilpin's image of "a region of limitless plenty" is evidently still alive and well, as is evident in the development of the miniaturized version of the pioneer homestead—the suburban subdivision and the exurban ranchette popping up on previously undeveloped hillsides, pastures, and prairies.

One Person's Eden Is Another Person's Sprawl

The consequence of individual households' seeking the collective suburban dream was what many critics label *sprawl*. "Sprawl is spread-out development that consumes significant amounts of natural and man-made resources, including land and public works infrastructure of various sorts."[6] One chief argument against sprawl is that it does not pay its own way.[7] By some estimates, the cost of providing public infrastructure and services to sprawl development is twice the amount of the new taxes they generate, leaving other taxpayers, current and future, to cover the difference.[8]

With the growth of the environmental movement, the impacts of losing open space as well as agricultural and fragile lands were added to the cost equation, as evident in the 1974 analysis *Cost of Sprawl* conducted by the Real Estate Research Corporation for the President's Council on Environmental Quality. This report, updated in 2002, argues that "sprawl provides lower fiscal benefits than compact development," and that "overall housing costs are greater under sprawl development." The study acknowledged, however, that sprawl developments also provide less-expensive suburban housing at the peripheries of urban regions and that it can help reduce congestion by allocating more trips *between suburbs* rather than *between suburbs and central cities*. Because sprawl provides us with a safe and largely controlled environment, the report suggests, it "also allows households to choose a variety of community settings in which primarily single-family housing is available and local governments are small and accessible. Americans are generally satisfied with this choice."[9]

The southern and western census regions of the United States have experienced the most rapid rates of growth in the country over the past four decades, most of it accommodated in low-density suburban subdivisions. The relatively low cost of land, in part reflecting low agricultural land values, has served to encourage sprawl-type development. In the period from 1960 to 2000, the number of housing units in the South and the West increased by 133 percent, whereas housing in the Northeast and the Midwest increased by only 57 percent. Projected population growth to 2025 is expected to continue favoring the southern and western regions. Half of the eight states in the Rocky Mountain West rank among the top twenty states in terms of projected increases in households and employment (Arizona ranks fourth; Colorado, ninth; Nevada, fifteenth; and Utah, nineteenth).[10] Similarly, four metropolitan areas in the Rocky Mountain West rank among the top twenty in terms of growth by 2025 (Phoenix-Mesa, ranked sixth; Denver-Boulder-Greeley, tenth; Las Vegas, fourteenth; and Salt Lake–Ogden, twentieth).[11]

With respect to projected sprawl by 2025, four of the most rapidly growing Rocky Mountain West states rank among the top twenty (Arizona, ranked second; Nevada, sixth; and Colorado, seventh). Utah, which ranked nineteenth in projected growth, is expected to rank only thirty-first in projected sprawl.[12] Of the four metropolitan areas in Rocky Mountain West that are projected to rank among the top twenty in terms of growth by 2025, three ranked among the top ten in terms of projected sprawl (Phoenix-Mesa, ranked first; Denver-Boulder-Greeley, fifth; and Las Vegas, sixth).[13] Again, only the Salt Lake–Ogden region is expected to achieve a more compact form of development while experiencing record growth.

Demand for Water

The demand for water is the most significant condition of suburban sprawl that raises strong sustainability challenges in the West, especially the Rocky Mountain West. Most population concentrations have developed in areas that are naturally semiarid. These areas have been made habitable by engineering the transfer of water over great distances and challenging landscapes by means of aqueducts, reservoirs, and pumping stations. As increases in demand for water parallel increases in population, competition for water rights have grown fierce. The Rocky Mountain western states experiencing record growth have also experienced record water consumption. In recent years, however, they have also experienced record droughts as well as devastating and costly forest fires.

All of the rapidly growing Rocky Mountain states and California are party to the 1922 Colorado River Compact. California is the single largest water consumer. It has long benefited from the fact that the other states in the compact have not needed their full allocation. By 1990, however, water demand in Arizona and Nevada for the first time required their total lower-basin allocation.

According to a recent report,[14] in rapidly growing southern Nevada the existing Colorado River water allocation along with ground water will meet that region's needs only until 2015. In Arizona and elsewhere, urban users have been turning to agricultural users to buy their water rights. Under Governor Bruce Babbitt, Arizona crafted a water basin agreement for the Valley of the Sun that basically created a market mechanism for the trading of water within the basin. It also prohibited transfers outside of the basin. Ironically, the discipline that such a market mechanism might have imposed was undermined by the opening of the federally constructed Central Arizona Project (CAP). The CAP channels additional Colorado River water to the valley, making it possible for wasteful patterns of consumption to continue unabated.

The growing competition for the region's major source of surface water is clearly being driven by the need to sustain population growth while maintaining agriculture. Some water districts along Colorado's thirsty Front Range have investigated purchasing agricultural water from the San Luis Valley in south central Colorado, which is one of the economically poorer parts of the state. The impacts on area agriculture are unknown, but the only water to be transferred would presumably be surplus.

Other communities, such as rapidly growing Parker, Colorado (between Denver and Colorado Springs), are investing in the construction of new storage-capacity reservoirs that retain runoff from the rainy season. Although this approach avoids the legal issues associated with transbasin transfers (such as the one proposed for the San Luis Valley), the costs of constructing such projects are typically passed on to new home buyers in the price of the house. Although the drilling of wells in more rural areas that lie outside a water district has long been an alternative practice, in Colorado a well must now have a one-hundred-year proven reserve, a standard that is becoming more difficult to achieve as water tables are drawn down.

Apart from the issues of trading water between agricultural and urban users, environmental impacts have to be considered, but are often placed last in the pecking order of priorities for water use. Because such large portions of western states are federally owned, any move to protect wildlife habitat affects the availability of water to support urban growth. A major new challenge coming largely from western federal lands concerns increased energy development. Part of that development includes the use of new rock-fracturing techniques that enables natural gas to be drawn from wells once considered almost depleted. Tens of thousands of new gas wells are now springing up. The water released through this new process unfortunately contains contaminants pumped into the wells to help release their gas. These chemicals are turning up in domestic water supplies in rural areas.

The Suburban Subdivision Then and Now

Although sprawl is most obvious when reviewed at a regional scale, it is best to look at specific practices and standards applied to the development of suburban subdivisions in order to understand the source, character, and appeal of sprawl. Sprawl advances not one house at a time, but by whole communities at a time. If the development of the suburban subdivision can be reformed to make it more sustainable, then the region as a whole might benefit. By *sustainable,* we mean that one generation avoids consuming so much of the environmental resources of a place that the succeeding generation is left worse off.[15] Achieving more sustainable suburbanization requires modification of the prevailing approach to development largely transplanted from older regions where there were fundamentally different environmental conditions. It also requires reform of land-use regulations and taxation laws that have perpetuated this dominant approach.

The pattern of suburban development in western cities following World War II lagged behind practices in the more industrialized urban regions of the East.[16] In the East, the magnitude of demand could justify the building of whole new communities, such as Levittown, New York, that leapfrogged over farm land and created urban-density developments surrounded by meadows and cultivated fields.[17] In the West, where demand was initially lower, postwar subdivisions were more modest in scale. They continued to be developed at the edges of the already developed urban areas, reflecting the fact that jobs were still largely concentrated in the central cities. This contiguity also reflected the fact that the central cities were often the providers of water resources to the new subdivisions. In Denver, for example, accessing city water meant following subdivision design requirements imposed by the municipal utility, which also included extending the existing street grid.

Population in the Sunbelt began increasing rapidly in the 1960s, but really took off in the 1970s. Suburban developments spread apace with new design standards. The overall size of subdivision developments increased. Effort to extend established street grids was abandoned as new subdivisions expeditiously were designed with internal curvilinear and cul de-sac street systems engineered to maximize the yield of buildable lot areas. Lot and house sizes increased, bringing densities down but increasing the linear miles of roads as well as water, sewer, and electric lines. Hence, the distance to schools, shopping, and services increased, ushering in a more automobile-dependent lifestyle.

In the 1970s, many municipal officials wondered how to accommodate the future residential growth expected to occur in or on the outskirts of their jurisdictions. Their planning departments, often working with outside advisors who sometimes included local real-estate developers, established comprehensive land-use plans. Although some eastern states required such plans from their municipalities, states in the Rocky Mountain West, where strong home-rule traditions prevail, did not. In most states throughout the United States, county comprehensive plans are not required, so developers can build in unincorporated areas and then request annexation into a nearby municipality if it can supply needed services.

Private developers created the master planned community (MPC) as a counterpart or alternative to municipal comprehensive plans. These communities typically embodied several suburban subdivisions, each of which could be built out by a separate developer or by individual home builders. Having multiple subdevelopers and builders not only spread financial risks and commitments, but also enabled the conception and marketing of more diverse house styles, floor plans, lot sizes, and price ranges.[18]

Parcels designated for commercial uses typically were developed by yet other companies that specialized in retail real estate. MPCs, depending on the municipality in which they were being developed, also included varying levels of public amenities such as parks, recreation centers, golf courses, schools, libraries, commercial areas, and even small office parks. They could be annexed by a municipality or incorporated as their own government. More often they provided government-like services in a privatized form, which were eventually turned over to the governance by homeowner associations.

MPCs cemented the automobile-dependent lifestyle. A mother with stroller, for example, could no longer easily walk to neighborhood stores or playgrounds. They were too far away, so she packed the children into the car and drove to wherever she needed to go. MPCs gave rise to the "soccer mom" phenomenon—parents who had to drive their children to organized recreation, music practice, or scout meetings.

By the 1980s, the suburban development market became increasingly popular, competitive, and segmented. Developers began to design, plan, and build larger projects with themes or characteristics directed toward specific sectors of the population (e.g., family-oriented communities, seniors-only golf course communities, "lifestyle" communities for those without families who wanted minimal private outdoor spaces). Developers hired marketing companies to design elaborate advertising campaigns emphasizing these themes and features.

Increased demand for larger tracts (e.g., ten to twenty-five square miles) and cheaper land from the 1980s to the present led developers to acquire properties that were no longer adjacent to or even near established urbanized areas. The resulting leapfrog development pattern was in part made possible by the ease with which special districts, such as metropolitan districts, could be created. A special district is a unit of government created specifically for the purpose of providing a single or occasionally several services along with their necessary capital infrastructure (e.g., fire protection, library, water, sewage, roads). Colorado, with its development-oriented laws, spawned the second-highest number of special developer districts in the nation (Washington State developed the most). Although such districts can legally participate in the public-debt market by issuing their own bonds, they are typically established with little public scrutiny. For example, in Colorado, county commissioners must approve the establishment of special districts within their jurisdiction, but they exercise no oversight of those districts once created. A private developer can establish separate districts as a strategy to pay for any number of capital improvements, passing the debt onto the bond market and ultimately to the homeowners who find the debt burden attached to their annual real-estate tax assessment.

Although the MPC typically provides most of its own *internal* amenities and services, most developers do not consider as part of their responsibility the costs associated with the development and maintenance of *external* infrastructures to which their community implicitly connects and demands services (water, electric, and transportation services). Many states outside of the Rocky Mountain West have adopted the "development of regional impacts" (DRI) policy in order to place this financial burden on the developer, but DRIs are usually not applied in this region. Some counties have tried to establish their own equivalents of DRIs,[19] but they are usually stymied if the impacting development is outside of their jurisdiction.[20]

The ultimate form of leapfrog development is the "exurb." Compared with suburban subdivisions, with densities of two to six houses per acre, exurban developments are being built to densities as low as one house per thirty-five acres. In the Denver metro area, housing was being developed in the 1990s at one-third the density of the previously built urban area. But when exurban development was added, density figures really plummeted. Allen Best reports in *High Country News* that 8 percent of the metro area's population occupies one-third of its land. Moreover, "between 1960 and 1990, Colorado's semi-rural areas gained population three times more rapidly than its towns and cities."[21]

Exurban development is being fueled both by second homeowners and by people willing to commute more than an hour each way to work in order to have a rural setting for their homes. A good example is Custer County, which is exurban to both Colorado Springs and Pueblo, Colorado. Between 1990 and 2000, Custer County's population increased 80 percent, whereas the state's population increased by a more modest 31 percent. By 2000, the county had slightly more than 3,500 residents, but it had 9,000 plotted lots.[22]

Because many of the nation's most rapidly growing areas are in the West, the low-density pattern of development will have its most powerful impacts on that region. The Brookings Institution projects that by 2030 the highest rates of urban fringe and exurban development will be in Arizona, Nevada, and Utah, followed closely by Idaho, Colorado, New Mexico, Oregon, and Washington.[23] Although slower-growing Frostbelt states maintain better densities, the pattern is nationwide. The metro-Cleveland region, for example, has the same population as it did in 1960, but it now occupies twice the land area.[24]

The Expeditious Landscape

Many planners, design professionals, educators, and lay consumers argue that we can and should do a better job of planning and stewarding urban growth in the West. They believe that it is desirable, if not simply imperative, to provide alternative landscape-development paradigms to accommodate future urban growth. These new approaches need to reflect better the diverse yet unique cultural and physical attributes of the region while simultaneously providing affordable, attractive, and safe communities responsive to the needs and wants of a diverse population.

Toward this end, the academic and the development worlds have begun working together. In Denver, for example, the Challenging Suburbia Initiative was developed at the University of Colorado College of Architecture and Planning to engage faculty and students with practicing professional architects, landscape architects, planners, engineers, land developers, home builders, and public-sector officials in a discourse about how to accommodate projected urban growth. The imperative motivating this collaboration was investigation of alternative ways to accommodate the projected 50 percent increase in Colorado's population over the next two decades. Where will or should this growth take place, and in what urban form, density, and configuration? Are there alternatives to the "business-as-usual sprawling subdivision" that has consumed, and continues pervasively to consume, ever-growing amounts of the western landscape?

One component of the Challenging Suburbia Initiative was interdisciplinary graduate-level design studios that merged architecture, landscape architecture, and planning students together with the practitioners of suburban developments. The challenge given in one such studio was to plan a residential community on a twenty-acre site.

During the first week, students were assigned the task of designing a subdivision plan to accommodate sixty homes on a twenty-acre site. They were instructed to design the subdivision as "development as usual" following then-current municipal-development standards at a density of about 2.3 dwelling units per acre. Unbeknownst to the students was the fact that this site had already been developed about ten years earlier by a very prominent local developer and was currently inhabited by sixty families. Whereas *some students* tried to incorporate considerations of sustainability into their designs—such as water consumption and solar orientation—most did not. All of the students, however, predictably found it relatively easy simply to lay out the subdivision using standard street width, turning-radius requirements, and standard lot sizes without having to worry about the residents' water- and energy-consumption bills. Accommodating such considerations, they concluded, would take more time and require more thought and expertise then the one-week assignment permitted.

Over the ensuing weeks of the semester, the students and their professional mentors designed other possible community-development plans for this twenty-acre site. One developer was extremely impressed with one group's idea. Instead of development at 2.3 dwelling units per acre, the group designed a community plan at 6 units per acre. In their proposed plan, the homes were oriented to maximize solar gain in the winter to reduce the cost of heating the home. The plan also proposed a landscape planting plan and building design that would minimize solar gain and water consumption in the summer. Unfortunately, although applauding the students' solution for its creativity and delivery, the developers said that this project would be impossible to build today given established practices and processes. For example, many of today's subdivision standards require substantial irrigated lawn areas, minimum lot sizes, and property setbacks that minimize opportunities for creative siting and design.

As the practitioner-mentors explained, the standard subdivision design has a great deal of inertia behind it, resulting in what participants in the design studio came to call the *expeditious landscape*. Its form, economics, and development processes are formulaic and, under normal circumstances, highly predictable. Daring to deviate from the standard, according to "common knowledge," is fiscally perilous. This conclusion was reinforced at the 2003 Challenging Suburbia Forum directed by the Colorado Community Design Network. In attendance were the builders, developers, design professionals, and municipal planners in the business of creating today's suburbia. All agreed that there is a huge disconnect between, on the one hand, the conception and development of more economically, ecologically, and sociologically sustainable communities, and, on the other, the actual design, land-development, and building processes and practices in place today. One developer spoke up to say that proposing an "innovative" concept for a subdivision was the surest way to ensure significant delays in the project approval process. Most agreed that such delays have led to a "let's play it safe" mentality, meaning "let's continue the accepted suburban development pattern-as-usual. We understand it, we know how to process it, it's predictable and it's a safe [market] bet."[25]

The development community's and the buying public's aversion to risk have perpetuated the notion of the expeditious landscape. Why be exposed to more risk when the buying public and the public-entitlement process accept the business-as-usual formula? Residential development is a high-risk enterprise for all stakeholders—builders, developers, municipalities, and consumers. Vast sums of money are made and often lost. According to conventional thinking within the development community, deviation from the standard development model increases the developer's financial risk, which can be mitigated only with increased prices to the consumer. It therefore follows that it must be best to play it safe. Develop as usual. But is that the best strategy in the long run?

Let's examine the notion of development risk. Four major risk factors have impacted and continue to impact the development landscape:

1. *The time cost of money.* The longer it takes to bring a project through the development process—from entitlements to exactions, staff review, public scrutiny, and project approval—the greater the cost in terms of interest on development loans. A known "product," such as the standard subdivision, involves less scrutiny and therefore requires a shorter review and approval time. It's familiar. It raises fewer questions. Why? Because "we've done it a million times."

2. *Consumer demand.* Consumers and their mortgage institutions are comfortable with known products, such as the standard subdivision. Such

subdivisions have a proven and predictable track record as measured in terms of resale and property values. Consumer demand is increasingly fueled by speculators who buy homes just to "flip" them for a quick profit.[26] Such buyers favor a generic product and have little interest in alternative designs that offer operating-cost savings.

3. *Economy of scale.* Smaller, local builders and developers find it difficult to compete with much larger national players. The national development and building corporations have substantial financial backing afforded by their being part of publicly traded corporations. Access to Wall Street capital markets provides them with "cheaper money" for development and construction. These corporations have the financial means to endure the increasingly longer development-entitlement process and have the clout to buy building materials and appliances such as furnaces and stoves in huge quantities. As a consequence, they tend to be less responsive to variation in regional environments. They also tend to offer the same proven "development product" regardless of region or location. Although they work to stay competitive, they usually avoid radical development innovations because doing so is likely to increase their exposure to risk, especially during times when having to prove the value of something new to nervous stockholders and the money markets may at face value be unwise.

4. *Litigation and neighborhood protests.* Community opposition to a project in the form of Not in My Back Yard (NIMBY) protests and attendant litigation can significantly delay a development. Although one might expect that a community would welcome sustainable design alternatives, especially on vacant infill sites, opposition occurs when the community is faced with the possibility of increased densities as well as more congested roads, schools, and playgrounds. By contrast, developing a subdivision on a "green field" (open or agricultural land) is far less likely to provoke such opposition and its attendant delays.

In sum, adversity to risk and a desire for predictable returns on investments contribute to the production of the expeditious landscape. The *desirability* of the expeditious landscape and the potential rewards of the lifestyle that it has evidently produced have been idealized on television in what sociologist Dolores Hayden calls the "sitcom suburbs," referring to the places where the Nelsons (*Ozzie and Harriet*) and the Cleavers

(*Leave It to Beaver*) once lived and that are now occupied by "desperate housewives."[27]

People who buy into and live in the standard model of the suburban subdivision want it to look just like the sitcom suburbs while ignoring regional conditions. In a region well known for its low humidity, arid landscape, and broad thirty- to fifty-degree daily temperature differentials, Colorado Front Range residents eagerly spend thousands of dollars to import water-hungry green trees and shrubs from nurseries as far away as Missouri, Ohio, Oregon, and Pennsylvania. In order to avoid brown grass, westerners will pay the cost of pouring tens of thousands of gallons of water on their manicured blue grass lawns. In a region that receives more than three hundred days of sunshine annually, Colorado Front Range residents continue to purchase natural gas and electricity in increasing quantities in order to heat their homes instead of demanding better-oriented and insulated homes or investing in solar-energy technologies.

The Inertia of Local Governments

In spite of the risk-aversion factors, an increasing number of developers have been and are willing to challenge the risks. These forward-thinking developers, design professionals, municipal leaders, and educators argue and actually demonstrate that it is in fact possible to provide better-designed and more sustainable communities. In the 1980s, George Writer, a Denver-based developer, built Willow Creek, a thoughtfully planned and designed community that provides single-family and multifamily homes for hundreds of families. Internal trails offer pedestrian and bike linkages through both vegetated and open maintained and natural landscapes. Children take these trails to visit their friends, commute to school, and access playfields, tennis courts, and swimming pools. Seniors walk the trails daily. It is no wonder that today, more than twenty years since being built, Willow Creek homes resell quickly and at a premium. Willow Creek homeowners love the fact that their property values increase annually. When walking or driving through Willow Creek today, one admires this residential community's beauty and asks why more such communities aren't being built today.

The developer who wants to build a Willow Creek–style community *today* faces an uphill battle, however. One issue has to do with the competence of those charged with reviewing development plans. The second issue, voiced by the developers, is the increasing number of studies and reports required to justify development proposals.

According to Chris Fellows, a twenty-seven-year veteran Denver-area developer, the time required in the development process for the municipal entitlements, exactions, and approvals increased from ninety days in the 1980s to one year in the 1990s and then to three years. Reasons for this change include the fact that development activity in the region has increased tremendously over the past three decades. Innovative designs are likely to provoke even longer reviews. Local municipal-planning staffs charged with approving project proposals are already overwhelmed by the sheer number of applications. Fellows explains that "many municipal staff planners and technicians performing plan review functions are inadequately trained to begin with or have not had continuing education to keep up with emerging practices. Worse still is the lack of preparation of appointed planning commissioners or elected council members charged with making development approval decisions."[28]

Local, state, and even federal agencies require developers to produce expensive and often weighty environmental, traffic, drainage, and infrastructure impact studies in order to prove the viability of their proposals. In addition, developers must attend public hearings in response to additional demanding entitlement, exaction, and due process mandates. Demonstrating that a project is in the public interest is now an accepted part of the developer's costs of doing business. Developers argue that these efforts take more time and thus cause project delays, which ultimately increase the cost of development and home prices to consumers.

National versus Local Developers

Increased development costs and increased risks run on parallel tracks. The name of the residential development game, as in most high-stake businesses, is "Survival of the Fittest." In Denver prior to the 1990s, for example, local developers and builders—people who lived in the area, perhaps even grew up in the region—delivered nearly 90 percent of the homes built in the metropolitan area. Only about 10 percent of the homes were built by national, publicly traded builders. The local builder was often a member of a local community and quite often lived in the community he developed and in one of the houses he built. Most local builders cared about their reputations and worked to take care of their buyers. If they didn't, they eventually went out of business. A consumer who purchased one of their homes could make a local telephone call to speak directly with the builder to resolve a problem. The marketplace liked this model because it generally forged trusting relationships between the builders and the home buyers.

Things changed during the 1990s, however. The national economy was booming. The marketplace, particularly in the West, demanded new homes and wanted them quickly. Corporations, especially high-tech and service-oriented businesses, expanded into the West. For example, by 1999 Denver's southeast business corridor along Interstate 25, twelve miles from the downtown business district, boasted clusters of midrise office buildings including the Tech Center, Inverness, and Greenwood Village. This area accommodated more office workers than downtown did. Local builders did their best to keep pace with the demand for new homes for these employees, but met with fierce competition from the publicly traded national home-building companies backed by Wall Street investors who saw the West's market potential.

Many local builders, no longer wanting or able to compete, eventually sold their businesses to these large national corporations. By the late 1990s, the Writer Corporation based in Denver—one of the most highly respected and award-winning local building companies in the region—was sold to Standard Pacific Homes, a national building corporation whose stock is traded on the Big Board. D. R. Horton, another publicly traded national home builder, bought Denver's locally owned Melody Homes. By 2006, according to local Denver developer Chris Fellows, 90 percent of the new homes delivered in the Denver Metro area were being built by the large, publicly traded corporations.[29] That's quite a development paradigm shift over a little more than a decade.

This transformation happened quickly and easily. First, during the 1990s small local builders found it increasingly difficult, if not impossible, to keep up with market demand. Second, the entitlement process severely impacted local builders' financial resources by increasing the amount of time and work required to approve their projects. Third, the cost of money required to fund upfront development and construction costs rose sharply. A local builder had to borrow private money at an interest rate of 15 to 20 percent, whereas publicly traded building corporations could raise the same money from corporate sources at 3 to 5 percent or self-finance their own projects from past profits. Fourth, local builders couldn't compete with the larger corporations in their ability to procure building supplies and labor. A large national builder such as Pulte Homes or D. R. Horton could buy thirty to forty thousand refrigerators from GE in a year, whereas a local builder could buy at most a few hundred.

The large, publicly traded building companies' mission is to make strong returns for their investors. They execute a straightforward strategy: build and sell a great deal of product (homes) quickly and deliver them at the lowest cost possible and at the high possible price the market can stand. This strategy is accomplished by maximizing their buying power and developing the market-proven, business-as-usual normal subdivision products that they know both local planning boards and consumers will feel comfortable with, approve, and buy.

The result of national builders' efforts to maximize profits is that house you see everywhere. What D. R. Horton—"America's Builder"—builds in Raleigh, North Carolina, looks pretty much like what it delivers to consumers in Dallas, Texas; Eugene, Oregon; or Highlands Ranch, Colorado. The design, materials, construction methods, and siting of homes in these subdivisions take few clues from the natural or cultural characteristics of the different regions where they are developed. As long as energy costs remained low (a condition that may no longer hold), the use of high-tech, efficient heating, ventilating, and air-conditioning systems, double-pane glass, and somewhat more insulation allowed developers to ignore solar orientation, natural drainage patterns, and native plant materials already provided at a site. Simple adjustments to local conditions, which would save owners on their lifetime home-operating costs, would require more planning and design, which costs builders more time and money.

Transforming the Standard Model

What is a Rocky Mountain West home and community supposed to look like? One recent response has been the development of so-called neotraditional communities promoted by the New Urbanist movement.[30] Many communities following these standards have been popping up around the West. They are characterized by a rectilinear street grid aligned with tree lawns, street trees, sidewalks, front porches, and alley-loaded garages. Development densities are higher: eight dwelling units per acre compared with two to five dwelling units per acre. Community amenities and local shopping are often designed to be within walking distance.

Stapleton Redevelopment is one such New Urbanist community under development on the site of Denver's former Stapleton Airport. According to master developer Forest City, "When complete Stapleton's 4,700 acres will set a new standard for the rebirth of urban America: a new generation of neighborhoods where [*sic*] 30,000 residents and 35,000 workers will call home."[31] Stapleton's redevelopment was originally conceived to be state-of-the art sustainable development, employing building technologies and site planning that would achieve that objective. Forest City markets the community with an emphasis on sustainability. Sales, according to Stapleton staff, are considered very strong, indicating a captive and willing market within the boundaries of a central city. Stapleton is required to provide a certain percentage of its homes within an affordable price range.

Another, albeit smaller, New Urbanist–like development is Belle Creek located about ten miles northeast of Stapleton in Commerce City. Gene Myers, president of New Town Builders, a local building company that developed Belle Creek, concludes that challenging the conventional wisdom of the marketplace is risky business.[32] Belle Creek is surrounded by and competes for sales with several standard subdivision projects offered by the national building companies such as KB Homes, D. R. Horton, and Shae Homes. Given similar price points of the homes sold, Belle Creek's competitors offer larger homes on bigger lots. Belle Creek's sales have lagged behind those of it competitors. The market is voting with its consumer dollars.

The New Urbanism, however, is arguably the old urbanism spruced up to appeal to modern tastes. Like the old suburban subdivision of the 1920s, it has little to say about requirements unique to the Rocky Mountain West, nor is it a particularly meaningful attempt to understand the requirements of sustainable development. For example, front porches are a common element, but people stopped using their porches with the advent of air conditioning and TV. Back alleys get cars off the street,

FIGURE 3.2. New Urbanist–style homes at the site of the former Stapleton Airport in Denver feature front porches and back alleys.

but they add significantly to the amount of paved surface and hence increase the outdoor ambient air temperature in the summer as well as the polluted runoff carrying fertilizer, insecticide, and snow-melting chemicals.

In fact, it is difficult to find truly "green design" communities in the Rocky Mountain West. Village Homes, developed by Michael Corbett and Judy Corbett in Davis, California, offers an example of an established community (completed in 1981) that demonstrates how the application of appropriate design principles can make a huge difference in life-cycle costs.[33] The streets at Village Homes are oriented east to west so that all lots are oriented north to south. This siting allows houses to make maximum use of the passive solar design incorporated in their construction. Average energy bills are one-third to one-half of those in surrounding developments.

Street widths are narrow, reducing the amount of paved surface exposed to hot summer sun. Instead of lining both sides of the street with sidewalks, residents utilize extensive pedestrian and bike paths. The design of surface drainage systems saved $800 per lot, which was put back into landscaping. Resale of homes has been at a premium over other developments in the surrounding area. Consumers clearly see the value of the alternative.

Although it is difficult to find developments as progressive as Village Homes in the Rocky Mountain region, many municipalities have adopted so-called smart-growth principles that encourage sustainable design. Local governments such as those in Aurora and Fort Collins, Colorado, have revised building codes and zoning and planning regulations with the goal of enhancing both the appearance and the sustainability of new residential communities. Some of the changes in regulations and codes are motivated by local citizens' concern for the rising costs of heating and cooling, increased traffic congestion, and limited water supply. More citizens—as measured by increasing attendance and participation at planning-commission hearings and smart-growth conferences, letters to the editor, editorial columns, and feature stories in local newspapers— are worried about quality-of-life issues for themselves and future generations. They are less focused on the initial cost of housing and more on the life-cycle costs of living in a home. These same citizens are motivating local governments to adopt sustainability practices in the delivery of municipal services (e.g., using vehicles powered by natural gas and changing bulbs to ones that consume less energy) and in the construction of public facilities and landscapes.

Some Recommendations

The standard model of subdivision and community development will be perpetuated until it is no longer economically attractive. Unfortunately, consideration of the short term and short profitability, for both developers and consumers, has largely eclipsed concern for economic as well as ecological sustainability over time. Gilpin's image of unbounded resources for development in the West still trumps Powell's image of stewardship. But there are ways to shift images, specifically among four key stakeholder groups—local governments, developers, consumers, and, previously not mentioned, universities.

Local Governments

We have suggested that local governments (municipal and county) play a key role in perpetuating the standard model of suburban development. They do this through their zoning and building codes as well as through their associated review processes. They must be convinced that alternative, sustainability-based subdivision design can be more fiscally beneficial than the standard models. Studies dating back to the mid-1970s demonstrate, however, that taking only this one step is clearly inadequate. Professional staff, appointed commissioners, and elected officials have to become more sophisticated regarding alternatives and how to evaluate them. In the Rocky Mountain West, many communities provide models for alternative patterns of development, but what is missing is peer-to-peer education about the advantages of these alternatives and how to reform ordinances and processes to help support new forms of development. At a more proactive level, local governments can help level the playing field for smaller, regionally based developers who are willing and able to build alternative, sustainability-based communities, but who are fearful of absorbing the associated financial risks. Because one of those risks consists of protracted review time resulting from submission of innovative alternatives, local governments should work with qualified developers on more of a partnership basis to make sure the latter receive expedited reviews and should begin employing effective development agreements. Local governments might also provide incentives to such developers in the form of reduced fees for design features that result in lower public-sector maintenance costs over the life of the subdivision and lower use of public utilities.

Ultimately, state governments need to be involved in supporting local governments in these efforts. Unfortunately, the states of the Rocky Mountain West have not been especially strong leaders in this area, although they are coming along. The state of Florida, which has had strong state-wide growth-management requirements since the mid-1970s, offers an example of what can be done. One Florida statute defines what constitutes a "quality community development." Any developer who meets these requirements is assured of an accelerated review. This is no small incentive because the review and permitting process in Florida can take years.

States can also assist in transforming the market by providing measures of the cumulative impact of major new developments on the surrounding region. Right now each local government considers—within the limits of its technical abilities—what kinds of impacts a new development will produce. States are in a better position to develop the methods to outline impacts and to provide accounting of those impacts. Ironically, Colorado developed such methods when faced with a rapid energy development boom in the late 1970s and early 1980s, but it has never considered employing such analysis to review the impact of rapid population growth in general.

Developers and Builders

Along with local governments, developers must shift their perceptions and practices. Instead of marketing the selling price of their homes, they can do a great deal more to make consumers aware of the life-cycle costs of owning one of their homes. Such a shift would not only assist the initial buyer in making a choice, but serve as a selling point for resale. Fortunately, some developers have taken this approach, such as the builders in the Stapleton redevelopment project in Denver, who pitch their advertising significantly around sustainability features. Local governments can do more to assist both regional developers and national builders such as

Stapleton's Forest City, who are willing to provide more sustainable developments. Partnerships to achieve this goal require not only greater sophistication on the part of the local planning bureaucracy, but also developers who are capable of working effectively with local governments.

Consumers

Consumers must redirect their preferences by refining their economic assumptions about housing costs. Because Americans move so frequently (about once every five years), the individual home buyer tends to be as oriented toward the short-term investment as most developers are. But as the cost of running a home (energy, water, maintenance, and so on) increases, the monthly budget realities of poorly designed homes and communities become more apparent. Imagine opening the pantry door of a new home and finding a sticker there—similar to those provided on major new appliances—indicating the annual operating cost of a home and comparing it with the national range for similar homes. Consumers also need assistance in factoring in the costs of mobility when they make their housing and community choices because transportation is the second-largest household budget item. At the federal level, Fannie Mae now provides both energy- and location-efficiency mortgages that take into account lower life-cycle costs by providing more favorable rates to households purchasing qualified homes.[34]

Consumer education should include awareness of what design features to look for in a home and community, such as what makes for better solar orientation, site drainage, landscaping, materials and systems maintenance, and of course, livability. Such education is especially important for people new to the region and unaware of its unique characteristics. Just as people are informed about how to adjust their baking recipes for Rocky Mountain altitudes, they should also receive an orientation on living in this region.

Universities

Because this chapter is authored by two university professors whose teaching and research activities focus on questions surrounding urban planning and design, it should come as no surprise that we feel that higher education must assume a greater role in future efforts to "heal the West," at least as far as urban development is concerned. We who teach in a design profession have at least two responsibilities: to prepare students for careers in the professions as they are currently being practiced and to prepare students to be able to face the challenges of their chosen professions as they are presented today and as they emerge in the future. The first is relatively easy in that current practice, accreditation standards, and licensure tells us what students are required to learn. Meeting the needs of present and future challenges that might confront design professionals is more daunting.

Those of us in higher education have an opportunity to lead by developing the new knowledge and capabilities that take practice to a higher level of competence and excellence in dealing with planning and design questions for the West. Design education must undertake a much more rigorous research agenda fueled by the questions that surface as we attempt to deal with urban growth pressures and to accommodate the needs of an always changing and demanding society. This agenda will demand that universities do far more in terms of convening the disparate groups that seek to accommodate growth. This means universities will and should conduct more forums such as the Colorado Tomorrow Conference held in 2004 and 2005 that put us in contact with experts, raise critical questions, and encourage people to talk about how best to move forward. Doing so will require universities to become active participants in the discourses surrounding urban growth. It will require universities to involve the development community in the classroom not only to share best practices but also to work together in developing, documenting, and evaluating new practices.

The success of the design studios at the University of Colorado at Denver reveal how students interacting with the development community can identify critical questions and lay the foundation for research and development. Enhanced strategic partnerships aimed at information exchange and inquiry in areas of research, development, and application of new design technologies will enable designers and decision makers to generate, visualize, and evaluate alternative development scenarios for existing and proposed infrastructures, natural resources, existing social fabrics, economies, and government processes. The opportunities to develop technologies and processes that maximize energy efficiencies while minimizing consumer costs, for example, should motivate the development community, local municipalities, and consumers to work with academics and scholars, especially as today's students become tomorrow's decision makers.

Looking for a "Healing Image"

We began this chapter by contrasting two images of land development in the Rocky Mountain West: Gilpin's image of a limitless plenty that invites unbridled development and Powell's image of fragile, arid lands that require careful stewardship. Whereas Powell's image was based on an accurate assessment of reality, Gilpin's image is the one embedded in real-estate development ads selling the Rocky Mountain lifestyle. But the challenges now go well beyond what Powell envisioned, in part because he was largely ignored outside of federal lands.

Changing the image of suburban living in the Rocky Mountain West will require a combination of reeducating all parties involved and shifting economic priorities and incentives. Universities and professional associations can play a significant role in advancing the process of reeducation. Likewise, local governments in partnerships with local developers can and should play a more proactive leadership and competent service-oriented role in the economic and regulatory arenas. Efforts along these lines are already evident around the region, but they remain minuscule compared to the juggernaut driven by national developers and unintentionally pushed along by local governments.

The Rocky Mountain West needs a new and regionally appropriate image of livability with accompanying sustainable land-development practices. This image must highlight the region's environmental, economic, and cultural realities.

Part 2
Recovering What's Been Lost, Healing Injury

4

Reversing the Trend of Habitat Loss in the American West

THE UNCERTAIN PROMISE OF ECOLOGICAL RESTORATION

Sharon K. Collinge

The History of Habitat Loss in the American West

The landscapes of the American West have changed dramatically over the past four hundred years, and no one can miss the great irony in this transformation. Wildness defined much of the appeal and attraction of the West, and yet our ancestors transformed the wildness to meet the demands of their—and now our—appetite for convenience.

Western settlers found strong, towering trees they could turn into fuel, houses, and timber for framing mine shafts. They found fertile prairies that could grow wave after amber wave of grain. They also found some inconveniences—grizzly bears and wolves that ate their livestock, lands too arid to grow crops without irrigation, and soggy wetlands they couldn't use for farms or home sites. In deftly using these resources and creatively overcoming these inconveniences, colonists transformed the West into a safer, more habitable place for comfort-oriented humans, turning rock, soils, plants, and animals into economic resources.

And now many have noticed the costs incurred by these activities. Conversion of native forests and grasslands to clear-cut ground and agricultural fields has left little territory available for native plants and animals to thrive. Those spaces that remain tend to be small, isolated remnants of land that can support only a few, reduced populations of prairie songbirds and forest-dwelling mammals, for instance.

Consider these figures. The World Wildlife Fund estimates that only 5 to 9 percent of the grasslands in eastern Wyoming and Montana and in western North and South Dakota remain undisturbed by human activities (Ricketts et al. 1999). These grasslands were home to enormous herds of bison and contained among the highest numbers of bird species in North America. The conifer forests running north to south through Colorado have declined by 70 to 80 percent due to logging, hard-rock mining, oil and gas development, and residential construction. In fact, habitat loss and fragmentation are the greatest forces behind the decline of species in North America, causing risk to more than 85 percent of the plants and animals on the endangered species list (Wilcove et al. 1998).

The grasslands of the Central Valley of California, one of the most biologically diverse ecosystems of the American West, have declined by an estimated 99 percent since European colonization (Ricketts et al. 1999). Within these grasslands are temporary wetlands called *vernal pools* because of their magnificent displays of flowers during the spring. These pools fill with water during the winter rainy season and then erupt with color during late spring as rainfall ceases and the pools dry. The great western naturalist John Muir wrote of this landscape: "The Great Central Plain of California, during the months of March, April, and May, was one smooth continuous bed of honey-bloom, so marvelously rich that, in walking from one end of it to the other, a distance of more than 400 miles, your foot would press about a hundred flowers at every step" (1894, 339). But Muir also foretold and lamented this landscape's fate as a consequence of the region's economic progress: "The time will undoubtedly come when the entire area of this noble valley will be tilled like a garden, when the fertilizing waters of the mountains, now flowing to the sea, will be distributed to every acre. . . . Then, I suppose, there will be few left, even among botanists, to deplore the vanished primeval flora" (350).

Muir's projections of the future were quite accurate—indeed, the conversion of California's vernal pools to housing developments and agricultural fields has caused substantial habitat loss and has resulted in federal protection of dozens of vernal-pool species under the Endangered Species Act (ESA). Because of legal requirements set forth by the ESA, vernal-pool mitigation often mandates restoration or creation of pools to compensate for their loss. Later in this chapter, I delve into the world of these biological gems to illustrate both the uncertainty and the promise of such efforts.

Questions about Ecological Restoration

Because habitat loss and fragmentation cause sharp declines in the abundance of native species, efforts to restore native ecosystems to historic conditions should enhance native diversity. Ecological restoration is understandably gaining support among ecologists and environmentalists as a hopeful remedy for degraded landscapes. As scientists and activists exhort the public to tread this path of reparation for our past sins, three basic questions come to the fore. First, should we even bother to restore these native habitats? Our predecessors in the region devoted boundless energy and effort to make the substitute West a safer, easier, more convenient place to live, so should we try to reverse all their hard work? Second, if we decide that we should restore native habitats, is it even possible to do so? Our scientific know-how may or may not enable us to write a prescription for reassembling the scattered pieces into a coherent whole, and restoration may be an uncertain promise, given the complex structure and function of native ecosystems. And third, even if the scientists achieve their goals and decipher the mysteries of restoration, will the citizens of the American West choose to put this understanding to work? We may or may not lack the legal requirements, the financial incentives, and the political motivations to make restoration a working reality.

Such thorny questions invite ethical argument, scientific discussion, and economic debate. In addressing the first question, advocates of restoration may well respond that we must restore native habitats because humans should not be the cause of species declines and extinctions. At the least, we should not diminish the natural heritage we will pass on to posterity. In addressing the second question, field scientists study the complexity of ecological systems in an attempt to define simple rules that will help us restore native habitats (see, for example, Jordan, Gilpin, and Aber 1987). It is still too early to tell if we can return native habitats to the way they were, but some efforts provide a sprinkling of optimism. Regarding the legal and political motivations that underlie restoration, our strongest societal motivation for restoration rests on the ESA, which declares that it is illegal to harass, capture, or kill endangered species unless provisions are made to increase the survival of endangered populations or species in some way. These provisions usually include creating or restoring habitat for the species in a similar, nearby place. Even though this legal requirement has produced many efforts at restoration, in most cases there is only equivocal evidence that the endangered plants and animals find their new homes appealing enough to stay a while.

In this chapter, I delve into the topic of habitat restoration by exploring the three questions posed here. I first briefly investigate the issue of whether society should engage in ecological restoration or whether our anthropogenically created landscapes offer desired substitutes. Then, drawing on my own research with vernal-pool habitats in California grasslands, I pursue in detail the question of whether ecological scientists currently have the knowledge to restore native ecosystems effectively. I end with a brief discussion of whether sufficient legal, economic, and political incentives are currently in place to achieve ecological restoration in the American West. I recognize the impossible task of definitively resolving these issues within the context of this chapter or, for that matter, in this book, but my intent is to raise these issues to provoke thought, dialogue, and—I hope—action.

These three questions similarly arise in discussing issues of restoration featured in other chapters of this volume. In particular, conversations about restoring cultural resources such as language, ritual, and history are often permeated with similarly challenging questions. Andrew Cowell's chapter describes motivation and methods for maintaining both the spoken and the written native language in Native American nations. Brenda Romero discusses the cultural importance of the *matachines* dance ceremony for the persistence of New Mexican Pueblo culture. And Len Ackland explores the complex ethical arguments involved in restoring societal memory of nuclear proliferation and production during the Cold War. Each instance raises critical issues of ethical argument, scholarly know-how, and societal motivation to restore these cultural resources.

But how do problems associated with cultural restoration relate to those associated with ecological restoration? I argue that despite restoration's divergent targets, there are at least two distinct similarities in the restoration of ecological entities and cultural entities. The first similarity relates to our scientific or scholarly understanding of the restoration target (e.g., a species or a language) in the broader context of the ecological or cultural community. As discussed in detail later in this chapter, restoring a species within an ecosystem typically requires restoration of the processes that generate or maintain appropriate habitat conditions for that species. Without restoration of those processes in which that species is situated and on which that species depends, its long-term persistence is unlikely. For example, successful wolf-restoration efforts discussed in Hannah Gosnell's chapter require plenty of prey for wolves in the surrounding habitat. Likewise, restoration and long-term persistence of the Arapaho language or the matachines dance depends on restoration of the cultural context in which these entities are embedded.

A second, perhaps more dire similarity between cultural and ecological restoration is that the political will to take action for both types of resources is often analogous to emergency-room medical practice. In other words, action is taken only in desperation when the species or language is nearly gone. But efforts akin to preventive medicine—such as actions taken to thwart decline or loss of the resource—will likely be much more effective and much less expensive, but perhaps also less obviously heroic.

Should Habitats Be Restored?

When European settlers came to the American West, many were intimidated by the threats posed by the vast wilderness. Grizzly bears and wolves routinely visited camps and dwellings, and the lack of water made the cultivation of crops a risky proposition. Our predecessors in this region industriously made the West a safer, easier, more convenient place to live by controlling predators and devising complicated and highly effective water-delivery systems.

Predators were a particular worry for western ranchers whose goals included safely raising sheep and cattle. The livestock industry successfully lobbied the federal government to introduce predator control, and by the mid-1920s the gray wolf (*Canis lupus*) had been effectively extirpated from most of the western United States (Dunlap 1991). In 1961, a Canadian biologist named Douglass Pimlott wrote: "The wolf poses one of the most important conservation questions of our time. Will the species still exist when the twentieth century passes into history? Or will man have exterminated the wolf as a final demonstration of his 'conquest' of the wilderness and of wild things that dare to compete or conflict with him?" (quoted in Dunlap 1991, 173).

With the passage of the ESA, however, the gray wolf became a legally protected species, and plans were made for its recovery. By 1980, the

FIGURE 4.1. Gray wolf (*Canis lupus*). (Photograph by Gary Kramer, U.S. Fish and Wildlife Service)

U.S. Fish and Wildlife Service completed a draft recovery plan, which acknowledged that there were still a few places where wolves might be reintroduced (Dunlap 1991). In 1995 and 1996, gray wolves were trapped in Canada and released in Yellowstone National Park despite resistance from many ranchers adjacent to the park. By 2005, more than 170 wolves lived in the park.

The wolf-reintroduction project is certainly one of the most contentious of restoration efforts in the American West. This program underscores the

question of whether we, collectively as a society, should engage in ecological restoration. Many people question whether we should reverse the
efforts of those citizens and government agents who successfully eradi-
cated this predator from the western United States in order to achieve
clearly defined goals of safety and livestock production. But advocates
of restoration make an equally compelling ethical argument—that we
should restore native habitats and native species because it is unethical
for one species (humans) to cause the extinctions of other species. They
argue that at the least we should pass on our natural heritage to posterity
in the best condition possible. The point is that the pursuit of ecological
restoration is a key question in any restoration effort and must be faced
straight on by all parties in deliberations of restoration actions.

Can Habitats Be Restored?

Once a decision is made to embark on an ecological restoration project,
the harsh reality of how to do so emerges. To restore a native ecosystem
is a complex task; it is not as if one can purchase off the shelf a complete
habitat ready for installation. Ecological scientists have long known that
any native habitat involves a complex web of interactions, but only relatively recently have they attempted to restore or re-create intact habitats.
Studying ecological complexity, they try to define simple rules that will
help us restore native habitats. It's too early to tell if we can return such
habitats to the way they were, but some efforts provide a sprinkling of
optimism.

   One of the first and most difficult issues to grapple with in initiating a
habitat-restoration project is the decision regarding the appropriate reference condition to target in the restoration effort. In terms of the metaphor of healing highlighted throughout this book, this decision essentially
requires restorationists to determine the qualities that would constitute
a healthy ecosystem. Most habitat-restoration projects in North America
in general and the West in particular use a pre-Columbian baseline. In
other words, most projects' goal is to restore habitats to the conditions
that were likely present prior to settlement of the continent by Europeans. The choice of this baseline notably carries with it the assumption
that before colonization by Europeans, habitats existed in an agreeable
and healthy state, and that Euro-Americans inflicted the wounds that we

observe in many places today. Hence, although this choice of an appropriate baseline seems rather benign, it is laden with political, social, and even scientific assumptions.

Perhaps the best way to demonstrate a complete scientific understanding of a native habitat is to try to create it from scratch. One of the most famous cases of ecological restoration is an effort initiated and led by Aldo Leopold at the University of Wisconsin arboretum in 1935. Leopold and others took the first steps to transform a former pasture into a tallgrass prairie. Over the next decades, scientists learned essential aspects of prairie ecology that were not previously known. For example, they learned that periodic fires play a critical role in maintaining prairie species. Prior to the addition of fire, the restoration project failed to produce plant communities that mimicked nearby intact prairie ecosystems. Most initial attempts at ecological restoration do fail, but by carefully observing those failures, scientists learn critical lessons.

Successful restoration of a native habitat requires restoring both the structure and the function of the original ecosystem. The term *structure* typically refers to the assemblage of species found in the original community, and restoration efforts should strive to include most or all of the species present prior to the degradation or loss of that habitat. The term *function* typically refers to those species' interactions with the abiotic (nonliving) environment as well as with other species that occur in that habitat. For example, successful restoration should include restoring the plant species in a community (structure), but also the key insect pollinators that facilitate reproduction of those plant species (function).

If restoration efforts are successful at restoring both structure and function to an ecosystem, then the tangible societal benefits that ecosystems provide can balance the economic costs of restoration. "Ecosystem services" include valuable processes that natural systems perform and that ultimately enhance human well-being. For example, intact wetlands provide natural flood control, native bees perform pollination of crop plants free of charge, and soil microbes decompose organic wastes.

But how do scientists and restorationists go about restoring both the structure and the function of native ecosystems? In some cases, restoration may require little action. Restorationists may choose to adopt the "let nature take its course" strategy, leaving the native habitat alone to recover on its own from its losses. At the opposite end of the spectrum,

PASSIVE

"Let nature take its course"

ACTIVE

"Plant, weed, water, fertilize"

C O N T I N U U M

FIGURE 4.2. A conceptual diagram of active and passive approaches to restoration. At the passive end of the continuum, little effort is required to return the ecosystem to its native state. At the active end, extensive human efforts are required to restore the system. Restoration efforts may fall anywhere along this continuum.

restoration of a native habitat may require intensive intervention. The site to be restored may need to be planted, watered, weeded, and fertilized in order to recover its previous condition. It may not be entirely clear where a specific restoration project falls along this spectrum of passive to active approaches. Ecologists may be able to evaluate several key factors to determine which approach to use to restore structure and function in a specific place: the substrate at the site, the natural-disturbance regime, dispersal of key species to the site, food availability for animals that will inhabit the site, animals' behavior, and competition, especially from non-native, invasive species.

The substrate at a site includes the mineral and organic soils as well as the organisms that live within the soils. If the substrate is intact, little intervention may be necessary. But if the substrate has largely been destroyed, then major efforts may be required to import appropriate soil and soil organisms. For example, gravel-mining operations in riparian zones often remove vegetation and topsoil from a site to access the valuable gravel below the surface. Because it takes literally decades for soil formation to occur naturally, the successful restoration of the riparian vegetation to a mined site after removal of these layers may require importing nutrient-rich topsoil and even inoculating the soil with the mycorrhizal fungi that form critical partnerships with many plant species, facilitating the transformation and uptake of nutrients from the soil to plant roots.

Disturbance to ecosystems comes in many forms, including both natural and human-caused events. Many species have evolved in the context of natural-disturbance regimes, including periodic fires, floods, and grazing by native herbivores. In some instances, successful restoration may necessitate adding back to the ecosystem a previously eliminated natural disturbance. For example, scientists have documented a history of periodic fires in the ponderosa pine forests of the western United States. These fires were typically of low intensity and served to eliminate many pine seedlings from the forest floor, thereby producing relatively open, parklike ponderosa pine forests. The policy of fire suppression in western forests over the past one hundred years has resulted in forest stands that are quite different, with high densities of small-diameter trees. To restore these forests requires the reintroduction of periodic, low-intensity fires, and many land-management agencies regularly engage in prescribed burns as a means of returning these forests to their previous structure and function. In other cases, restoration may require the elimination of a particular disturbance. Fragile cryptobiotic soil crusts in the Great Basin are essential to nutrient capture in these stressful desert ecosystems, but are also highly sensitive to trampling by domestic livestock and recreationists. The restoration of the crusts thus requires the elimination of these human-induced disturbances.

To restore native species to a degraded habitat successfully, those species must be able to travel to and establish themselves at the site. The likelihood that an animal or plant will reach a site largely depends on the site's context: Is it surrounded by native habitats, such that colonists will easily disperse to the site? Or is it surrounded by completely modified habitat, such that the nearest native habitat is miles away? If native plants and animals' dispersal to a site is limited, then restorationists may need to intervene by transporting individuals of the desired species to the new habitat. For example, in most prairie-restoration efforts, scientists collect seeds of native plant species from an intact prairie habitat and transport them to the restoration site. This active approach is required because it is highly unlikely that the seeds will disperse to the restoration site without such intervention.

The reintroduction of animals, in particular predators, to areas where they have been extirpated presents the unique challenge of food availability. For example, in the late 1990s Canada lynx were introduced to southwestern Colorado in an effort to restore this species to the southern part of its range. Nearly half of the lynx introduced the first year were dead by the following spring. Critics of the project asserted that the Colorado Division of Wildlife, the agency responsible for the introduction, had not sufficiently assessed the availability of snowshoe hares in the reintroduction area. Hares are the lynx's favored prey; hence, their abundance would significantly influence lynx survival. Current analyses by the Southern Rockies Ecosystem Project of the Southern Rockies' suitability for wolf reintroduction thus explicitly includes an assessment of the abundance of ungulates (deer, elk) available as prey for the wolves (Miller et al. 2003).

In addition to food availability, animals' behavior may significantly influence their success at relocation or reintroduction. Behaviors may include those involved in mating and feeding as well as those associated with interactions in social groups. Relocation of black-tailed prairie dogs (*Cynomys ludovicianus*) out of the path of development in the Colorado Front Range has been particularly problematic because of their highly social behavior. Prairie dogs live in family groups called coteries and spend much of their time alerting family members of impending danger. When predators such as coyotes or Red-tailed Hawks enter a prairie dog colony, family members emit alarm calls to warn their relatives to seek cover. In initial relocation attempts, relocation technicians did not make the effort to keep family groups together when moving them from one site to the next. As result, the prairie dogs spent most of their time at the new site attempting to relocate their family group, which made them more vulnerable to predation.

If all conditions are met for a restoration site, the successful establishment of the desired species may still not occur because of strong competition for resources from other species. This outcome happens especially when nonnative, invasive plant species displace native species by outcompeting them for resources such as water, light, or nutrients. For example, the invasive plant tamarisk, or salt cedar (*Tamarix* sp.), has significantly altered riparian zones throughout the American Southwest. Tamarisk has a deep taproot that enables the plant to draw water from greater depths under the soil surface than is possible for the native willows and cotton-woods. Thus, it effectively drains the subsurface soil of its water, leaving the native plants without sufficient water to survive. Moreover, tamarisk exudes salt from its leaf tips, altering the soil's salinity and rendering the soil less suitable for native species. To restore native habitat under such conditions requires the reduction or elimination of competing species that threaten the persistence of the desired native species.

The scientific foundation for ecological restoration is still fairly modest, but scientists are increasingly using restoration efforts to enhance our understanding of the ecological factors that influence the formation and persistence of native communities. The six factors cited earlier provide a framework for determining where a particular restoration effort may fall along the passive-active continuum of restoration approaches. I suggest that the consideration of at least these factors will usefully guide restoration efforts.

A Restoration Case Study: Vernal Pools in Northern California. Vernal pools are ephemeral wetland habitats that typically occur in areas with Mediterranean climates. During the wet winters, these basinlike depressions in the landscape fill with rainwater, supporting a diverse array of invertebrates such as fairy shrimp and tadpole shrimp. During the dry spring, flowering plants take their turn in the pools, producing a spectacular display of purple, yellow, and white. These vernal pools harbor high biological diversity but have declined in abundance by more than 90 percent due primarily to agricultural and urban development. They are thus currently found in very few spots in California.

Because of their rarity, conservation of existing vernal pools and restoration of pools that once existed will be critical aspects of maintaining the rich biological diversity supported in these habitats. For the past eight years, I have conducted research on vernal-pool ecology and restoration in northern California. My research contributes mixed messages to the conversation about restoring native habitats. My restoration efforts involved painstakingly collecting seeds of rare plant species from a relatively intact vernal-pool habitat and using them to jump-start 256 newly excavated vernal-pool basins near the same site (Collinge 2003).

This large-scale restoration experiment was designed to investigate if and how vernal-pool plant communities can be restored. Because it was known that the study site historically supported vernal pools, I assumed that the substrate was intact. For vernal pools to function, there must be a relatively impermeable clay layer underneath the soil surface that doesn't allow water to percolate through the soil. This substrate causes the water to pond for several months on the soil surface, creating the pool. No major natural disturbances were known for this ecosystem, so there was no need to reintroduce disturbance. Although naturally occurring pools existed at the study site, many vernal-pool plants have limited dispersal ability. Thus, I reasoned that planting seeds collected from the site would be essential for restoration. Finally, the upland areas surrounding the vernal pools are dominated by nonnative, invasive grass species. However, few of these species are able to tolerate the seasonal inundation of the vernal-pool basins and thus are not able to compete, so I made no attempt to control them.

In the eight years since the inception of this restoration experiment, I have visited the restored pools in the winter to record the water levels during the seasonal flooding of the pools and in the spring to record the plants present in the plots where I planted seeds of native species. Results thus far show that in some of the pools, the depth of water and the duration of inundation during the winter wet season mimic those found in the naturally occurring pools at the site. In these pools that exhibit the appropriate hydrological function, the native plants that I seeded into the pools are thriving. The rarest of the rare plant species, a federally endangered member of the sunflower family, grows only where I have planted it; it cannot colonize new pools on its own so far. In about one-third of the restored pools, vernal-pool plants do not have sustained populations because the environmental conditions (hydrologically speaking) do not appear to mimic real pools closely enough.

These encouraging but modest findings suggest that we may still be a long way from having on hand a reliable instruction manual on vernal-pool restoration. In truth, it would be nice to work with less sense of urgency in timing. Wouldn't it be logical to halt further destruction of vernal-pool habitat until we learn more about the process of restoration?

FIGURE 4.3. Flowers of *Lasthenia conjugens*, the federally endangered plant species included in the vernal-pool-restoration experiment at Travis Air Force Base in northern California.

Will Habitats Be Restored?

For the moment, let's imagine that society has collectively decided that we should embark on ecological restoration and ecological scientists have achieved their goals to decipher the mysteries of restoration. Will the citizens of the American West choose to put this understanding to work? Or do we lack the legal requirements, the financial incentives, and the political motivations to make restoration a working reality? Once again, I admit that these questions are so complex that answers are elusive, but it is worth highlighting some key points to elicit consideration of these critical issues.

The ESA is arguably the strongest piece of environmental legislation in the United States because it prohibits actions that would harm endangered species or their habitats. It stipulates that human actions must avoid areas with endangered species. This rule seems simple enough, yet a key loophole in the act allows private landowners to obtain a permit to develop land with endangered species as long as they develop a plan to compensate for the damage to the species in some other way. This "other way" usually involves habitat mitigation or restoration. Either of these ways may be problematic, however, because, as I have argued, many uncertainties are involved in achieving successful ecological restoration. Moreover, despite the ESA's potential power, applying its authority in practice is often difficult. For example, William Lewis's chapter on using the ESA's regulatory strength in managing the Klamath basin illustrates the complexity of putting the ESA into practice. And the political assaults on the ESA by both the legislative and executive branches of government in recent years reveal this legislation's vulnerability to political battles.

Although the ESA is essentially a "top-down" force driving ecological restoration, many local restoration projects emerge from citizen-based, grassroots, "bottom-up" efforts that draw more on local ethical, aesthetic, and even economic motivations than on legal mandates. These ecosystem-restoration efforts may be the most hopeful restoration actions of all because they are motivated by intangible notions of what is right, beautiful, and ultimately beneficial to our own health and well-being. If we so choose, such values can serve as our guideposts for the next four hundred years of human habitation in the American West. As an example, nonprofit conservation groups such as The Nature Conservancy and the Predator Conservation Alliance have launched broadscale efforts to restore grasslands throughout the Great Plains to provide permanent homes for charismatic species such as bison, pronghorn antelope, Burrowing Owls, Ferruginous Hawks, prairie dogs, and black-footed ferrets. Their ambitious goals are not only to increase the numbers of these species but also to restore the functioning grassland ecosystems of the Great Plains in particular sites.

Perhaps even more impressive is the sheer number of restoration projects in progress, most of which literally occur in the backyards of people who are committed to their local environment. Several scientists recently joined efforts to create a database of river- and stream-restoration projects. They found more than thirty-seven thousand such projects in the United States alone (Bernhardt et al. 2005; Palmer et al. 2007; see list of projects at http://www.restoringrivers.org)! The architects of this database underscore the critical part played by local communities in successful restoration: "Citizens can and do have an incredibly important role to play in river restoration" (Palmer et al. 2007, 478).

To restore or not to restore is ultimately, of course, our collective choice as local, regional, and global communities. Increasingly aware of what has been lost, we are making many efforts now to rehabilitate, remediate, or repair our damaged environments and cultures. In the sense of healing, the aims of these actions are to identify the wounds inflicted on these ecosystems and cultures and to return them to health. I suggest that the assessment or diagnosis of the patient in question requires thoughtful consideration of the critical ethical, scientific, and political issues involved. If we approach such efforts with broad and inclusive perspectives, I believe that the promise of restoration will be sincere, meaningful, and long-lasting.

Acknowledgments

The ideas presented in this chapter have been greatly inspired by the words and deeds of Andrew Cowell, Fritz Gerhardt, Dan Janzen, Patty Limerick, Yan Linhart, Jaymee Marty, Jenny Ramp, Buzzy Jackson, and the other authors in this volume. I thank the Air Force Center for Environmental Excellence and the U.S. Fish and Wildlife Service for financial and logistical support of the vernal-pool-restoration experiment at Travis Air Force Base, California.

Literature Cited

Bernhardt, E. S., M. A. Palmer, J. D. Allan, G. Alexander, K. Barnas, S. Brooks, J. Carr, S. Clayton, C. Dahm, J. Follstad-Shah, D. Galat, S. Gloss, P. Goodwin, D. Hart, B. Hassett, R. Jenkinson, S. Katz, G. M. Kondolf, P. S. Lake, R. Lave, J. L. Meyer, T. K. O'Donnell, L. Pagano, B. Powell, and E. Sudduth. 2005. Synthesizing U.S. River Restoration Efforts. *Science* 308:636–37.

Collinge, S. K. 2003. Constructed Vernal Pool Seeding Experiment Aids in Recovery of Contra Costa Goldfields (California). *Ecological Restoration* 21:316–17.

Dunlap, T. R. 1991. *Saving America's Wildlife: Ecology and the American Mind, 1850–1990*. Princeton, N.J.: Princeton University Press.

Jordan, W. R., III, M. E. Gilpin, and J. D. Aber, eds. 1987. *Restoration Ecology: A Synthetic Approach to Ecological Research*. Cambridge: Cambridge University Press.

Miller, B., D. Foreman, M. Fink, D. Shinneman, J. Smith, M. DeMarco, M. Soulé, and R. Howard. 2003. *Southern Rockies Wildlands Network Vision*. Golden: Colorado Mountain Club Press.

Muir, J. 1894. *The Mountains of California*. New York: Century Company.

Palmer, M., J. D. Allan, J. Meyer, and E. S. Bernhardt. 2007. River Restoration in the Twenty-first Century: Data and Experiential Knowledge to Inform Future Efforts. *Restoration Ecology* 15:472–81.

Ricketts, T. H., E. Dinerstein, D. M. Olson, C. J. Loucks, W. Eichbaum, D. Della-Sala, K. Kavanagh, P. Hedao, P. T. Hurley, K. M. Carney, R. Abell, and S. Walters. 1999. *Terrestrial Ecoregions of North America: A Conservation Assessment.* Washington, D.C.: Island Press.

Wilcove, D. S., D. Rothstein, J. Dubow, A. Phillips, and E. Losos. 1998. Quantifying Threats to Imperiled Species in the United States. *BioScience* 48:607–15.

Recovering the West

MEXICANS AND THE MEMORY OF TOMORROW'S LANDSCAPE

John–Michael Rivera

THE LANDSCAPE OF the United States is transforming. In 2001, the U.S. Census Bureau published *Mapping Census 2000: Geography of U.S. Diversity,* a special atlas to map the 2000 census population, in which the populations of ethnic peoples were cartographically located, marking what were once predominantly white American lands of the United States as ethnically diverse landscapes (Brewer and Suchan 2001, 43). The history of America's landscape is once again changing. What is of importance to me today is the rather large section of the atlas on Latino population changes. Represented in shades of purple, Latinos now make up a significant and recognizable portion of the United States. Buried within the map's population statistics and color coding are the real cultural lives of at least thirty-seven million Latinos. The focus of this chapter is the group of Latino people who constitute nearly 60 percent of this map: Mexicans, most of whom are living in what we geographically call the West and the Southwest.[1] In shades of purple, the map superimposes a new demographic reality on the landscape of the United States; Latinos, especially Mexicans, are now the largest minority, and they soon will perhaps take over the map: a "brown tide is rising" (Santa Anna 2002, xv).

In its cartographic representation of the Mexican population within U.S. territory, however, this map elides and naturalizes something— namely, the emplacement of Mexicans and the historical and cultural location they have held in what is now the United States. In the cartographic and demographic representation of the present and future place that Mexicans hold and will hold in the United States, the map temporally locates them within the here and now of the landscape; it suggests that the "browning of America" is a contemporary phenomenon.[2] Kirsten Gruesz Silva describes this moment as a contradictory unfolding event

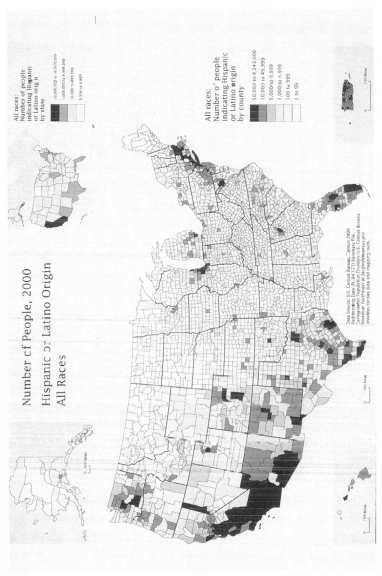

FIGURE 5.1. A census map of the United States in 2000 demarcating populations of "Hispanic or Latino origin." (From Brewer and Suchan 2001, 62)

created within the national public spheres that masks the historical significance of the Latino culture in the United States (2003, 55–56). According to Gruesz Silva, however, Latinos were anticipated in the unfolding of a particular set of relations between the United States and Latin America before they were "born" in the 2000 census (57). She reminds us that buried within the memory of the landscape, deep within the historical logic of the census atlas itself, is the transcontinental period of Manifest Destiny that would lead to the Mexican-American War of 1846–48 and the signing of the Treaty of Guadalupe Hidalgo, which in time would constitute Mexicans as hyphenated political subjects, "Mexican-Americans," and would secede millions of acres of lands to the United States and define the map's borders.

It is not surprising, then, that the geopolitical roots of this hidden cultural history of Mexicans buried within the census map can be found in yet another census atlas, the *Statistical Atlas of the United States Based on the Results of the Ninth Census, 1870,* produced by Francis Walker in 1874 (and thus referred to here as the Walker atlas or map). The first map in it is from the "American Progress" section of the Walker atlas, which was based on the first major U.S. census after the Mexican-American War. This map is particularly important because it was the first to mark cartographically and demographically the "manifest destiny" of a country that found progress through the geographic expansion of democracy and the future projection of Euro-Americans across the continent. But again something is missing in this map as well. The West is represented as unpopulated; it is space, not place; it is terra incognita.[3] Of course, the problem with this cartographic masking is that there were nearly 175,000 Mexicans in the West and the Southwest at the time the map was commissioned. In the nineteenth-century culture that read this map, Mexicans and Native Americans were not representable; therefore, they did not warrant a color on the landscape of the map. Mexicans were to hold no place in the future territory of the growing body politic. They were not part of the land and thus not a civic people. They did not signify a color, for they were not full citizens, but rather only "semicivilized citizens" (Almaguer 1994, 2–34). In the 1870 census map, "American" progress alone is signified, the westward expansion of Anglo history. In effect, this progress had to elide the genocide of Native Americans and the imperial acquisitions of Mexican lands.[4]

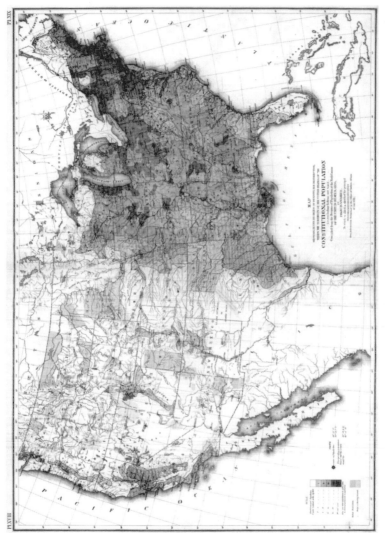

FIGURE 5.2. A census map from 1870 marking U.S. Manifest Destiny cartographically and demographically. (From Walker 1874)

But I juxtapose these two maps not just to tell the cartographic story of imperialism. The masking of the legacy of conquest may instead work for us. As such, I want the subjugated knowledge of the maps to help us recover an atlas of Mexican American peoplehood—a geography that recovers a new history connecting these two periods. In this chapter, I propose to remap and explore how Mexican Americans first entered the political landscape now defined as the United States and then how Mexican Americans in the United States would forever change its complexion through their cultural practices. These two maps act as springboards for the cultural history I delineate for you, which is the cultural emergence of Mexican Americans and their asymmetrical relationship to the constitution of the U.S. body politic. I tell the story of their lived experience within the natural landscape and of their search to recover place and belonging. These population maps are more than detail, longitude, area, and scale of land; they mark or do not mark the place of Mexican subjectivity, political identity, and culture.

I use these two census maps as a backdrop to render two moments of U.S. geographic change that have had a profound effect on the cultural landscape of the United States: first, the mid-nineteenth-century Manifest Destiny era that would produce the Walker map and define the territories of the West and its people as terra incognita in order to consolidate the western region into the eastern United States; and, second, today's turn of the millennium, the era the media is calling the "browning of America," a moment when the transitional imperatives of the North American Free Trade Agreement (NAFTA), neoliberalism, and George W. Bush's "compassionate conservatism" are once again relocating and restricting the places that Mexicans are able to reside in the United States. I want to juxtapose these two periods in history, these two important liminal moments of American geographic and cultural change, not to show the stark differences in the two periods, but to reveal the common struggles that Mexicans have had both then and now, as well as to explore how important Mexicans have been in the transformation of the U.S. landscape. In studying these two periods, I recover with you the lives that lie buried in the colored landscape of the maps, revealing the history and the archives of people who, despite their ambivalent position in U.S. culture, were always on the western map, creating a literary and cultural history for hundreds of years.

Terra Incognita: The Space of the Mexican Question

Seven years ago I read something that caught my attention in the nine-teenth-century California newspaper *El Clamor Público:*

> The United States' conception of freedom is truly curious. This much-landed freedom is imaginary. Civil Freedom is the right that links all citizens to society so that they can do as they please when it is not to the contrary of the established laws. But here in this fabulous country, he who robs or assassinates most is he who enjoys freedom. Certain people have no kind of freedom—this freedom, we say, is that which the courts deny to all individuals of color. It is enough that these institutions are unique in a country that tries to consume everything due to its "Manifest Destiny." . . . The latter is that which affects our Californian and Mexican population directly. They particularly distin-guish us by the title Greasers. (Ramirez 1855, my translation)

I had just begun my work as a research assistant of the periodicals portion of the Recovering the U.S. Hispanic Literary Heritage Project (hereafter the Recovery Project): Envisioned by Nicolas Kanellos, who also founded what has become the oldest and largest Latino press in the United States, Arte Público Press, the Recovery Project is a ten-year archival endeavor to recover the lost or forgotten literary tradition of Latinos in the United States from the Spanish colonial period to 1960. It is important to remember that for centuries, Mexican and Latino literary history has been buried or destroyed. Because of prejudice or simply a lack of understanding of the history and importance of Mexican literary production, libraries themselves participated in the erasure of these voices and deemed them unworthy of archival preservation. Nevertheless, to date, the Recovery Project has managed to locate more than fifteen hun-dred newspapers published by Latinos. As of today, they have also located more than seventeen thousand fiction and nonfiction narratives written by U.S. Latinos, many of which are from the nineteenth century.

Searching through library archives and private collections in both Mexico and the United States, we all felt that the Recovery Project was more than simply an archival endeavor; it was a political recovery of our lost heritage, an act of remapping the literary landscape in the United

States. With each uncovered voice, we slowly were able to recover a lost segment in our literary and cultural history. Indeed, this newly recovered literary landscape has changed how we understand literary production and the very idea of the archive. What I came to understand is that Mexican American literature and culture have a long tradition in the United States, that this history did not emerge in the mid-twentieth-century civil rights movement (El Movimiento), but in the colonial period itself, and that it experienced its own renaissance in the nineteenth century, the same period when U.S. democratic culture was expanding its geographic boundaries into Mexican and Native American lands. It is perhaps no surprise that questions of land, the politics of Mexican American inclusion, and Mexican and American statecraft would be of concern to the Mexican American writers of the period.

The quote that began this section is of particular importance because it marks a foundational theme prevalent in many of the archives we located: the relationship among race, landscape, and democracy. Writing this editorial just seven years after the Treaty of Guadalupe Hidalgo was signed, Californio newspaper editor and political philosopher Francisco Ramirez astutely questioned the geographic contradictions of American democracy: "freedom," he wrote, is "curious" precisely because its connotations elide the racial ideologies of Manifest Destiny that underpin its spatial development in the United States. The racialization of the newly constituted "Mexican American," therefore, develops because of the profound contradiction resulting from the effects of Manifest Destiny. American democratic culture's belief in the expansive rhetoric of Manifest Destiny results in an irresolvable tension between an ideological conception of race and a modern political system called democracy that espoused universal freedom, equality, laws, and "natural" rights for all the nation's citizens. In this way, Ramirez was one of the first Mexican American cultural workers to locate an inextricable relationship among the country's land hunger, the spatial ideas inherent to the project of democracy, and the racialization of Mexican Americans as a collective people. Although contesting the founding sentiments of Thomas Jefferson, Thomas Paine, and Alexis de Tocqueville, Ramirez's comments are located in a long line of political thinking about democracy's relationship to the land. However, unlike these political thinkers, whose desire was to locate and normalize a white "virgin landscape" for democracy, Ramirez revealed the contested nature of the relationship between land and democracy that develops when racialized peoples stand in the way of the new nation's geopolitical quest across the continent.[5] As he emphatically noted, discourses of land expansionism such as Manifest Destiny lead to a cultural understanding of Mexicans as "greasers" and thus not fit for democracy.[6]

Indeed, the term *greaser* was deeply tied to the landscape. In an 1899 *Atlantic Monthly* article titled "The Greaser," William Lighton argued that it is in the "strange" and incomprehensible landscape of the West where the "least comprehensible of our national character lives," the "greaser." What one must ask of this *Atlantic* essay is what makes the western landscape so strange yet such an object of attention to the eastern public implied in the narrative: Is it the incomprehensible land itself or the greaser who lives upon it? It is within this strangeness and otherness of space that the rhetorical and political dimensions of terra incognita emerge. Rising from the collision between the "strangeness" of the unknown space and that of the unknown greaser, a pervasive inquest known as the "Mexican Question" asked how the United States could territorially incorporate and profit from a strange land while simultaneously excluding the Mexicans on that land from the body politic.

It is not surprising that the first widespread use of the phrase "the Mexican Question" (and of the source of its popularized meaning) was in the writings of John O'Sullivan, the very same man who coined the powerful expansionist phrase "Manifest Destiny." Indeed, his popular magazine *The United States Magazine and Democratic Review* would publish both the essay "The Mexican Question" (O'Sullivan 1845b) and the well-known essay inaugurating the phrase "Manifest Destiny" in the same summer of 1845 (O'Sullivan 1845a). For O'Sullivan, the Mexican Question developed from Manifest Destiny's rhetoric of geopolitical progress. In the end, the Mexican Question became an ambivalent inquiry into Mexicans' rights and status that developed from both the anxiety and the promise that terra incognita brought to the nation's manifest designs and its capitalist desire to control natural resources. To reiterate, this nineteenth-century "Mexican Question," which became associated with the desire to locate and understand Mexicans' democratic rights and racial status, emerged within the imperialist and expansive rhetoric of terra incognita.[7]

For an emerging nineteenth-century U.S. democratic culture, the Mexican Question's geopolitical designs would become increasingly important when the Treaty of Guadalupe Hidalgo was signed in 1848, for Mexican "greasers" had in theory been given the democratic status of citizen within the U.S. body politic. Let us not forget that the treaty was the first U.S. document to address the civil rights of Mexicans within a geographic discourse. Articles 8 and 9 granted Mexicans the legal right to be included in the body politic as "Americans" at the same time that it geographically defined the Mexican lands, borders, territories, and property rights. In the end, the treaty became the first document that constituted both Mexicans as public subjects in the United States and Mexican lands as public domain.

Under the treaty's provisions, Mexicans in the United States were afforded the ability to enter the public as citizens and as property owners, while still maintaining their private traditions as Mexicans who were Spanish-speaking Catholics. However, as Deena González has so convincingly argued, the treaty offered only a semblance of democratic inclusion and land rights (1998, 132). And as Martha Menchaca (2001) argues, Mexicans Americans' mixed-race background historically placed them in an ambiguous racial and legal position in the public sphere. Let us not forget that at varying times in U.S. history, the nation's legal, political, and literary spheres constituted Mexicans as white, mixed blood, and "racially other," all of which affected the constitution of Mexican peoplehood in the United States.

After the Mexican-American War, Senator John C. Calhoun would add to the complicated racialization of Mexicans when he made a statement to Congress that was later printed in the *Congressional Record,* arguing that Mexicans represented "a motley amalgamation of impure races, not [even] as good as Cherokees and Choctaws." He continued to ask the American public whether they could "incorporate a people so dissimilar in every respect—so little qualified for free and popular government—without certain destruction to our political institutions. We do not want the people of Mexico, either as citizens or [as] subjects" (1849, 17). Senator Calhoun's anxiety that the inclusion of Mexican "mongrels" would destroy the fabric of American democracy is not historically isolated to the years in which the treaty was formed. From President Polk to dime novels to newspapers and journals, hundreds of narratives about Mexicans since the Treaty of 1848 circulated under the ambivalent phrase "the Mexican Question," asking whether Mexicans posed a threat to the founding ideals of American democracy or if they were even fit for those ideals.[8]

It is important to point out, however, that Anglo-Americans were not the only cultural group to define the geopolitical and embodied contours of the Mexican Question. The first book recovered by the Recovery Project, María Amparo Ruiz de Burton's *Who Would Have Thought It?* ([1872] 1995) explicates through a bitter satire the hypocritical logic of the Mexican Question. What is now believed to be the first novel to be published in English by a Mexican American begins with this paragraph:

> And finally, impelled by that liking, the doctor betook himself to California, which is full of "*natives.*" And as a just retribution for such perverse liking, the doctor was well-nigh "roasted by the natives," said the old lady. Whereupon, in behalf of truth, I said, "Not by the natives, madam. The people called '*the natives*' are mostly of Spanish descent, and are not cannibals. The wild Indians of the Colorado River were doubtless the ones who captured the doctor and tried to make a meal of him." "Perhaps so," said the old lady, visibly disappointed. "To me they are all alike,—Indians, Mexicans or Californians, they are all horrid. But my son Beau says that our just laws and smart lawyers will soon '*freeze them out.*' That as soon as we take their lands from them they will never be heard of anymore, and then the Americans, with God's help, will have all the land that was righteously acquired through a just war and a most liberal payment of money. (11; emphasis in original)

The opening scene reveals the novel's central theme: the problems of locating what was in the nineteenth century referred to as the "Mexican Question" in an antebellum American culture that based its racial and geographic imaginary on black/white and South/North binaries. That this opener centers on the eating of white northern peoples, "the roasting" of the New Englander Dr. Norval, by racial others imagined as "cannibals," announces that the ways in which the eastern politics of defining the Mexican race, the "greasers" in the West, is inextricable from attendant geopolitical discourses of the human body. Indeed, the reader is here introduced to the protagonist, an orphan named Lola Medina, whose metamorphic body represents the novel's exposition of the Mexican Question.

Amparo Ruiz and the novel come into even sharper focus when we consider that in 1869, the year she began writing her book, she also wrote a letter to Mariano Guadalupe Vallejo, an equally important national figure, in which she discussed how the gendered and racial presuppositions of Manifest Destiny had affected her. As she stated, "Ah If I were a man, What a sorry thing a woman is." "Providence and Manifest Destiny," she claimed, "should make up for having made her a woman, ugly and poor." Under Manifest Destiny, she no longer had any enthusiasm for this continent. "Where are my twelve acres of land!" she ended. Born in Baja California in 1832, Amparo Ruiz came from the landed classes and would through her lifetime lose these lands. Her proletariatization would begin in 1849, one year after the signing of the Treaty of Guadalupe Hidalgo, when she married Colonel Henry S. Burton, who was sent to Baja California to quell a Mexican uprising. After their marriage, Amparo Ruiz went with Col. Burton to the Northeast, where she began her literary career as a novelist. Her emplacement in the Northeast would affect her tremendously, and *Who Would Have Thought It?* captures her experiences of New England well.

Occurring during the backdrop of the Civil War, western expansionism, and eastern industrialization, the plot of *Who Would Have Thought It?* unfolds when Dr. Norval saves Lola from Indian captivity in the western territories and brings her back to his New England home. Because Lola's Indian captors have dyed her body, her racial and cultural identities in New England are entirely ambiguous. In effect, Lola's metamorphic body is terra incognita, an indefinable landscape. As the story progresses, however, we learn not only that her true identity is "Mexican American," but also that she has inherited gold and diamonds that her mother acquired while they were in captivity and lands that her father owned in the West. The remainder of the novel traces her life and focuses on how she becomes a part of New England culture and the Anglo middle class.

The trajectory of Lola's assimilation into Anglo-American culture and of her "worth" and position in New England corresponds precisely to the fading of the dyes on her body, for as they fade, she undergoes numerous changes in racial status, which overlap with and effectively generate her simultaneous acquisition of material wealth and cultural capital. Yet as Lola's body and her location in the United States change, so too does the economic position that the Norvals hold in New England culture, metaphorically representing how Anglo-America and the northern United States economically prospered after the Mexican-American War of 1846–48 when they expanded into the West. But it also reveals how Mexican women's bodies became associated with land expansionism, associated with "landscaping," as they became yet another geographic space to shape and control. Herein lies the gendered dimension of the Mexican Question.

This dimension would also have a biographic precedence. Amparo Ruiz's own marriage and the thematic coupling between Lola and Julian, a northern soldier, were very common, and they were yet another way that Anglo-Americans gained control of Mexican lands. In fact, Burton, Amparo Ruiz's husband, was an avid card player, a lousy one, and he gambled away all of her lands. After his death, she spent most of her life fighting in the courts, unsuccessfully, to regain her lands. Because of newly imposed Anglo laws that robbed Mexican women of their property rights, she no longer had rights to her land as she had had under Spanish and Mexican law.

I highlight Amparo Ruiz and her work because her focus on Mexican American women in the novel and her own person in her letter to Vallejo reveal a critical and arguably protofeminist response to a much larger masculinist geographic discourse that was incredibly popular in nineteenth century U.S. public spheres. While Amparo Ruiz lived, countless Anglo-American novels and works represented the relationship between Mexican women and the land. From dime novels to newspaper articles in which the recurring figures of La Malinche and Califas are rendered, Mexican women became central to U.S. geopolitical designs.[9] Two important representations illuminate the masculinist landscaping of Mexican women: the Tallis illustrated map of the Southwest and Mexico (Tallis and Rapkin 1851) and John Gast's landscape painting *American Progress* (1872).

Of particular importance to me in the Tallis map is the marginal emplacement of the naked Mexican woman in the bottom left-hand corner. The cartographic practice of placing symbols on maps was common in the seventeenth, eighteenth, and nineteenth centuries. Instead of Mexican women, however, sea monsters would often encompass the margins. The placement of dangerous or potentially resurgent elements to the map margins circumscribed the fear of threats to the virgin land. According to this map, Mexican women were yet another space to fear

FIGURE 5.3. John Tallis and John Rapkin, *Tallis Illustrated Map of Mexico, California, and Texas,* 1851, 9.5 by 13 inches. (From Tallis and Rapkin 1851)

and thus to occupy and control. Circumscribing them, then, would ensure that the land would remain virgin or empty, a space waiting to be filled or dominated. Clearing (or mining) space in the West in effect became a tool to establish whiteness—or to differentiate eastern expansionists from Mexicans.

Indeed, clearing space for whiteness through controlled representations of women's bodies is perfectly illustrated in John Gast's painting *American Progress.* Here a white woman becomes the manifestation of Manifest Destiny itself, clearing the landscape of "foreigners." Equally important is the fact that Mexican women did not hold the same relationship to the land that white women did. Mexican women, like the land, were conquered or marginalized outside of the landscape; in Gast's *American Progress,* it is white women who clear the land of ethnic peoples.[10] It is no small coincidence that Amparo Ruiz's book *Who Would Have Thought It?* was published the same year that Gast's painting was

FIGURE 5.4. Thomas Gast, *American Progress*, 1872, oil on canvas, 17¾ by 21½ by 1¾ inches. (Courtesy of the Museum of the West, Autry National Center)

commissioned and publicly displayed throughout the eastern United States. The painting served as a visual display that would help in the selling of the West to the eastern public. In fact, Gast's painting was one of the most popular landscape portraits of the period, and prints of the painting were sold throughout the United States. Attached to many land advertisements of the nineteenth century, it was meant to entice Anglo-Americans to venture into the West and the lands of California where Amparo Ruiz lived.

Despite the thousands of newspaper articles, novels, and cultural works written by Mexican Americans such as Maria Amparo Ruiz and Francisco Ramirez who voiced their dissatisfaction with U.S. geopolitical designs, the pervasive and enduring logic of Manifest Destiny would in the end clear the land in an attempt to erase its memory and wipe Mexicans clean from its soil. The progressive goal of expansion, after all, was to wipe the earth clean, to create terra incognita, so that it could be resettled. Here we can surmise how the relationship between wiping the natural landscape clean was deeply associated with wiping the cultural and literary heritage of a people from that landscape. The atlas of American letters created during that expansionist period in literary history, what scholars have called the American Renaissance, also had to be terra incognita, mapped solely through the aesthetics of a white nation. But land, too, has memory.

Terra Cognita: Locating the Recent Past

Today, in our global age, terms such as *civic belonging, place,* and *landscape* take on such modernist, nostalgic, and essentialist connotations that I am almost afraid to utter them. But, you see, I have a memory of the land, a memory that is deeply rooted in the past. I remember countless stories about my grandparents and parents, all of whom at one time in their lives spent many days laboring on the white American lands in El Campo, Texas. My Mexican family has had a long history with lands that are now geographically defined as the United States. Either picking cotton or working on rice farms, they formed a relationship to the land that is not isolated. They spent their lives trying to escape the memories of the fields or lands they had lost in the war, only to realize that the fields and lands are always with the family, emerging in the stories they tell. Escaping the fields had a special meaning: it signified that we had made it to a better place and we now belonged. Mexicans' relationship to what are now U.S. lands has been bittersweet. For Mexicans, land and geography symbolize bodily and psychic pain, frustration, exclusion, racialization, and the past I related in the previous section. Yet, at the same time for them, land represents belonging, freedom, ownership, rights, *la raza, familia,* hope, and love. This struggle to make land a place instead of a space has been one of the culture's most enduring creative struggles. Tomás Rivera captures this struggle so eloquently in his beautifully crafted novel *Y no se lo trago la tierra (And the Earth Did Not Devour Him)* (1993) when he shows that land is the creative temporal force behind Mexican American culture; it is where all stories begin and end—it is where the future unfolds.

How do you recover and confront what has been so powerfully contradictory in Mexican American culture? How do Mexicans find and remember a place in and belong to an American landscape that does not presently include them in its technological vista? I return to the imaginative power of culture. Here we find Judy Baca's visual work *La memoria de nuestra tierra: Colorado* (The Memory of Our Land: Colorado), which perfectly illustrates how the discourse surrounding place, political inclusion, and belonging continue to affect our past and future understanding of Mexican American culture in the United States. Dedicated in 2000, *La memoria* is the last public-art mural the city of Denver installed in Denver International Airport (DIA). Funded by Denver's Public Arts Council and the Chicano Arts and Humanities Council, a grassroots community organization, the digitally produced ten-by-fifty-five-foot *La memoria* is in the central public space of DIA's main terminal. What I find so appealing about the piece is that it visually merges the public spaces of DIA, the state of Colorado, and the nation by merging Mexican lands and Mexican images with the expansionist history of the United States. In this way, it helps the public remember the imperial past that Ramirez and Amparo Ruiz address in their treatises on democracy's racial and geographic contours. *La memoria* is timely because today U.S. democratic culture is once again in crisis as its national landscape is demographically "browning." It is instructive because, like Ramirez's editorials and Amparo Ruiz's novel, both written during a founding moment of Mexican and Anglo relations, it shows that Mexicans continue to engage the public spheres and nineteenth-century geopolitical issues in order to challenge a U.S. democratic culture that questions their political and cultural position on U.S. lands.

Engaging the public in order to revitalize twenty-first-century democracy, *La memoria* uses digital technology to confront a U.S. public that has excluded and forgotten the geopolitical design of American democracy through what Judy Baca refers to as "public memory." Baca's conception of public memory further substantiates Raul Villa's argument that "narratives of place" reveal that "the persistence and power of memory is crucial, being simultaneously effective—as practically informing *history* in the politics of communal defense" (2000, 235). In this way, *La memoria*'s evocation of public memory is an act of civic recovery that brings forth a political message: Mexican lands and people are not antithetical to the democratic ideals of America. For *La memoria,* blood and soil bleed into one another, creating a new res publica within what were once Mexican lands. The mural serves as a model for understanding the possibility of a truly inclusive democracy. In doing so, it radically expands democracy's inclusive and universal ideals through the recovery of land

and of the Mexican political and cultural workers who once resided on the land, like the newly recovered writers Ramirez and Amparo Ruiz. As I discussed earlier, because of the loss of property rights in the years that followed the Treaty of Guadalupe Hidalgo, these workers' civil right to enter the U.S. political system was affected, and therefore their voices were historically relegated to the dustbins of democratic and literary history. They have only now been recovered in this age of the browning of America. In the end, *La memoria* helps us both to remember Ramirez's and Amparo Ruiz's literary contours of democracy and to recover a place in the American landscape where Mexicans belong.

Recovering Mexicans and Chicanos who have shaped the American landscape, *La memoria de nuestra tierra* interweaves the Colorado landscape with digital images of Aztecs, Mexicans of the Mexican Revolution, Chicana workers, farmers, miners, immigrants, Native cultures, and the Chicano public figures César Chávez, Rudolfo "Corky" Gonzales, and Reies López Tijerina, who were involved in the land-recovery movement of Aztlán during the Chicano civil rights movement. Merging the landscape with historical memory and public figures who have fought for Mexican American civil rights since the nineteenth century, Baca's work blurs the distinction between the land and Mexicans, between the public and the private, between civil rights and land rights in order to make a new place for the Mexicans of today and tomorrow. The Mexicans in the work haunt the brown and gold landscape of mountains, canyons, and plains; they are specters in the memory of the land. The digitally enhanced ghostly photographic silhouettes shimmer when the light from the sun penetrates DIA's mountainous architecture, and the translucent images of these Mexicans symbolically represent their absence from America's history.

La memoria's visuality is particularly important considering that in the media Mexicans have once again become the object of discussions concerning their place in the U.S. political landscape. Take, for example, the collaboration of media giants CNN, ABC News, *Time,* Time.com, and America Online in a month-long investigation into the future of American democracy: the making of "Amexica." "The border is vanishing before our eyes, creating a new world for all of us," *Time* magazine declared on the cover of its special issue on the browning of America ("Welcome to Amexica" 2001). On the cover, under the headline, a *Time* photojournalist captures two Mexican children. Staring at the public through sunglasses, the children become haunting images, silently representing the new demographics of an American nation whose economy is fueled by NAFTA's contradictory empire-building and neoliberal ideals.

As Anglo-America gazes upon these photographs at the newsstands, in supermarket lines, and in their homes, they question how to include these people into their lives and how this inclusion will affect their world. Changing the name *America* to *Amexica* (without the proper accent), *Time* freezes the attention of the middle-class and mostly white public in a moment of linguistic terror. The word *America*, which has historically symbolized democratic freedom, liberalism, terra cognita (known and mapped landscape), and free-market capitalism, morphs into a new symbol, one changed by the linguistic inclusion of the word *Mexican*. Terra incognita once again reveals itself within the linguistic meaning of *Amexica*, and yet another Mexican Question emerges.

After the 2001 visit of Mexico's president Vicente Fox, President George W. Bush, the Spanish-speaking and self-defined "friend of the Mexican people," discussed legislation that would continue to affect this complexion of the United States. After Fox's appeal to a joint session of Congress in September 2001, asking for dual citizenship for Mexicans residing in America, Bush stated that he wanted to accommodate his friends in Mexico and that if "[Mexicans] are willing to do jobs others in America aren't willing to do, we ought to welcome that person [*sic*] to the country and we ought to make that a legal part of our economy" (qtd. in Editorial 2001).

Covered by every news channel, newspaper, and talk show, Bush argued that Mexicans would do the work that Anglo-Americans would not. They would groom Anglo lawns, raise their children, clean their homes, and pick their produce. Therefore, Bush insisted that Americans should include Mexicans into America as laboring citizens; after all, they were already participating in the economy by working the land. According to Bush's "compassionate conservatism," the geopolitics of Mexican American inclusion and their increased numbers in the United States is a fiscal matter: it is good for the U.S. economy. As such, the border between the two nations should become a porous space that will allow Mexican laborers to cross so that they can work U.S. lands. Despite the fact that America was entering a recession, he argued that their presence would only help, not hinder, our progress as a nation.

Bush's comments maintain the common solidarity of America by selling two different types of political identities within the nation's borders. On the one hand, Mexicans are "included" in the public not through traditional republican ideals of property ownership, but rather through their collective racialized existence. Mexicans are a laboring prosthesis in the United States. On the other, America is not a democracy of universal equality and egalitarianism; rather, it is a capitalist democracy built on the backs of racial others whose political subjectivity is as laborers tied to the U.S. capitalist mode of production, not as free citizens of the state. As such, the prosthetic, laboring Mexican enables Anglos to normalize themselves as a class and citizen designation drastically different from that of Mexicans in the United States. Mexicans are the working arms of the body politic, whereas Anglos remain the reasoned mind of U.S. democracy. Anglos can enjoy the land, not work it. Moreover, under Bush's proposal, even if Mexicans become the predominate population in the United States, as the 2000 census map indicates, they will merely be second-class citizens who work the land by picking produce or grooming lawns. In effect, Bush creates third-world rights for Mexican workers, not inclusion for them as citizens within the U.S. first-world geographic border.

Bush's answer to the Mexican Question, the browning of America's landscape, and the making of "Amexica" form a more leisurative Anglo-America that benefits from the labor done by Mexican Americans, whose citizenship remains dubious. When *Time* magazine, George W. Bush, or the published figures of the census suggest that we are soon to have "Amexica," this assertion poses a challenge to U.S. inclusivity and thus to white America's common solidarity. Although the presuppositions of democracy warrant Mexican American inclusion, such inclusion is counter to a nation's desire to create a country whose people know one another, trust one another, look alike, and feel a sense of solidarity with one another.

And yet for more than fifty years the media has been defining Mexicans as the sleeping giant, objectifying a people according to a rhetorical logic of absent presence. Despite the fact that Mexicans are within the U.S. borders and immigrate every day to help maintain the U.S. global economy, the U.S. public spheres have rhetorically created an ephemeral existence for Mexicans in the past 150 years. The short-lived memory concerning Mexicans in the public spheres creates a cyclical inquiry into the rights and status of Mexicans in the United States. As I have been suggesting, the inquiries recently developed from the demographic "browning of America" are not new: they are nothing more than yet another question about the absent presence of Mexicans on the U.S. landscape that began in the nineteenth century.

Today, Mexicans' relationship to the U.S. nation is mediated through the free-market rhetoric of NAFTA and conservative anti- or pro-business immigration legislation. Media venues in the age of NAFTA do not want to remember that Mexico has geographically and economically participated in the rise of the United States as an imperial and economic power. U.S. borders are still patrolled under Operation Gatekeeper, as are the discursive borders of the public sphere. Parochial discourses of America's economic exceptionalism inform the national public's lack of memory. The result is that Mexicans remain objects of inquiry within the media, never able to represent themselves fully in the nation.

For Mexicans in the United States, however, the land has an alternative public memory. And this is exactly why *La memoria*'s recovery of the landscape is so important during this moment. As a site that visually represents the temporal past of Mexicans and their land, *La memoria* places the private history of Mexicans within a late-capitalist space, an international airport that defines time according to transnational and global flight schedules. With each shimmering landscape panel, the mural reminds the Denver public of its inability to remember the past. In one of the busiest airports in the world, the mural has an infinite number of public subjects to impress and thus is a landmark in Chicano public art in that its geopolitical strategies of publicity make Mexicans in the United States *the* public site of civic debate for an infinite number of publics, either local or national or global. The mural's initial spatial act of publicity "browns" DIA's white architecture, but as a public site creating public memory for local, national, and global spaces, the mural also "browns" Colorado, the United States, and the world through historical images that are literally reflected out of the digitally inscribed photos and landscape. The mural, then, inevitably expands democratic culture with each passenger's gaze, creating public memory of the land where there was once none.

The mural conveys the idea that Mexicans are not passive subjects being discussed and shaped by and for white America. Although white

America constitutes one of the many publics the mural addresses, Baca also personally reached out to more than four thousand members of the Mexican American public, held classes and seminars, talked to their political leaders, and created public spheres in which Mexicans in the United States could actively engage in her vision of the mural. In every way, the mural was a public act, created out of the history of Mexicans who are demographically changing the complexion of America's landscape. Through *La memoria,* Mexicans' presence in the United States of this NAFTA era is no longer an amnesiac inquiry that objectifies or normalizes them and their land for global capitalist flows. *La memoria*'s Mexicans are no longer outside of the map. The land has memory, and so too should we all.

The recovery of the recent Mexican past will be an ongoing archival endeavor that has yet to be fully realized. The demographic numbers of the 2000 census mark an important moment in the United States that has yet to reveal its cultural effects on the everyday realities of Mexicans and Anglos. The period when Mexican Americans emerge from the shadows of capitalism is still unfolding with every page unearthed by the Recovery Project. In the end, then, it is in the realm of culture that Mexicans in the United States will uncover the paths that will help us map our recent past and create the future history of Mexican America. Through archival projects such as the Recovering the U.S. Hispanic Literary Heritage and the recuperative visual work of Judy Baca, Mexicans in the United States will show that their heritage in America has roots deep within the very bedrock of America.

Literature Cited

Almaguer, T. 1994. *Racial Faultlines: The Historical Origins of White Supremacy in California*. Berkeley and Los Angeles: University of California Press.

Amparo Ruiz de Burton, M. [1872] 1995. *Who Would Have Thought It?* Edited by Rosaura Sanchez. Houston: Arte Público Press.

Brady, M. P. 2002. *Extinct Lands, Temporal Geographies: Chicano Literature and the Urgency of Space*. Durham, N.C.: Duke University Press.

———. 2003. Full of Empty: Creating the Southwest as "Terra Incognita." In *Nineteenth Century Geographies: The Transformation of Space from the Victorian Age to the New Century,* edited by Helena Mitchie, 251–65. New Brunswick, N.J.: Rutgers University Press.

Brewer, C., and T. A. Suchan. 2001. *Mapping Census 2000: The Geography of U.S. Diversity*. Washington, D.C.: U.S. Census Bureau, U.S. Department of Commerce.

Calhoun, J. C. 1849. Statement to the U.S. House of Representatives, July 29. *Congressional Record* (no other information available).

Casteñeda, A. 2003. Malinche, Califia y Toypurina: Of Myths, Monsters, and Embodied History. Unpublished paper.

Editorial. 2001. *Washington Post*, September 7.

Gaspar de Alba, A. 1997. *Chicano Art: Inside/Outside the Master's House—Cultural Politics and the CARA Exhibit*. Austin: University of Texas Press.

González, D. 1998. *The Treaty of Guadalupe Hidalgo, 1848: Papers on the Sesquicentennial Symposium, 1848–1998*. Las Cruces, N.M.: Doña Ana Historical Society.

Gruesz Silva, K. 2003. Utopia Latina: The Ordinary Seaman in Extraordinary Times. *MFS: Modern Fiction Studies* 49, no. 1: 54–83.

Lighton, W. 1899. The Greaser. *Atlantic Monthly* 83, no. 500 (June): 986–1021.

Menchaca, M. 2001. *Recovering History, Constructing Race: The Indian, Black, and White Roots of Mexican Americans*. Austin: University of Texas Press.

O'Sullivan, J. 1845a. Annexation. *The United States Magazine and Democratic Review* 17, no. 85 (July–August): 234–54.

———. 1845b. The Mexican Question. *North American Review*, 434–45.

Perez, E. 1999. *The Decolonial Imaginary: Writing Chicanas into History*. Bloomington: Indiana University Press.

Ramirez, F. P. 1855. Editorials. *El Clamor Público*, no specific dates.

Rivera, T. 1993. *Y no se lo trago la tierra (And the Earth Did Not Devour Him)*. Bilingual ed. Houston: Arte Público Press.

Rogoff, I. 2000. *Terra Infirma: Geography's Visual Culture*. New York: Routledge.

Santa Ana, O. 2002. *Brown Tide Rising: Metaphors of Latinos in Contemporary American Public Discourse*. Austin: University of Texas Press.

Stephanson, A. 1995. *Manifest Destiny: American Expansion and the Empire of Right*. New York: Hill and Wang.

Tallis, J., and J. Rapkin. 1851. *Tallis Illustrated Map of Mexico, California, and Texas*. From *The Illustrated Atlas*. London: John Tallis and Co.

U.S. Census Bureau. 1997. *Statistical Abstract of the United States*. Washington, D.C.: U.S. Census Bureau.

———. 2000. *Census 2000*. Washington, D.C.: U.S. Census Bureau.

———. 2001. *Survey of Minority-Owned Business Enterprises*. Washington, D.C.: U.S. Census Bureau.

———. 2007. *Current Population Survey*. Washington, D.C.: U.S. Census Bureau.

Villa, R. 2000. *Barrio-Logos: Space and Place in Urban Chicano Literature and Culture*. Austin: University of Texas Press.

Walker, F. A. 1874. *Statistical Atlas of the United States Based on the Results of the Ninth Census, 1870, with Contributions from Many Eminent Men of Science and Several Departments of the [Federal] Government*. New York: Julius Bien.

Welcome to Amexica. 2001. *Time* magazine, June 11.

6

Healing with Howls

REWILDING THE SOUTHERN ROCKIES

Hannah Gosnell

SOMETIME AFTER JANUARY 15, 2004, a two-year-old female member of Yellowstone National Park's Swan Lake Pack known as Wolf 293 set out on her own to look for a mate with whom she might start another pack in a new territory. Perhaps because it was winter, her instincts told her to head south and keep to the lower-elevation valleys and foothills, where she would be able to find game along the way. After traversing the length of Wyoming, she was spotted by humans near Steamboat Springs, Colorado, and again farther south near Idaho Springs. She must have noticed increasing signs of human activity along the way, as anyone driving south from Wyoming inevitably does, but she still forged on, looking for other wolves. Her five-month, five-hundred-mile journey came to an end on June 7 when she was hit by a car and killed while trying to cross Interstate 70, a major highway bisecting the state of Colorado.[1]

Wolf 293's premature death is tragic in and of itself, given how far she had come, the futility of her search for other wolves in Colorado, where the last wild wolf was killed in 1935, and the missed opportunity to make it a few hundred miles farther to New Mexico, where she may have found the wolves she was looking for. But even more troubling is what her demise suggests about the condition of the Southern Rockies.

Coloradoans have been wildly successful at attracting newcomers to our state for more than a hundred years, and we have a vibrant economy and culture to prove it. But along the way we have destroyed native species and ecosystems and have carved up the landscape so much that even if we decided to change our minds and welcome back wide-ranging carnivores such as the wolf, they probably would not do very well here. As the population in the Southern Rockies continues to grow—demographers anticipate a Colorado population of 6.2 million by 2050—so too will the rate of habitat loss and fragmentation, the leading causes of biodiversity loss.² Given that many people are attracted to the Rockies for their wilderness qualities, it is ironic that their arrival inevitably and inexorably contributes to the "dewilding" of the region. Wolf 293's death raises the question, What kind of future do we want for the region? If we decide on a wild future, how do we do it? How can we "rewild" the Southern Rockies?

The Big Picture: Healthy Ecosystems Need Carnivores

In 1949, Aldo Leopold published "Thinking Like a Mountain," an essay about his journey toward an understanding of the critical role that large predators such as the wolf play in mountain ecosystems and the problems that arise when they are eliminated. The essay recounts his experience shooting a wolf with some fellow hunters and gathering around the fallen animal:

> We reached the old wolf in time to watch a fierce green fire dying in her eyes. I realized then, and have known ever since, that there was something new to me in those eyes—something known only to her and to the mountain. I was young then, and full of trigger-itch; I thought that because fewer wolves meant more deer, that no wolves would mean hunters' paradise. But after seeing the green fire die, I sensed that neither the wolf nor the mountain agreed with such a view.³

Leopold went on to describe the negative ecological effects of overbrowsing by deer on "wolfless mountains," where no natural predators exist to cull their populations. Wildlife biologists like Leopold have since then sought to understand better and explain the complex relationships between predators, prey, and the ecosystems in which they live.

Many carnivores, such as Wolf 293, are "keystone species," meaning that their influence on ecosystem function is disproportionately important relative to their low abundance.⁴ The keystone-species concept posits that although all species interact, "the interactions of some species are more profound and far reaching than others, such that their elimination from an ecosystem often triggers cascades of direct and indirect changes on more than a single trophic level, leading eventually to losses of habitats and extirpation of other species in the food web."[5] Conversely, the presence of large carnivores in a system can enhance its functionality. The extirpation and reintroduction of wolves in Yellowstone National Park illustrates this point perfectly.

Wolf 293 was part of the Swan Lake Pack, one of approximately fifteen wolf packs that have recolonized the Greater Yellowstone Ecosystem after nearly seventy years of absence, bringing some stability back to the ecosystem.[6] Without wolves, elk were free to congregate along streams all day, eating willows at an unsustainable rate, which had a negative impact on riparian ecosystems, much like the overbrowsing by deer observed by Leopold in the 1930s. The damage to riparian areas in Yellowstone resulted in a diminished food supply for beaver and a loss of habitat for nesting bird populations.[7]

The reintroduction of wolves in 1995 created what wolf biologists have called an *ecology of fear*.[8] Elk no longer spend as much time in open streambeds now, thus reducing the stress on willows, which in turn has created favorable conditions for the return of the beaver. The number of beaver colonies in the park's northern range, for example, increased from one prior to wolf reintroduction to seven in 2003.[9] Beaver, acting as "ecosystem engineers," initiate their own trophic cascade of positive effects when they build pools of slow-moving water around their dams and create habitat for otters, muskrats, insects, moose, and many bird species. The reintroduction of wolves in Yellowstone has also helped scavenging species such as ravens, magpies, and grizzly bear, who eat leftovers from wolf kills.[10]

A major benefit of supporting natural processes such as predation is that they minimize the need for human management. Once large predators are restored, the thinking goes, other keystone species and natural processes will recover on their own.[11] So reintroducing wolves to a system can save time, money, and frustration over the long run. The Greater Yellowstone Ecosystem is healthier now with wolves, but to what extent can lessons learned there be applied elsewhere? If our goal is anything more than an isolated zoo, we need to think about what will happen when Yellowstone wolves such as 293 seek to expand their territory and find less-welcoming environments to the north and south. What is it about Yellowstone that allows wolves to thrive? In a word, space.

Large carnivores need large, intact, protected swaths of land to thrive. National parks and federally designated wilderness areas are the best we can offer, but they are few and far between, relatively speaking. Given that it would hardly be reasonable to expect all activities, development, and roads to cease along the length of the Rockies in the name of creating wolf habitat, connectivity between core protected areas becomes critically important. With adequate connectivity, wide-ranging mammals can be accommodated and the locking up of entire landscapes avoided. Without connectivity, wolves such as 293 do not stand a chance.

A Vision for Continental Connectivity and the Role of the Southern Rockies

Recognition of the importance of big wilderness and connectivity for ecosystem health dates back to the late 1960s with the development of the theory of *island biogeography,* which focuses on the species-area relationship.[12] Researchers identified a positive correlation between the size of a preserve and species diversity, noting that small habitat remnants not only hampered the movement of wide ranging species, but were also vulnerable to "edge effects" and invasion of exotic species.[13] In 1985, William Newmark published a paper documenting his finding that the rate of local extinction in U.S. national parks was inversely related to their size. He noted a loss of mammal species in all but the largest North American park complexes.[14] According to this line of thinking, even Yellowstone National Park, at 3,472 square miles or approximately 2.2 million acres (larger than Rhode Island and Delaware combined), is considered inadequate to provide sufficient "demographic resilience" and "genetic-evolutionary fitness" for animals such as wolverines and grizzly bears in the absence of linkages to other wildlands.[15] In the early 1980s, the principles of island biogeography were adopted by a new group of scientists—conservation biologists—interested in the practical application of science to the cause of conservation.[16]

Birth of the Rewilding Concept

In 1991, Michael Soulé, often called the father of conservation biology, suggested a San Francisco meeting of a few leaders in the conservation world, including Earth First!er Dave Foreman. Tired of the defensive,

"putting-out-brushfires" approach to conservation that so many organizations relied on with mixed results, and cognizant of the complexity
and scale of the problem of biodiversity loss, Soulé wanted to develop a
hopeful, proactive, hundred-year vision of what North America should
be. The group agreed that Earth is now clearly in a mass-extinction event
caused almost entirely by the impact of humans (see David Armstrong's
chapter in this volume). Stemming this alarming tide of extinction, they
decided, would require conservation vision and action at local, regional,
and continental scales.

The group of scientists and activists envisioned a continent where
pre-Columbian animal migrations could take place via an interconnected
network of wildlands. They identified four major "MegaLinkages": the
Pacific—from Baja California to Alaska; the Appalachian—from Florida to
New Brunswick; the Boreal—from Alaska to the Canadian Maritimes; and
the Spine of the Continent—from Central America to Alaska through the
Rocky Mountains and other ranges.[17] Foreman and Soulé cofounded the
Wildlands Project in 1992 to implement their vision: "rewilding" North
America. *Rewilding* is defined as "the scientific argument for restoring
big wilderness based on the regulatory roles of large predators."[18] Central
to the rewilding approach are what Soulé calls "the three Cs": cores,
corridors, and carnivores. In a 1998 article, Soulé and fellow conservation biologist Reed Noss outlined the reasoning behind the rewilding
approach to conservation:

> Our principal premise is that rewilding is a critical step in restoring
> self-regulating land communities. Recall that viable populations of
> large predators require both large core areas and connectivity, thus
> bolstering the resilience and viability of reserve networks. Also, large
> predators initiate chains of far-reaching and manifold ecological inter-
> actions; in the absence of these keystone species, many ecosystems
> will become degraded and simplified. Extensive networks of cores
> and habitat linkages also sustain a vast range of natural processes, thus
> minimizing the need for human management. Once large predators
> are restored, many if not most of the other keystone and "habitat-
> creating" species (e.g., beavers, prairie dogs), "keystone ecosystems,"
> and natural regimes of disturbance and other processes will recover
> on their own.[19]

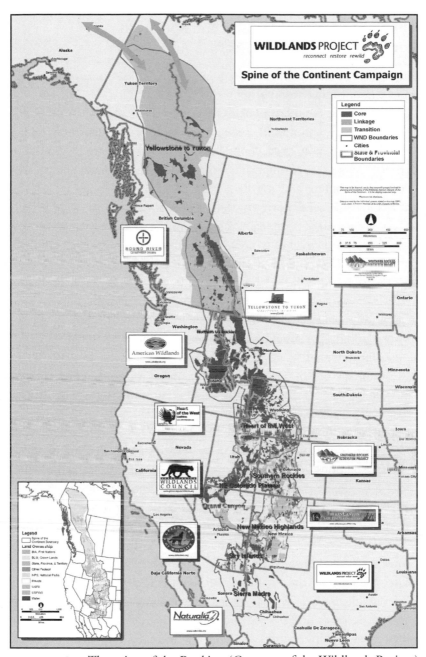

FIGURE 6.1. The spine of the Rockies. (Courtesy of the Wildlands Project)

The Southern Rockies and the Southern Rockies Ecosystem Project

During the 1990s, a number of regional organizations formed to implement the rewilding vision around the continent. One of them was the Colorado-based Southern Rockies Ecosystem Project (SREP). Founded in 1992, SREP is a nonprofit conservation biology organization working to protect and restore large, continuous networks of land in the Southern Rockies Ecoregion.[20] Comprising most of western Colorado and parts of southern Wyoming and northern New Mexico, the Southern Rockies are roughly 500 miles north to south and 250 miles east to west at their widest, for a total of about 63,000 square miles, or more than 40 million acres—an area the size of Maine, New Hampshire, Vermont, Connecticut, Rhode Island, and Massachusetts combined. The Southern Rockies encompass ten major river basins (including the Colorado, the Platte, and the Rio Grande) and straddle the Continental Divide. There are no major cities in the region, but obviously it is greatly affected by the cities surrounding it—Albuquerque, Santa Fe, Denver, Colorado Springs, Fort Collins, Grand Junction, and Casper.

The Southern Rockies are especially famous for Fourteeners (mountains higher than 14,000 feet) and high alpine ecosystems, but include many other major native ecosystem types as well (approximately thirteen of them, including old-growth ponderosa pine forest, old aspen forest, low-elevation riparian communities, sagebrush shrublands, and montane grasslands, among others). This diversity is a result of the region's dramatic topography—elevations ranging from 4,300 feet along the Colorado River near Grand Junction to 14,433 feet on Mt. Elbert. The average elevation in the ecoregion is 9,670 feet above sea level.

In spite of all the region's grandeur, only 11 percent of it is strictly protected as wilderness areas and national parks and monuments. Like most of the West, the Southern Rockies Ecoregion is mostly publicly owned, with the U.S. Forest Service managing the largest share—about 7 million acres, or 42 percent—but most of that land is open to multiple uses such as logging, grazing, mining, and recreation. In terms of strictly protected areas, there are fifty wilderness areas and six national parks and monuments, with Great Sand Dunes being the most recent addition to the park system. Most of the strictly protected land, however, is in alpine

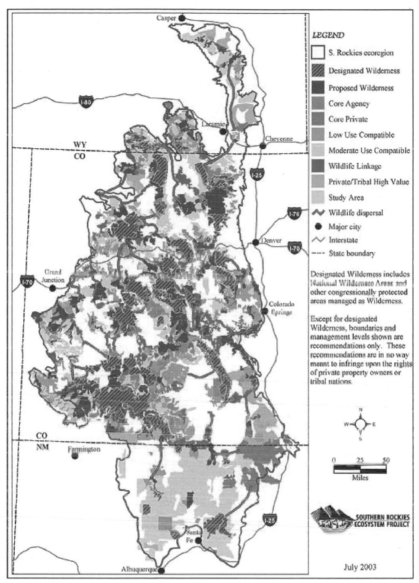

FIGURE 6.2. A general outline of the Southern Rockies Ecoregion.
(Courtesy of the Southern Rockies Ecosystem Project)

and subalpine environments. One of SREP's major findings in its 2000 *State of the Southern Rockies Ecoregion* report was that because of this alpine bias, our current system of preserves does not adequately protect the region's major ecosystem types.[21]

On a more positive note, however, when one takes into consideration all the unprotected roadless areas with wilderness value in the ecoregion as well, it is fair to say that about one-quarter of the ecoregion remains in a wild condition. There are roughly 9.6 million acres in roadless areas, but only 40 percent of those acres are protected as parks and wilderness. Roadless areas are important to conservation efforts not only because they provide linkages between core protected areas but also because many of them contain middle- and lower-elevation ecosystems that are not well represented in our current system of preserves. A number of leading conservation biologists have documented significant linkages between roadlessness and biodiversity.[22] Similarly, the threats to carnivore survival posed by roads (habitat loss, avoidance issues, barrier effects, vehicle collisions, increased accessibility to wild areas by poachers) have been well documented.[23] Not only do roads themselves represent a threat to carnivore survival, but the access they provide to human settlements increases the likelihood of conflict with humans, which often results in mortality for the carnivore.[24]

Protecting roadless areas in the Southern Rockies is an important first step in the restoration and preservation of a wild Southern Rockies, but it is important to note that even if we were magically and permanently to protect all the roadless areas tomorrow, we would still be left with a fragmented landscape. An aerial view of the region would reveal that 93.8 percent of these areas is within two-tenths of a mile from a road.[25] Years of piecemeal development without attention to the bigger picture have resulted in a landscape that is difficult for large mammals to navigate, and we are starting to reap the cumulative effects in the form of biodiversity loss and incidents such as the death of Wolf 293.

In an effort to combat this short-sighted "expeditious" approach to development (see the chapter by Alan Wallis and Gene Bressler) with a proactive, achievable, landscape-scale vision for protecting and restoring the Southern Rockies, analysts at SREP used computer modeling and expert opinion to design a viable wildlands network for the ecoregion. Using geographical information system software to perform analysis of

FIGURE 6.3. A wildlife bridge. (Courtesy of Digital Animation Services)

plant communities, key species' suitable habitat, and existing protected areas throughout the region, they established both where protected cores and linkages should be located and how large the network should be. They then incorporated existing citizen management and wilderness proposals for public lands to shape the network design map, which is at the heart of SREP's overarching vision for the Southern Rockies. This process has enabled SREP and its partners to pinpoint the natural landscapes that are most critical to rewilding the Southern Rockies. In essence, the wildlands network design is a potential roadmap for animals such as Wolf 293 —but only if the relevant lands identified are adequately protected.

Implementing the Wildlands Network Design

Rewilding the Southern Rockies and ensuring long-term ecological health in the region will involve a three-pronged approach: (1) preserving remaining roadless areas as core protected areas; (2) ensuring appropriate use and adequate protection of key linkages between core areas to facilitate landscape permeability and connectivity; and (3) reintroducing wolves and other missing carnivores to the ecoregion.

Protecting Roadless Areas

In January 2001, just two weeks before leaving office, President Bill Clinton took a big step toward accomplishing the first of these necessary actions by signing into law the Roadless Area Conservation Rule ("Roadless Rule") to prohibit timber harvesting and most new road construction in areas inventories by the Forest Service. The rule aimed to protect 4.43 million of the 6 million previously unprotected acres of roadless wildlands in Colorado. The "Roadless Rule" was the result of years of deliberation and the input of approximately 2.5 million comments from Americans all around the country, including thirty-six thousand comments from Coloradans, 90 percent of which were in favor of protecting roadless areas. Unprecedented in its overwhelming popularity, the rule garnered ten times more public comments than any other federal rule in history.

With the election of George W. Bush in 2000, however, the fate of the Roadless Rule came into question. Soon after taking control of the White House, the Bush administration issued a directive postponing the effective date of all federal rules not yet in effect, including the Roadless Rule. On May 9, 2002, twenty-six senators sent a letter to President Bush asking him to uphold the rule. Citing concerns about the economic impact the Roadless Rule might have on western states, however, the Bush administration proposed to replace the rule with a state petition process that would allow the governor of any state with inventoried roadless areas in national forest to petition the secretary of agriculture to adopt regulations for management of a given roadless area. If the secretary accepted the governor's petition, the Forest Service would initiate a state-specific rulemaking. Without the Roadless Rule's restrictions and in the absence of a state petition, management of roadless areas would revert to the direction contained in local forest-management plans. According to a Wilderness Society analysis published in 2005, forest plans nationwide allow road building in 34 million acres of inventoried roadless areas, or about 59 percent of the 58.5 million roadless acres. Thus, under the new rule, most roadless areas would be vulnerable to new road construction for logging, energy development, and other commodity uses unless individual governors proactively attempt to seek protection in each state.[26]

In July 2004, the U.S. Forest Service initiated a comment period for the Bush administration's new proposed rule. By the close of the comment period, more than 1.7 million comments—including a letter from New Mexico governor Bill Richardson and eight other governors—opposed the administration's draft rule and supported the reinstatement of the original Roadless Rule. In spite of public pressure, the Bush administration eventually repealed Clinton's Roadless Rule formally in May 2005, replacing it with the state petition process. In response to this action, Montana governor Brian Schweitzer wrote in a letter to President Bush: "Shifting the responsibility for management of the nation's roadless areas to the states is an attempt to pass the buck. . . . Four years ago, when the 2001 roadless rule was being considered, Montana went through an exhaustive public process conducted by the Forest Service. . . . Our Montana values and the importance of these mountain areas have not changed."[27]

In August 2005, Governor Ted Kulongoski of Oregon and three attorney generals from California, Arizona, and Oregon filed a lawsuit against the Bush administration for dismantling restrictions in the Roadless Rule, alleging a threat to forests, fisheries, and drinking water.[28] Several other states later joined them in this lawsuit. At the same time, individual governors, including Republican governor Arnold Schwarzenegger of California, began to petition for protection of their state's roadless areas under the new guidelines. On September 20, 2006, Judge Elizabeth LaPorte of the U.S. District Court Northern District of California ruled that the administration had illegally repealed the Roadless Rule, and she reinstated it nationwide, except in Alaska's Tongass National Forest. This decision was later upheld by the Ninth Circuit Court. In May 2007, more than 150 Democratic and Republican members of Congress introduced legislation that would codify the original Roadless Area Conservation Rule, thereby permanently protecting 58.5 million acres of roadless national forest land in thirty-nine states. The fate of the Roadless Rule is not certain, however, as opposing states continue to file lawsuits challenging the rule.

The Bush administration's determined efforts to stop the protection of roadless areas out of concerns about economic impacts deserve closer examination. Contrary to the administration's claims, studies have shown that such protection would be economically as well as ecologically beneficial to states such as Colorado. In 2001, for example, 82 million Americans sixteen years or older, or 43 percent of the adult population, enjoyed some form of wildlife-related recreation. In doing so, they injected $108 billion into the national economy (1.1 percent of gross domestic product), supporting hundreds of thousands of jobs.[29] This figure does not even include the economic benefits of popular sports such as hiking, biking, backcountry skiing, and horseback riding. According to the Outdoor Industry Association, Coloradoans spend an estimated $200 million annually on outdoor gear.[30] The Forest Service's own statistics demonstrate that extractive industries on Forest Service lands generated $9 billion in 1999 and 153,000 jobs nationally, whereas conservation activities (wilderness, recreation, and the protection of endangered species) generated $27 billion and 669,000 jobs nationally.[31] And a Wilderness Society study found that, on average, one job is supported by 550 acres of designated wilderness in Colorado, slightly less than twice (1.7 times) the number of jobs in the state related to the logging industry.[32] These figures suggest that protection of the core wildlands identified by SREP as critical to the health of Southern Rockies ecosystems will not be an economic burden; on the contrary, it will preserve the qualities that attract people—and jobs—to the region.[33]

Cultivating Linkages Between Protected Areas

As important as core protected areas are, however, they are of little value if they are isolated from one another, separated by a sea of roads and residential and commercial development. In addition to protecting core areas, we must also think intelligently about and act to protect critical corridors or linkages connecting them. What are the best "Band-Aids" for the arguably "sick," disparate landscapes of the Southern Rockies? How can bits of pristine, protected habitat be stitched together in a way that keeps the ecosystem alive and healthy? One way is by proactively identifying feasible corridors on private, developable land that are capable of being protected in one way or another, for example by local land-use policy or conservation easements. "Clustered" residential development that concentrates houses in one part of a parcel while leaving open space, or a commons, where critical wildlife habitat exists is one example, but requires developers and planners to move beyond the expediency discussed in Wallis and Bressler's chapter.

Mitigating the habitat fragmentation caused by busy highways represents another such approach, one that SREP is actively pursuing. In partnership with the Colorado Department of Transportation (CDOT), The Nature Conservancy, and Colorado State University, SREP recently launched Linking Colorado's Landscapes, a campaign to identify and prioritize wildlife linkages across the state of Colorado. The goal is to provide transportation planners, community leaders, and conservationists with a statewide vision for reconnecting habitats that are vital for maintaining healthy populations of native species.[34]

The second phase of this project concentrated on twelve of the highest-priority linkages and was designed to provide in-depth assessments of highway permeability for wildlife where highways transect these linkages.[35] To complete the linkages assessments, SREP partnered with transportation engineers and biologists from state and federal transportation and resource agencies to develop guidelines and recommendations for improving safe passages for wildlife across these stretches of highway using the best available techniques. CDOT and the Federal Highway Administration intend to use these linkage assessment reports to improve transportation and mitigation planning in these high-priority corridors.

These twelve locations are not the only places where CDOT is focusing attention on wildlife connectivity needs. It has installed crossing structures for the endangered Canada lynx (*Lynx canadensis*) in several locations around the state that are undergoing highway-expansion projects. In addition, in collaboration with the U.S. Fish and Wildlife Service, the U.S. Forest Service, and the Colorado Division of Wildlife, CDOT recently completed an analysis of the Interstate 70 transportation corridor and identified thirteen key wildlife-crossing areas. Among them is West Vail Pass, which serves as one of the last remaining forested connections for wildlife moving north–south through the heart of the Rocky Mountains. Heavily developed resort areas, high levels of recreational use, and streams of passenger and freight traffic severely constrict wildlife movement through this linkage.

To mitigate these barriers, one of the nation's first vegetated wildlife overpasses, also known as a wildlife bridge, is being proposed at this location. Construction of this bridge, which seems likely, will be nationally significant due to its progressive, multiagency approach to wildlife management and landscape-scale conservation. Seven "span bridges" currently allow wildlife passage under Interstate 70 in the Vail area, but there is no wildlife fencing along the highway to encourage use of the structures, and a five-mile gap between crossing opportunities occurs near the top of the pass. The wildlife bridge is proposed somewhere within this five-mile gap. According to SREP, "Fencing will tie together the existing underpasses and the wildlife bridge. This addresses the landscape permeability needs of the entire Vail Pass landscape, providing multiple opportunities for safe passage within this eight mile stretch." In November 2005, $420,000 was allotted to CDOT for preliminary analysis and design of the bridge. In February 2007, CDOT posted a Scope of Work for those funds to determine the exact location of the bridge at West Vail Pass, after which preliminary engineering designs will be completed.[36] Agency support for wildlife connectivity is critical to the survival of wildlife populations at both a local and a regional scale, as are innovative partnerships such as the one between SREP and CDOT. The West Vail Pass Wildlife Bridge Project illustrates how seemingly disparate organizations such as SREP, CDOT, federal agencies, and other partners can work together to develop solutions to the problems surrounding fragmented landscapes where many different stakeholders are involved. Indeed, SREP's vision and approach are now being adopted in other regions around the West.[37]

Reintroducing Wolves to the Southern Rockies

Finally, if we are to ensure a wild future for the region, we must support the reintroduction of wolves to the Southern Rockies. In 2001, an independent survey of voters in Colorado, New Mexico, and Arizona revealed that two-thirds of respondents support the restoration of wolves to the Southern Rockies, but the political opposition to such a plan remains strong.[38] The arrival of Wolf 293 in 2004 suggests that wolves are willing and able to get here, but whether they are allowed to stay and whether they are ever invited back are issues still being debated.

In February 2004, acknowledging the likelihood of wolves' eventual migration to the region from Greater Yellowstone, the Colorado Division of Wildlife began to develop a wolf-management plan. The agency held meetings around the state to inform the public about the planning process and to gather public input on the issue. All six meetings were well attended, and comments were overwhelmingly in favor of welcoming and supporting the wolf.

The agency next appointed a working group composed of scientists, agency personnel, conservationists, sportsmen, and livestock producers to develop a draft wolf-management plan. Two major issues to be discussed were (1) whether wolves would be tolerated and allowed to stay as they migrated in on their own; and (2) whether they should be actively reintroduced to the state, keeping in mind that reintroduction on non-federal lands would require approval of the state legislature. The group met several times around the state, with the goal of producing a draft plan by the fall of 2004, but contentious debate among its members made progress difficult. It was not until the group met for the fourth time in a remote place on the Western Slope for two days that progress began to be made. According to one working group member, something about being "stuck" with each other overnight forced them to begin to appreciate the humanity in one another, and formerly ideological positions began to soften—an important lesson for other efforts to heal the "tattered" relationships referred to elsewhere in this volume. The working group agreed upon and produced a draft plan in the spring of 2005, then asked the public to comment on it. In May 2005, the Colorado Wildlife Commission eventually adopted the plan, which allows wolves that migrate into the state on their own to remain.[39]

A few months later, in February 2006, district wildlife managers with the Colorado Division of Wildlife captured brief video of a suspected wolf about ten miles south of the Colorado-Wyoming border near the town of Walden after a landowner reported the sighting.[40] Under the new law, this wolf will be allowed to stay if it so chooses. But waiting for wolves to find their way here one by one and hoping they will reestablish themselves is not the most effective approach to healing a broken ecosystem. Many conservationists and wildlife biologists argue strongly for active reintroduction to the ecoregion, the approach taken in the Greater Yellowstone Ecosystem to the north; however, prospects for such proactivity in the more heavily populated Southern Rockies are uncertain at best due to political opposition.

Wildlife managers at Rocky Mountain National Park in northern Colorado recently removed from consideration a potential plan to restore a self-sustaining wolf population to control problematic elk populations in the park. In the spring of 2006, the park released the Draft Elk and Vegetation Management Plan Environmental Impact Statement (DEIS), which considers four alternatives that would guide park management for the next twenty years.[41] In addition to wolf reintroduction and "no action," the park considered a culling plan that would have U.S. National Park Service staff shooting three hundred cow elk in the park annually for four years and sixty-five cows in each of the following sixteen years, as well as a fertility-control plan that would involve capturing and giving cows fertility shots or darting them with a drug in the wild. Both of the latter alternatives would also involve fencing of riparian areas and "elk-redistribution techniques" to relieve pressure on willow habitat.[42] Rocky Mountain National Park received approximately 2,700 comments on the DEIS, then narrowed the alternatives being considered to ones involving culling. The park released a final plan in December 2007, and the Record of Decision for the Final Elk and Vegetation Management Plan was signed on February 15, 2008, by Mike Snyder, intermountain regional director for the National Park Service. Park staff will now focus on implementing the twenty-year plan, which includes a variety of conservation tools including fencing, redistribution, vegetation restoration, and lethal reduction of elk. The park's Web site, as of July 2008, notes that "[i]n future years, the park will, using adaptive management principles, re-evaluate opportunities to use wolves or fertility control as additional tools."[43]

The adoption of human-induced, herd-reduction approaches—in essence, an endorsement of a "substitute West" (see Sharon Collinge's chapter)—is surprising because a recently completed five-year study of the impact of the park's elk herd on vegetation noted that past efforts to cull the elk by shooting them had done little to relieve the pressure on aspen and willow. The study also noted the great success Yellowstone National Park has had with aspen and willow regeneration via wolf reintroduction. As discussed earlier, the key seems to be that wolves keep elk moving, reducing their tendency to overbrowse a particular area. Recruiting humans to cull elk rather than working to restore a self-sustaining, functional ecosystem driven by carnivores is a bit like the aspirin approach described in the introduction to this volume.

Concluding Thoughts

When Michael Soulé and Dave Foreman first put forth their vision of rewilding North America by restoring keystone species and landscape connectivity, Paul Ehrlich recalls, their ideas were met at first with amusement, "but these goals have now been embraced broadly as the only realistic strategy for ending the extinction crisis."[44] Indeed, even key federal and state agencies such as the National Park Service, CDOT, and the Federal Highway Administration have shown interest in and outright support of some of the central rewilding concepts and their application to the Southern Rockies—namely, the critical role of carnivores and connectivity.

In spite of rapid growth and development in the Southern Rockies and continued opposition to wolf reintroduction, at least a few key pieces of the puzzle appear to be coming together in recent years. SREP has completed a science-based vision for a wildlands network that, if implemented, will go a long way toward ensuring the future of a wild, intact, connected Southern Rockies. Moreover, wolves are apparently eager to repopulate the region if we will only welcome them with adequate room to roam.

Soulé and Noss have observed that the biggest obstacle to rewilding is an unwillingness to imagine it. Indeed, who would have imagined that federal and state agencies would seek out the advice and guidance of an organization (SREP) founded in large part on the ideas of former Earth First!er Dave Foreman? Who would have imagined that the National Park Service would (for at least a brief moment) contemplate the reintroduction of wolves as a pragmatic management tool in the relatively densely populated Southern Rockies? And perhaps most improbable, who would have imagined that lone wolves from northern Wyoming would make their way more than five hundred miles to the Southern Rockies? Remaining open to the possibility that nature might have the ability to moderate and perhaps even heal itself might save us time, money, and wasted effort on elaborate management schemes focused on "fixing" only one small part of a much bigger, hard-to-understand system. As Sinapu director and wolf advocate Rob Edward has observed, the science surrounding the feasibility of wolf restoration is not at issue. "Wolves will be happy anywhere there's enough elk or deer to eat. . . . The only other thing they need is a little human tolerance."[45]

Ironically, Wolf 293 was found the week before the Colorado Division of Wildlife Wolf Management Working Group was to meet for the first time. At first, the timing seemed too coincidental, and there was speculation that the corpse had been relocated from Greater Yellowstone to Interstate 70, perhaps as a hoax or to bring attention to the subject. But a necropsy showed that the wolf had made it to Colorado on its own volition, surpassing everyone's expectations. The immediate effect was to change the conversation from "What should we do if wolves come to the Southern Rockies?" to "What will we do *when* wolves come?" After much consternation, the working group decided that migrating wolves should be allowed to stay, but still looming on the horizon is the much larger and politically trickier question of whether wolves should be actively reintroduced to the Southern Rockies.

As Rob Edwards observes, "The North Park wolf shows that there is still a tenuous connection between Colorado and the Greater Yellowstone wolf population," but energy development in southern Wyoming and residential development in northern Colorado increasingly puts that connectivity at risk. Edwards suggests that we reintroduce wolves to the Southern Rockies "so that the next wolf that wanders down from Wyoming has a welcoming committee."[46] For now, many questions still surround not only wolf reintroduction, but also protection of roadless areas in the region and establishment of usable linkages and corridors. How we answer these questions may determine the region's future.

A Scholar Intervenes

MATACHINES, RITUAL CONTINUITY,
AND CULTURAL WELL-BEING

Brenda M. Romero

THIS PERSONAL NARRATIVE explores the ways in which the ceremonial dance drama *los matachines* (mah-tah-CHIN-ehs) of New Mexico has positively embodied cultural and spiritual relationships between people historically at odds, yet in close coexistence. It is personal because, as a scholar, I chose to intervene by continuing the role of the Hispano musician for the *danza* (music and narrative dance event) in the Pueblo of Jemez when the old Hispano fiddler passed away in 1988. He, like his father, his grandfather, and many others before him, had fulfilled spiritual obligations by playing his violin in the Pueblo in honor of the Virgin of Guadalupe. As a New Mexican Hispana scholar, I felt myself to be a part of the forces helping to heal the old intercultural wounds, not only because I could help in this traditional manner, but also because I could keep the danza from declining at a crucial juncture for the Jemez people.

In writing this chapter, I also reflect on my cultural identity with regard to mainstream and white cultures, as well as to my scholarly identity. First, continuing a vintage Hispano tradition is in itself an act of resistance against hegemonic processes of erasure evidenced by mainstream attacks, including English-only and anti-immigrant legislation, on anyone of a Spanish-speaking culture. Second, the kind of applied ethnomusicology that my work represents is only beginning to be valued in the academy because scholarly intervention of humanitarian value has been legitimized only in the hard sciences and much less so in the humanities. For those of us who work with indigenous communities, however, it is essential to conduct community-based work if possible. I went to the Pueblo with research handbook in hand, leaving it for the Pueblo library at the end of my work there.[1] Healing the West must be a conscious act of intent. The context of this chapter describes another attempt to heal old wounds, this time between Hispanos and Euro-American latecomers, whose hegemonic concerns have generally limited a historical understanding of this region's people.

When the Spaniards colonized the Americas, they brought with them a handful of profane, carnavalesque traditions that were forms of entertainment most often seen in Catholic feast-day processions and accompanying celebrations. Once in the Americas, however, the visual similarities to indigenous ritual music and dance events made such imported traditions good substitutes for the "pagan" rites that were systematically eliminated along with other manifestations of indigenous religion. The matachines—from the Italian word *mattaccino,* "buffoon"—are the descendants of one particular type of danza that is rarely seen in Spain today. The genre is characterized by a double-file dance drama pantomimed to music (with two notable exceptions), found in various locations throughout New Mexico, in the Southwest in general, and in more places than one can count throughout the northern and central parts of Mexico. Versions exist in Colombia, Brazil, Puerto Rico, and no doubt other parts of Latin America.[2] They survive in New Mexico in local Hispana/o and Indo-Hispana/o (Chicana/o) guise, and in some of the Pueblos in indigenous guise, offering transparent examples of how the genre typically reflects local traditions following centuries of reinterpretation, although various elements have remained more or less stable over time from Colombia to New Mexico.[3]

I began to conduct doctoral fieldwork in the Pueblo of Jemez in December 1987, seeking to understand what musical and cultural values the process of syncretism had reinforced, if any; what the two versions were all about; where the music came from; and whether this dance had Moorish origins. There had been much speculation about this latter aspect because of the ceremonial dress and masks the matachines dancers wear (discussed later) and because the term *matachines* could be a corruption of the Arabic term for masked dances, *mudawajjihin* (literally meaning "they wear faces" and "they face each other").[4] The most likely etymology, however, is the Italian word *mattaccino:*

> According to Forrest, the first references to the Matachines are found in Italy and the likelihood is much greater that the real derivation of

the word is the Italian *mattaccino,* meaning "charlatan, jester, mimic, odd fellow; strolling player" (*Cassell's Italian Dictionary* 1979). The root of the word is *matto,* "mad" or "fool," and it derives from the Latin *mattus* or *matus* (Forrest 34), from the Sanskrit for "mad" or "to be drunk." Among the Romans it meant "drunk," "intoxicated" (*A Latin Dictionary,* 1962).[5]

Elsewhere I have discussed the early Spanish matachines contexts as closely tied to the commedia dell'arte in the fifteenth and sixteenth centuries. A different source cites the etymology (perhaps dubiously) thus: "The name comes from the Italian word 'mattinate' [*sic*] (mornings), going long hours, until morning, having fun. . . . Fun loving, irreverent, with the sling ready for throwing eggs . . . going around in groups, disapproved by the majority, wild and contemptuous."[6] Interestingly, the Italian *mattinata,* when applied to a spectacle, means "matinee, afternoon performance."[7] These definitions imply that the term *matachines* might certainly have originally referred to the musicians as strolling players, with various applications to the character(s) of the burlesques that accompanied or were encompassed in the dance and theater event itself. The polysemic nature of the term is mirrored in the nature of the historical dance-drama-pantomime that is los matachines.

The rare and interesting history of relationships between New Mexican Hispanos and local indigenous peoples reveals as much that is instructive as is destructive.[8] Establishing the oldest European settlements in the United States beginning in 1598, Hispanos brought the hated *encomienda* system, requiring tribute from the colonized and subjugating the First Nations of New Mexico in many of the same ways that the French, the English, and other Europeans were to do throughout the United States a century or so later. Not everything the Spanish brought was evil, however, and we can count among the positive contributions the introduction of European musical instruments and music that flourished in seventeenth-century New Mexican mission life. This influence declined abruptly with the Pueblo Revolt of 1680, the only successful indigenous revolt of the colonial period in Latin America.[9] The rebellion was a crucial Native victory because the Spanish were never again to invade the inner sanctum of Native beliefs and practices, and for many today, the two religions, Catholic and Native, exist side by side and together.[10] Even after the encomienda system was outlawed, however, it was replaced by a *repartimiento* system, levies assigned on a weekly basis, which did not begin to break down until the end of the eighteenth century.[11] Nonetheless, gradual understanding between regional First Nations peoples and Hispanos developed in contexts of mutual interest over the course of four hundred years. Religious rituals and expressions of spirituality were the most significant of such mutual interests for all concerned. The Catholic Church, both physically and spiritually, became a nexus of foreign encounter with the region's indigenous peoples.

The early polyphonic mission music that thrived in the Pueblos during the early colonial period never returned because the belief that fueled the Pueblo Revolt was that Catholicism and its rites (of which music was an integral part) had chased away the traditional Corn Mothers. As Ramón A. Gutiérrez states, "Taking the decade of drought that preceded and followed the Pueblo Revolt, we can understand the ecological factors that fueled village factionalism and internecine warfare."[12] The Spanish Reconquest of the region challenged the former early colonial way of life. No doubt the cost of replacing the destroyed musical instruments—indeed, whole ensembles—with new ones from abroad for every mission was only part of the problem because teaching the new religious music was no longer possible now that the Natives had made their point. Instead, priests and nuns—most of them white—eventually began traveling from Santa Fe to the various mission and community churches to sing for High Mass, carefully scheduled so that all the small parishes could hold Mass on important feast days. From my youth in the 1950s, I remember Gregorian chants sung by choirs of priests and nuns for Midnight Mass, the warmth of the soft adobe-textured walls of the Hispano village church, the excitement of incense, and the sounds of church bells. And so it was in the Pueblo village churches by the 1950s, albeit with some hymns in Native languages after 1960, when the church abandoned the use of Gregorian chant in favor of colloquial musics.

Aside from hymns, the only other performance tradition traceable to the Spanish that survives in *both* Hispano and Pueblo contexts in New Mexico is the matachines danza. The matachines was similar enough to indigenous dance rituals to make it an easy vehicle for religious conversion. For Hispanos, the matachines was also musically light-hearted, with high-stepping and precisely timed choreographies that were (and still are) very much in contrast to the melancholy of the religious *alabados* provided by male Penitente sects. For Pueblo people, the *matachina* (as they refer to it) was accepted as a new tradition through which Catholicism and Christianity could be revered via the honoring of patron saints, much as the Buffalo Dance eventually came to the Pueblos as a way of honoring the Plains First Nations religion based on White Buffalo Calf Woman. Because Catholicism was imposed on and permeated the culture, Catholic feast days continue to be celebrated with a Mass followed by Native dancing. For many Puebloans, however, dancing on those days is the extent of Christian reverence. The matachina is enacted on only two days of the year—on the feast day of the Virgin of Guadalupe and on New Year's Day, a secular holiday—and thus is only a small part of the annual Native traditional observances. It is important to note that the Eurocentric notion of monotheistic allegiance to a particular deity as person (or perhaps person as deity) is distinct from the indigenous spiritual concept of ritual power capable of addressing multiple spiritual forces. First Nations people typically believe in a multifaceted polytheistic Creation in which ritual causes things to happen. It was common in pre-Conquest times to "borrow" or "receive" or barter for a song or ceremony considered to have special powers, such as healing. In this worldview, the Catholic Mass was just one more possible source of spiritual power, but it was not the only one. Thus, today it is still common for many to participate in both the Catholic Mass and the Corn Dance on the same day, each having its own meanings and practices, but without psychological conflict. The source of powerful songs and rituals is spiritual; songs and rituals are therefore powerful formulas for meaningful action. The matachina, as music and dance ritual, is one among many rituals that help to maintain harmony and balance for the Pueblo people who keep the tradition.

In the danza's dual music/cultural role began the proliferation of matachines variants and meanings throughout Mexico and New Spain, largely evident in today's Greater Mexico and Colombia.[13] New Mexico is an interesting case because it is the only place that "Spanish" versions survive, and the processes of reinterpretation through which the danza has been transformed into a more indigenous tradition (as is widespread in Mexico) are still transparent.[14] In 1993, I was enticed to write a doctoral dissertation on matachines by the two versions of the danza in the

Pueblo of Jemez, New Mexico (after first learning that in the Pueblos it is called "matachina"). The Turquoise moiety version is accompanied by guitar and violin, whereas the Pumpkin moiety version is accompanied by male chorus and drum. The latter is one of two versions, the other in Santa Clara (Tewa speaking), that include Pueblo musical reinterpretations of the Iberian model—changed to conform to local formats and beliefs—and words, at least that I am aware of. In Cochiti (a Keres-speaking Pueblo), the tradition has recently declined.

For the dissertation, I wanted to learn something about the significance of the performances of the two same-named but different-looking and different-sounding Jemez matachina versions. Being cognizant that the music for matachina in the Pueblos was often supplied by Hispano (male) musicians, I asked upon the death of the Hispano fiddler for Jemez if the Pueblo would allow me to play the repertoire for them the next year, and they agreed.

As I conducted fieldwork, I analyzed the different cultural groups I was studying as a means of locating the matachines within particular cultural settings and dynamics, including my own because I am originally from Rio Arriba County in northern New Mexico, the area the Spanish first occupied in 1598. I first compared the violin and guitar matachina in the Towa-speaking Jemez Pueblo to the violin and guitar matachina of the Tewa-speaking San Juan Pueblo.[15] I then compared and contrasted the matachina in San Juan Pueblo with los matachines in the Hispano town of Alcalde, New Mexico, just a few miles across the river from Lyden, the village where I grew up. In the end, however, the Pueblo of Jemez would not allow me to discuss Jemez in the dissertation until the elders had had a chance to weigh the dissertation's content in the course of the forthcoming year. As a single parent, I could not afford to wait another year to complete the dissertation, so I published only the San Juan/Alcalde comparison for the dissertation. I apparently had also failed to obtain permission to conduct research from each subsequent governor (they rotate annually),[16] which was disconcerting for my Pueblo collaborator Randolph Padilla (1952–2004), who was the Pueblo governor the year I became the fiddler and from whom I attained the initial necessary permissions. As a prominent Pueblo educator, he felt that my contribution to the Pueblo had gone unrewarded, and he took the slight personally. He was also at that time one of two lead matachina dancers from the

Turquoise Kiva (the moiety's ceremonial organization). In the end, the Pueblo did not allow me to publish my findings, but these findings have informed all of my matachines research since that time.

Los matachines is a narrative of conquest idealized, ritualized, and reinterpreted. It is always a reminder of the cultural dysfunction that has resulted from the dynamics of conquest and colonization. Not only does this reminder refer to Hispano subjugation of Natives, but also to the Anglo subjugation of Hispanos in New Mexico and the Southwest that began in the mid–nineteenth century. Pueblo cultures, too, subjugated bands of people they defeated in war, but they also empowered them by making their leaders heads of internal spiritual entities or societies.[17] The dysfunctional leadership introduced by Europeans took various forms and had various consequences, including ongoing racism from the dominant culture and, equally vicious, internalized racism among those who have been subjugated over time. What is internalized racism or oppression? If expressed as a personal struggle, it can be described thus: because I have been oppressed for so long, I begin to construct the oppression as part of the way I think; I carry it with me, I oppress myself, and even if I don't, I am reminded of my "place" in various subtle ways.

Other manifestations of the dysfunction include the loss of cultural cohesion, accompanied by large social problems such as drug and alcohol addiction and escalating suicide rates among the many who are struggling to regain a sense of wholeness in the context of colliding worldviews. Every cultural group has its own worldview, which is really a system of interrelated beliefs and practices that reflect basic premises based on geographical, mythical, philosophical, and many other vantage points—a cultural construction of what and how things work and why. Some people are descendants of the proud conquistadors and the rich landed immigrants they became before they too were conquered. Others were here for millennia before being conquered. All struggle to rise up to life's challenges.

This is not the first time in history that people have been challenged, but continue on. What did people do in other historical and ancient times in order to continue? In this part of the world, they invoked ancient remedies that included enacting rituals in which music and dance played central roles in communicating and negotiating with great powers that could be observed in nature—for instance, in the form of electrical storms. More often than not, these powers were mysterious and unseen, but undeniable. Ritual music and dance were and continue to be ways of directing human desire in a formal manner to those unseen powers, a way of uniting minds and souls to achieve harmony with forces inherent in place and beyond. All blessings and prosperity come from this harmony.

For Hispanos, ritual in the form of the Catholic Mass was also always essential to well-being and prosperity. Music was central to this experience, but by the time the Europeans arrived in the Americas during the Renaissance, both the Protestant and Catholic Churches had abolished dance in worship.[18] Popular (i.e., profane) dance in sacred contexts continued as part of the spiritual conquest of the Americas, however.[19] Church authorities allowed profane dancing only in processions for religious celebrations where religious themes were also commonly presented in dramatic enactments. Los matachines involve music as a central component, more so than the Mass, and their sound can change to reflect elements of particular cultural significance. Not only can the dancers look more indigenous in the Pueblos and more "Spanish" in the Hispano towns, but the music may also sound more Native or more Hispano depending on the musicians playing the guitar and violin.

Among the results of two cultures living in close proximity to each other, the indigenous concept of place—*tierra sagrada,* or sacred land—in particular spread to those who conquered the Indians at the same time that Catholicism became a regular part of Pueblo life. Many instances of intermarriage also contributed to peaceful intercultural relations, and although the Anglo-imposed reservation system perpetuated a geographical distance, it also helped to preserve distinct musical traditions.

The work I did in Jemez can be contextualized within a larger ideological frame that emerged through the civil rights and Chicano movements of the 1960s and was an outcome of applied methodology. Bear in mind that applied anthropology has always been cast in an inferior role within academia, although within ethnomusicology there is a growing body of applied scholarship (this seems to be true in anthropology as well). As I write, I realize that remedy, repair, restoration, and mitigation are interrelated cultural processes that retain some elements of culture and not others, and that achieve their ends through whatever means necessary. My role in this narrative represents both one of the ways in which individuals act as harbingers of such cultural processes and the potential for intervention in other spheres where academics can help facilitate healing.

Offering myself as ethnographic subject, I can say that I am a typical example of an individual who lost (or was deprived of) her cultural cohesiveness and is in the process of reclaiming it. With so many others, I suffered through the usual generic public-school curriculum where I was never privy to learning either about my Navajo and Pueblo friends' cultures or about my own Hispano culture—at least, not that I can recall. I returned to New Mexico at the age of twenty-seven following a seven-year absence. My experiences living in California, Australia, and Ecuador combined with ideas I had learned in Chicano studies courses at the University of California at Berkeley in the early 1970s during the height of the César Chávez farm labor movement. The result was that I had a somewhat mixed, if not mixed-up, identity by the early 1980s. Some things were very clear in my mind, however. In particular, a high school friend whose parents were members of the Baha'i faith had brought me to a sense that the world is in a spiritual crisis and that it was my moral and spiritual obligation to find myself in the company of people of different races—a Baha'i injunction. In learning to navigate the Anglo world, however, I found my own culture becoming Other. I returned to New Mexico after three years in Australia (the home of my then husband) for a formal education on my own cultural history and background, only to find that what I wanted to know was boxed away in university archival collections—as if my culture were merely a remnant of the past. (What, I ask, is so surprising about the high numbers of Latino school dropouts? Latino life takes place elsewhere, with its own forms of meaningful status denied in mainstream U.S. institutions.)

U.S. history books had always told the story of Anglo-Americans spreading unquestionably legitimate cultural forms and concepts across "America," claiming the continent with one simple linguistic gesture and then imposing English-only laws. Compare this situation with that in Switzerland, where there are four official languages and dialects of those languages from city to city! But there is a way in which the very oldest aspects of culture reach into a timeless past and color the very manner in which one perceives space. I knew from the very touch and taste of things that I was a part of this land in ways that I did not fully understand; I knew without a doubt that this was *mi* tierra sagrada in ways that Australia was not. I began the process of reconstructing my own history by applying for a graduate school grant that would allow me to spend as much time in the university music archives as I could possibly want, listening to the wavering husky voices of the old-time Hispano musicians who reminded me of the uncles I heard as I was growing up. I began to sing my favorites of the old songs, restoring a connection with my roots through my own performances and ethnomusicological investigations. Take, for example, "La cautiva Marcelina" (Marcelina, the Captive):[20]

> *La cautiva Marcelina*
> *ya se va, ya se la llevan,*
> *ya se va, ya se la llevan,*
> *para esas tierras mentadas,*
> *a comer carne de llegua,*
> *a comer carne de llegua.*
>
> *Coro*
> *Por eso ya no quiero en el mundo más amar*
> *de mi querida patria me van a retirar.*
>
> *La cautiva Marcelina*
> *cuando llegó al aguapa*
> *cuando llegó al aguapa,*
> *volteó la cara llorando,*
> *matarón a mi papá,*
> *matarón a mi papá.*
>
> *Coro*
>
> *La cautiva Marcelina*
> *cuando llegó al ojito,*
> *cuando llegó al ojito,*
> *volteó la cara llorando,*
> *matarón al Delgadito.*
>
> *Coro*
>
> *La cautiva Marcelina*
> *cuando llegó a los cerritos,*
> *cuando llegó a los cerritos,*

volteó la cara llorando,
matarón a mis hijitos,
matarón a mis hijitos.

Coro

Marcelina, the captive,
she is going, they are taking her
she is going, they are taking her
to those infamous lands
where they eat mare's meat
where they eat mare's meat.

(Chorus)
Because of this I no longer wish to live in this world
from my beloved homeland they are taking me away.

Marcelina, the captive
when she arrived at the cattail marsh,
(repeat)

she turned her head, crying
"they've killed my father."
(repeat)

(Chorus)

Marcelina, the captive when she arrived at the spring
(repeat)
she turned her head, crying
"they've killed Delgadito."
(repeat)

(Chorus)

Marcelina, the captive
when she arrived at the little hills
(repeat)

she turned her head, crying
"they've killed my children,"
(repeat).

Captivity ballads such as "La cautiva Marcelina" and other songs referred to as *inditas* raised many interesting questions in my mind about the nature of my ancestors' existence in New Spain. They also reminded me of how my great-aunt Delubina carried to her death in 1978 an ancient fear of Indian attack! The attacks, largely by the Comanche, had stopped in the 1870s; although she was born in 1896, she never outgrew the reflexes of that fear. The text alone cannot convey the profundity that the melody to this song imparts.

In trying to piece together a context for some of these songs, seemingly written by Native people in the Spanish language, I learned about the *genízaros*—the New Mexican Indian slave class and their descendants—and their links to my part-Apache *madrina* (godmother) and my part-Dineh (Navajo) neighbor during my childhood. Around this same time, my mother admitted to me that I reminded her of the descriptions she had heard of one of her ancestors—and thus my ancestor—reputedly a Tiwa from the Taos/Picuris area. I began to feel as if parts of me, previously separated like pieces of a puzzle, were starting to come together, and I began to experience a greater sense of wholeness.

Also around this same time, I began to see operating among my Hispano peers in New Mexico the same momentum originating with the civil rights and Chicano movements that had motivated me. One very controversial figure, Adrian Treviño, who claimed to be related to Emiliano Zapata, was key to my learning about matachines. Yes, I had seen the danza as a child in San Juan Pueblo, but it was a vague memory, not as clear as my memories of the frightening Apache Mountain Spirit Dancers I also saw as a child at the Pueblo. I met Treviño in his capacity as volunteer at the John Donald Robb Archive of Southwestern Music at the University of New Mexico, where I was conducting special research. Treviño was beginning to make it a point to appear everywhere that los matachines were dancing. His interest was contagious. It suddenly seemed as if everyone were interested in the matachines, and the tradition appeared to move into revival mode in both Hispano and Pueblo contexts.

In retrospect, revival is more often than not a new lens that magnifies what has always been there, resulting in attaching value to something previously taken for granted. In this case, older, traditional New Mexican Hispanos often considered los matachines to be part of the *indiada,* meant pejoratively for "things Indian." Revivalist attention focused on matachines among Hispanos was exciting to me not only because it implied new life, new excitement for cultural forms in decline, but also because it implied a new consciousness and receptivity to our own Indo-Hispano heritage. I wanted to do something to dispel the discomfort I felt with the European colonial mindsets about Indian people that were still prevalent in many places. As a woman and a woman of color, I also identified with the Native struggle. When I completed my master's degree, I turned away from the Eurocentric biases inherent in the study of music theory and composition at that time and instead pursued the study of ethnomusicology at the doctoral level at the University of California at Los Angeles (UCLA). I had high hopes that ethnomusicology would be a doorway for Native and Hispano individuals to enter the halls of music departments (an attempt at repair that has taken many years to address successfully).

At UCLA, I had the honor of studying with Dr. Charlotte Heth, Cherokee, one of a handful of Native ethnomusicologists in the United States. She introduced me to Susan Guyette's book entitled *Community-Based Research: A Handbook for Native Americans* (1983). I was deeply moved by this book's pragmatic approaches to working with Native peoples and its emphasis on working *for* the people in some way, whenever possible. I didn't realize then how soon I would have the opportunity to put these ideas into practice.

The significance of los matachines has multiplied and moved away from the part they played in the strategies of conquest, and the danza has come to imply ritual/ceremonial contexts as opposed to secular group dance contexts. The matachines *danzantes* in double-file formation are characterized by the tall *coronas* (crowns) they wear, from which multi colored ribbons fall. Scarves cover each dancer's mouth, neck, and back, and a bead or cloth fringe covers the eyes. The combination evokes the image of a Near Eastern desert tribal costume.

Very little has been written about the matachines in Spain, where it seems to have been considered a profane amusement among the common people and not without its objectionable elements. The church outlawed such profane dances in processions in the sixteenth century, in part because they became occasions for what the church deemed excessive shows of elegance and probably because the danza's burlesque elements could too easily parody the theocracy and the interminable poverty in

FIGURE 7.1. A ceremonial headdress of the Tuaregs of the Ahaggar
Mountain region in Algeria. (Detail of an illustration in Henri Lhote, *Les
Touaregs de Hoggar (Ahaggar)* [Paris: Payot, 1955], 305)

Spain prior to 1492.[21] Written narratives among Hispanos in the northern New Mexico–southern Colorado region still describe the evangelical function of the Catholic-imposed versions. In general, however, today's matachines danza honors Catholic saints or is danced ceremonially on important occasions in some places. In addition to the two lines of danzantes, the matachines troupe includes the Monarca, King (typically Cortés or Moctezuma), and the Abuelo, Grandfather, who symbolizes wisdom and tradition. In the New Mexico versions and in the *danza de la pluma* versions of the Mexican matachines, a young girl enacts the part of La Malinche as the first Christian convert of the New World. In New Mexico alone, the danza includes the young Toro, Bull, as a symbol of mischief and animal nature, who is typically castrated and/or killed at the high point of the drama. In the Pueblo of Jemez version, the bull is only subdued, rather than castrated or killed, because animals are honored in traditional ceremonial dances.[22]

I arrived at the Pueblo of Jemez to begin my fieldwork on December 12, 1987, the feast day of Our Lady of Guadalupe. I had become a devotee of Our Lady in 1983 when my sister was suffering from a fatal illness, so in some ways I felt "called" by Our Lady on this day. The fiddler for the Pueblo matachina, Adelaido Martinez, was also suffering from a terminal illness. I was able to find him at his home, however, and he and his wife, Maria Martinez Santos, were gracious enough to allow me to interview them. Adelaido died the following July, around the same time I had a dream that I would have to play the violin ten minutes a day. I returned to Jemez exactly a year later, on December 12, 1988, and again on January 1, 1989, when a marine home for the holidays at the Pueblo shot and killed one young person and permanently injured another. I became convinced that disruption in the ceremonial calendar contributed to disruption in the Pueblo in general.

According to anthropologist Victor Turner, "Processes, mediated by procedures, established ways of doing things, are set in train, the aim of which is to defuse tension, assess irrational deeds against standards of reasonableness, and to reconcile conflicting parties—having convinced them through showing them the damaging effects of their actions on group unity, that it is better to restore a state of peace than to continue in a state of hostility."[23] The matachina comprised an important set of procedures that had been absent for two years already, since Adelaido's death.

After all that Native people have lost, one more loss is not insignificant, especially one established in the ritual calendar with its attendant cultural processes. I approached Pueblo governor Randolph Padilla about the possibility of my learning the pieces so that the ceremony might continue, and he granted approval. (As previously mentioned, he was one of the lead matachina dancers at that time.) Of course, this opportunity was potentially an excellent field experience for me, but it was also a chance to return something to the people while working on my dissertation. All that year, I took lessons from the violin teaching assistant in the College of Music at the University of Colorado, transcribing the complicated little ornamental figures with her assistance.

At this particular time of year, when College of Music performance faculty and faculty in other applied areas such as art and architecture were conducting juries, I too had to perform for a jury. On the first occasion that I went to play for the December 12 feast day of Our Lady of Guadalupe, I entered the men's hall for the first time a couple of days beforehand. Men of all ages sat on the bench built out of the wall around the room and listened while I played the ancient melodies on the violin, accompanied by the Pueblo guitarist Daniel Culacke, who had been the matachina guitarist for decades (in spite of belonging to the Pumpkin Kiva). As I played each melody more or less intact, faces lit up, and the excitement built until it seemed that everyone was smiling. The war chiefs nodded, and we began the rehearsals in earnest. I subsequently played for nine years, during which time Daniel Culacke died and Adelaido Martinez's grandson took over on the guitar. An excellent musician, seventeen-year-old Lawrence Trujillo soon began to prepare the violin pieces with my coaching on the fastest and most complicated sequences. In the meantime, two other Pueblo members learned to play one or two of the melodies on the violin, and I began to defer to them on those pieces whenever possible. One of them, Kathleen Gauchupin, became a regular on the slow Monarca sequence. By September 1998, Lawrence, then nineteen, played all of the pieces for me, so, realizing that he was ready, I told him that I would not perform that year and he would have to play. He has done very well, deferring to Kathleen on one or two pieces for most performances. I, in turn, headed south to the international border to expand my research—again on December 12, the day on which the borderlands matachines are most active.

The matachines danza was originally introduced to evangelize the Indians, a point that is not lost to the Puebloans. Discussing the ways that symbols are often inverted to create ritual meaning, Victor Turner submits that

> One aspect of symbolic inversion may be to break people out of their culturally defined, even biologically ascribed, roles, by making them play precisely the opposite roles. Psychologists who employ the socio-drama method as a therapeutic technique claim that by assigning to patients the roles of those with whom they are in conflict, a whole conflict-ridden group can reach a deep level of mutual understanding. Perhaps ritual or dramatic symbolic inversion may operate in a similar way, breaking down the barriers of age, sex, status, class, family, clan, and so on to teach the meaning of the generic humanity; so that each person becomes the joker in the pack, the card who can be all cards, the method actor.[24]

Among Native people of North America in general, "received" rituals were typically performed in the past in order to acquire the power that they brought to their originating groups. A neighboring group sometimes still gives a song or dance to aid their friends with its healing power.[25] Seen as formulaic, such songs and dances were performed as closely as possible to the original versions. The Spanish (for their own reasons) took their roles as teachers of the dance seriously and coached the dancers on the "correct" (read "Spanish") form and dance steps.[26] Notwithstanding the formulaic aspect of things, both matachina music and ceremonial dress have changed over time to conform with Pueblo practices, which tends to confirm that enacting the Other's ritual defuses the Otherness, making Them more like Us through the mediation of the ritual itself, as Turner suggests.

The Pueblo myth-ritual complex appears to have allowed limited access by foreign or hostile groups and influences in such a way as to bring about at least partial resolution of intercultural conflict. Because Hispano towns and people surround the Tewa and Jemez Reservations, one would expect a certain level of hostility between the groups. This tension is perhaps best indicated by the "drum" version at Jemez, which has completely shed itself of Spanish characteristics in both music and dress, but has retained the dance and its associations with Catholicism.

FIGURE 7.2. The author playing the violin for the Pueblo of Jemez Turquoise Matachina at the Los Angeles Festival in September 1990.

At the same time, however, a number of Pueblo groups, including the Turquoise Kiva of Jemez, still perform the "Spanish" version, wearing a more typically Spanish-Mexican outfit and with violin and guitar accompaniment. This combination indicates acknowledgment of *mestizaje* in the Pueblos over the past four hundred years.

In 1990, the organizers of the Los Angeles Festival, directed by Peter Sellars and hosted by UCLA, requested that the Jemez Matachina be a host group for this important event that was breaking with the tradition of featuring only classical art music. The Pueblo elders gave their consent, which included consent to being filmed and photographed, but only because the festival was directed at the lofty goal of world peace. In the end, however, the more conservative Pumpkin Kiva group did not attend.

As previously mentioned, academia does not typically value scholarship with a conscience, suggesting that academia is rife with values so privileged that their colonial roots and mindset are ignored. I entered the matachina ritual world with the conscious intention of intervening in—of "repairing"—the historical picture that portrays Hispanos as racists and oppressors of the Indians. In spite of a foreground of Hispano oppression of Natives that Euro-Americans have in turn used as justification to oppress Hispanos, I encountered many accounts that show clearly that many New Mexican Puebloans and Hispanos developed positive social relations well beyond the ritual contexts of the Mass and the matachina. Since the 1980s, many others—notably literary folklorist Enrique Lamadrid and photographer Miguel Gandert, both of them at the University of New Mexico—have uncovered various contexts that acknowledge Native-Hispano interaction and mixing in New Mexico.[27]

Following the period of Americanization, after 1848, a gradual decline of Hispano culture accompanied the loss of land and water rights so that ceremonies and rituals such as los matachines were abandoned in many places. During World War II, this process was hastened by the absence of grown men to perform in the danza; thus, the Pueblo of Jemez took over the responsibilities of the danza from nearby Cañon, an Hispano town. The revival of los matachines among Hispanos today coincides with a sociopolitical movement to reaffirm Hispano culture in the face of growing tourism, loss of land, and loss of a sense of community. In Bernalillo, Alcalde, and other New Mexican Hispano settings, los matachines is also an active expression of faith, incorporating traditional Spanish theatrical devices as a form of social commentary. It is the only dance ceremonial allowed in rural New Mexican Catholicism. It is debatable whether los matachines would have survived among Hispanos had it not been for the symbiotic relationships established by Hispano musicians in the Pueblos, where dance rituals were part of the Pueblo organization itself and could serve as models of continuity for Hispano communities. That the tradition has survived and continues stronger than ever in some places is also a testament to the benefits it brings to those who participate and who greatly appreciate the lively, cheerful melodies.

A newspaper poll from a few years ago perhaps offers further proof that ritual is a powerful positive and integrative force: it stated that people who attend church live longer and that the more often they attend church, the longer they live! The Center for the American West at the University of Colorado recently hosted a conference on religion in the West. In Colorado, the largest group of people polled has no religion. Do secular rituals accomplish the same as organized religious ones? Who organizes and performs the secular ritual? Rock bands? Football teams?

Is it enough to reinforce the rituals that already exist? Can humans survive without rituals? I cannot answer these questions.

To complicate things a bit, the Tewa people voted in November 2005 to reinstate the pre-Hispano name "Ohkay Owinge," meaning "Place of the Strong People," in place of "San Juan Pueblo." Such a move sends a healing ripple across the ether to others whose very soul was renamed in the process of colonization.[28] Contemporary Hispanos can perhaps take vicarious consolation from this Pueblo act because Hispano culture is now suffering from similar colonizing attempts by redneck factions that would swindle away not only our land, but also our language and ties to Mexico. In recent times, conflicts have arisen when Euro-Americans living in New Mexican villages want to participate in the Hispano matachines.[29] Some Hispanos have opened their hearts to this idea, but others have not. Women were not always included in Hispano matachines, but today in Bernalillo women too dance. In Alcalde, Elaine Garcia organized an all-female group in 2005.[30]

Ramón Gutiérrez points out that a drought was significant in leading to the Pueblo Revolt of 1680.[31] Whether one sees the rebellion in a positive light, it teaches us that as global warming continues to take its toll, human reactions are likely to become more and more violent as a result of widespread feelings of despair and helplessness. But we can hope that a middle ground may gradually give way to a matachines that is inclusive of all ethnic groups, where healing can take the place of conflict and prejudice for those who are called.

Cleaning Up Abandoned Hard-Rock Mines in the Western United States

CAN AND WILL COMMUNITIES TAKE THE LEAD?

Joseph N. Ryan

BACK IN 1858, a party of settlers in horse-drawn wagons followed the South Platte River west across the Nebraska Territory to Pike's Peak in search of gold. They paused at Fort St. Vrain on the river for a view of the red sandstone peaks of the three-hundred million-year-old Fountain Formation that rise behind the valley that now holds Boulder, Colorado. These peaks, now known as the Flatirons, inspired the leader of the group, Thomas Aikins, a practical and focused man, to render this assessment of the locale's utility: "The mountains look right for gold and the valleys look good for grazing."[1]

Aikins's party proceeded to Four Mile Canyon, established a camp, and began mining the stream for gold. Using pans, rockers, and sluice boxes, they harvested gold "float" from the stream gravels and traced the gold back to quartz veins in the hills above Boulder near what is now the town of Gold Hill. Over the following decade, prospectors found gold, silver, and other metals, mainly in telluride (a mixture of gold, silver, and other metals with the metal tellurium), in the surrounding mountains. In what would become Boulder County, the mining districts and towns of Ward, Jamestown, Magnolia, Wall Street, Salina, Sugar Loaf, Sunshine, and Sunset were settled.[2] As in California a decade earlier, similar mining districts sprang up throughout the Colorado mountains as gold seekers worked Cherry Creek, Clear Creek, and many other Front Range streams.

The mines in Boulder County followed the steeply dipping fissures and faults in the granodiorites and schists of the Boulder Creek Batholith.[3] Unsuccessful prospectors quickly became the laborers who sunk

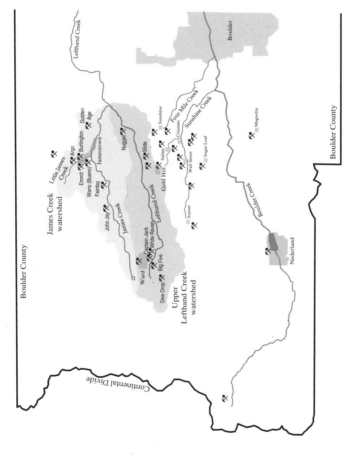

FIGURE 8.1. Western Boulder County, Colorado, showing the location of streams, mines, towns, and the upper Lefthand Creek and James Creek watersheds. The James Creek watershed is part of the Lefthand Creek watershed. The elevation ranges from 5,340 feet above sea level on the eastern edge of the map to more than 13,000 feet on the western edge of Boulder County.

shafts, blasted tunnels, constructed mills, and, over the years, removed about $230 million worth of gold from mines in Boulder County. The mines also produced tungsten, silver, lead, copper, zinc, fluorite, and uranium.

The City of Boulder grew rapidly to support the mining. It was established as a mining district in 1859, became the home of the University of Colorado in 1877, and was incorporated in 1878. Boulder's population reached one thousand in the 1870s, ten thousand in the 1910s, and fifty thousand in the 1960s, and it is now approaching one hundred thousand, not including the twenty-six thousand students that attend the University of Colorado. Meanwhile, only a couple of active mines lasted beyond the 1960s in Boulder County.[+]

Back in 1992, just after I graduated from the Massachusetts Institute of Technology with a PhD in environmental engineering, my wife, Martha, and I made our way to Boulder in a twenty-four-foot Budget rent-a-truck on Interstate 70. On the Boulder Turnpike just south of the city, we paused for a view of the Flatirons from a scenic outlook. But we weren't thinking of gold as we looked over the Boulder Valley, despite a definite paucity of riches after seven years in graduate school. Instead, I came to teach and do research at the university, and Martha came for a master's degree in fine arts. We came to do a little skiing, biking, and hiking, too. For us, Boulder meant higher education and recreation, not mining.

As proof of my ignorance of Boulder's mining history, it took me ten years to find "the lone figure dedicated to the miners of Boulder County whose stories are carried on the winds of time," the bronze statue of a miner by the east side of the Boulder County Courthouse.[*] It took me six years of driving the twenty miles from Boulder to our home in the Bar-K Ranch, a mountain subdivision at nearly nine thousand feet of elevation, to realize that I had been passing the abandoned head frames, shaft houses, mills, and waste-rock piles of the Jamestown Mining District. This mining district, also called Jimtown, was once the temporary home of some ten thousand miners, but only about three hundred now live in the town that the U.S. Postal Service insisted on calling Jamestown. So what did it finally take for me to recognize the mining history of Boulder County? The promises—or threats, depending on one's perspective—of a cleanup of the mines by the U.S. Environmental Protection Agency (EPA).

FIGURE 8.2. A view of Jamestown, Colorado, from the west in 2003.

In 2001, the EPA was making plans to add the former Jamestown Mining District and some other abandoned mines in the Lefthand Creek watershed to the National Priority List (NPL) under the Comprehensive Environmental Response, Compensation, and Litigation Act of 1980 (CERCLA). CERCLA is more commonly known as the "Superfund" law, and the NPL is the list of Superfund sites. Pollution from the abandoned mines had left many reaches of streams in the Lefthand Creek watershed lifeless and a water supply for fifteen thousand customers of the Left Hand Water District potentially at risk. Mining in Boulder County and throughout the montane West had left behind these landscapes wounded in the name of greed, progress, and national strength—landscapes in need of healing. The abandoned mines are echoed by landscapes injured more recently, such as Colorado's Rocky Flats, the now-decommissioned nuclear weapons plant discussed by Len Ackland in chapter 11, and California's Travis Air Force Base, the one-time and now again home of the vernal pools discussed by Sharon Collinge in chapter 4.

In addition to producing some 660,000 troy ounces of gold, Boulder County's mines and mills left behind a few million tons of waste rock and tailings. These mining wastes contain pyrite, an iron sulfide mineral. When pyrite is exposed to air and water, it releases sulfuric acid, lots of iron, and other metals. The iron oxidizes and forms the tell-tale "yellowboy" deposits on streambeds, described as the "gangrenous puss of deep earth wounds." Ore bodies that contain pyrite release sulfuric acid naturally, but mining accelerates the reaction by crushing and grinding ores. Crushing and grinding reduce the size and increase the surface area of the ore rocks, and these increases in surface area speed up the release of sulfuric acid and the metals. This process is called *acid mine drainage* or, if you want to recognize that some release of acid occurs naturally, *acid rock drainage*.

The sulfuric acid dissolves metals such as lead, copper, cadmium, and zinc into the water. These metals can be harmful to humans if they get into drinking water at fairly high concentrations. Even at very low concentrations, they can poison fish and other aquatic organisms. For example, the EPA allows drinking water to contain up to 1.3 milligrams per liter, or parts per million, of copper, but fish exposed to as little as 0.01 milligrams per liter of copper will die in a couple of days.

Boulder residents have had to reckon with the effects of mining on water quality since the 1870s.[6] Miners washed mill tailings into streams used for the water supply, and the heavy loads of suspended sediment made the water undrinkable. In 1874, the *Boulder County Herald* recommended the development of water sources farther up Boulder Canyon, above the mining areas, to support the city's growth. Contaminated water from Boulder Creek appeared to be the cause of the death of several watering horses in 1884. At an expense of $200,000, Boulder constructed its first reservoir in 1890, the beginning of a water system that collects water melting from snow that falls on the Continental Divide about thirty miles west of the city. I was surprised to learn that the City of Boulder, often hailed and envied for these well-protected water sources in times of endangered water quality and insufficient water quantity, developed these sources out of necessity, not through extraordinary foresight.

There is still a minute chance that mining pollution puts some Boulder County residents at risk. The Left Hand Water District, a drinking-water utility, taps Lefthand Creek to provide drinking water to about fifteen thousand customers in rural Boulder and Larimer Counties. The water flowing in Lefthand Creek does not contain any metals at levels harmful to humans; neither does the water distributed by the utility, but the

EPA believes that a catastrophic flood could carry metal-contaminated sediments into the treatment plant. Most of the metals now entering the streams of the Lefthand Creek watershed end up in the streambed sediments.[7]

Although the threat to human health is hypothetical, fish and other aquatic organisms (especially those that dwell in the streambed sediments) definitely have suffered from the effects of acid mine drainage in the Lefthand Creek watershed. The Colorado Water Quality Control Commission found only about half as many fish in the James Creek below its confluence with the Little James Creek as above the confluence, and no aquatic life at all in the Little James.[8] Bordering the Little James is a series of abandoned mines—the Wano, the Emmit, the Burlington, and the Argo—that generate acid and metals. In the spring of 2003, as snow from the largest snowfall in a century melted, Jamestown residents reported a fish kill in the James Creek. The fish kill coincided with a sudden release of contaminated water that had backed up in subsidence pits at the Burlington Mine. Because the streams in the Lefthand Creek watershed are designated as "cold water aquatic life, Class 1," meaning that they should be supporting trout fisheries, the Clean Water Act mandates cleanup of the abandoned mines that are releasing metals to the streams. But the fish can't demand that the watershed be healed, and parts of the watershed have been dead for so long that anglers have not voiced concerns. What drew more attention to the contamination in this watershed was the potential risk that the metals posed to humans—the fifteen thousand customers of the Left Hand Water District.

The result of more than a decade of water and soil testing was an EPA finding that many of the abandoned mines in the Ward and Jamestown areas were eligible for addition to the Superfund list.[9] Such findings come in the form of a Hazard Ranking System (HRS) score. Sites with HRS scores of higher than 28.5 are eligible for addition to the Superfund list; one of the abandoned mines in the Ward area, the Captain Jack Mine and Mill site, scored 50.52.[10] The EPA notified the public of its intention to add the Ward and Jamestown mines to the Superfund list in early 2001, and it moved to secure the approval of Colorado governor Bill Owens for the Superfund listing.

For many Jamestown and Ward residents, this announcement was the first they were made aware that the EPA was considering cleanups that would literally be done in their backyards, even though numerous federal and state agencies had been investigating metal contamination in the Lefthand Creek watershed since 1986. Over the spring and summer of 2001, the EPA conducted public meetings to gain support for Superfund listing, but some residents voiced strong opposition. A community group in Jamestown, the Citizens Advisory Group for the Environment (CAGE), led the opposition. CAGE's concerns regarding Superfund listing were valid and well known to communities at which the EPA had conducted Superfund cleanups in the past (for example, Leadville, Colorado).[11] The stigma of adding the Little James and James Creek abandoned mines on the Superfund list, CAGE members feared, would threaten their properties' value. They argued that Superfund coffers were currently nearly empty and that prospects of future funding were dim (and, indeed, in April 2002 Superfund did run out of the money raised by taxes on the chemical industry).[12] They contended that Superfund projects often spent more money and time on litigation than on cleanup, and the EPA ignored local opinions in its decisions. The residents mainly felt blindsided, and with the support of Boulder County officials, they pleaded for time to evaluate the EPA findings and to seek alternatives to cleanup by Superfund. In June 2001, the EPA acquiesced, even though public comment is not required until after sites are added to the Superfund list, and delayed for one year the request to list the sites.

To review the EPA decision, the Boulder County Board of Health formed a stakeholder group, the Lefthand Watershed Task Force, in August 2001. The task force included seven members: four community representatives from Ward, Jamestown, and Rowena; a representative and a customer of the Left Hand Water District; and an environmental consultant. It was charged with reviewing three decades of water- and soil-quality studies, the EPA HRS scoring, and alternatives for cleanup of the abandoned mines. Seven months later it reported to the Board of Health.[13]

The task force members unanimously concluded that the abandoned mines near Ward along a stretch of Lefthand Creek known as California Gulch merited Superfund listing. Mining had begun in California Gulch in the late 1890s.[14] Low-grade ores yielded gold, silver, lead, copper, and zinc. The area was mined intermittently through the twentieth century to the early 1990s.[15] At the upper end of the gulch, the Big Five Tunnel is

FIGURE 8.3. The Big Five Tunnel adit in California Gulch. Approximately five to ten gallons of water per minute flow from the Big Five Tunnel down a waste-rock pile, through a man-made pond, and into Lefthand Creek.

discharging acidic, metal-laden water to Lefthand Creek.[16] At the lower end of California Gulch, lead concentrations in the creek double as the creek passes by the waste-rock piles of the Captain Jack and White Raven Mines. Some of the metal concentrations in the creek exceed by more than ten times the aquatic life standards set by the state of Colorado.

Only a few people live in California Gulch. Some own their homes and land, and others may be squatting. One resident reported that her children used to come home wet up to their waists after playing in the Big Five Tunnel waters. The family pumped their drinking water from a shallow well located about thirty feet from Lefthand Creek. Another resident who has made the old Captain Jack Mill building his home had high levels of mercury in his bedroom. The California Gulch residents saw the need for a Superfund cleanup there. And as long as the Superfund site didn't extend into the nearby town of Ward, the residents of nearby Ward also supported the Superfund cleanup, even though the mayor described the town as "a lot of people [who] don't want a bunch of agencies involved in their lives and looking over their shoulders."[17] The Ward representative on the task force, Peter Gleichman, showed that the residents of Ward recognized their responsibility to future generations when he said, "We do not think that the actions of our ancestors should rain down upon our descendents."[18]

But the Lefthand Watershed Task Force could not reach agreement on a recommendation for the cleanup of the mine wastes along James Creek and Little James Creek, the two creeks that come together in Jamestown. A four-to-three majority of the task force declared that "the County should support further assessment and remediation of these areas using alternatives to Superfund." The minority felt that Superfund was the only viable option for cleanup. The alternatives to Superfund included "stakeholder-run initiatives," voluntary cleanups, and recruitment of government agencies other than the EPA into cleanup efforts. For the Lefthand Creek watershed, a stakeholder-run initiative would be a cleanup led by local community groups and other organizations (e.g., the Left Hand Water District) with concerns about the water quality of Lefthand Creek. Former mining interests with some level of responsibility for the abandoned mines would perform voluntary cleanups.

The task force majority pointed out that a voluntary cleanup of the Burlington Mine, which was suspected of being the major source of metals in the Little James Creek watershed, was about to be started. The Burlington Mine was operated in the 1940s by the General Chemical Company, which became a division of Allied Chemical Corporation. Honeywell International, Inc., later acquired Allied Chemical, and when Honeywell environmental managers learned that the EPA was considering addition of the Burlington Mine to the Superfund list, they initiated a voluntary cleanup with the Colorado Department of Public Health and Environment rather than be forced to pay for a Superfund cleanup. Despite the optimism generated by Honeywell's voluntary cleanup, the task force's recommendation was less an endorsement of stakeholder-run initiatives and voluntary cleanups than a condemnation of Superfund. Steve Edelstein, CAGE's founder and the Jamestown representative on the task force, reiterated his main concern about Superfund and its impression on real-estate appraisers, who "see a connection between Superfund and property values."[19]

In a move that must have surprised those concerned about a loss of local control in cleanup decisions, the EPA announced in March 2003 that it would adopt the Lefthand Watershed Task Force's recommendation for its remediation plans.[20] Only the abandoned mines in California Gulch were submitted for Superfund listing, and in September 2003 these mines were added to the Superfund list as the "Captain Jack Mill" site. A remedial investigation, the first step in a Superfund cleanup, was started in 2005 under the supervision of the Colorado Department of Public Health and Environment,[21] and it is still in progress. Subject to the availability of funds, the expected completion date for the Captain Jack cleanup is probably sometime in 2010. The entire Captain Jack cleanup is expected to cost $10 million. Just two days after the addition of the Captain Jack Mill to the Superfund list, the EPA announced that the Superfund money raised by a tax on the chemical industry, which expired in 1995 and was not renewed, had run out, and cleanup costs of $1.5 billion per year for the 1,239 Superfund sites around the United States would be borne by all taxpayers. Dave Williams, the Superfund coordinator for EPA's Region 8, stated, "We can't guarantee that the funding will be there, but because of the nature of Lefthand Creek in that it is a drinking water supply that serves fifteen thousand people, it will get a high priority on the national scene."[22]

That the EPA would not seek Superfund listing for the abandoned mines around Jamestown particularly pleased the task force majority and CAGE. They had stood up to the EPA in a fight for a peaceful life in their small mountain town as well as for their property values. But the satisfaction of victory was short-lived. The EPA made it clear that the stakeholder groups and voluntary cleanups touted in the task force report must make progress toward remediation of the Little James Creek mines. If progress were not made, the EPA would be forced to reconsider Superfund listing.

The task force recommended the creation of a stakeholder group to take on cleanup of some of the abandoned mines around Jamestown, and in early 2003 that group was formed—the Lefthand Watershed Oversight Group (LWOG). This group's membership is similar to that of the task force—it includes residents of towns in the watershed and representatives of the Left Hand Water District. The new group got off to a good start when it was awarded a watershed planning grant and a monitoring grant from the Colorado Nonpoint Source Council. The grants, a total of $75,000 over three years, were used to assess the sources of metals in the watershed and to develop priorities for cleanup.

After all those years of driving past the abandoned mines without noticing the water-quality problems they caused, I decided I could help, too. With grants from Honeywell and the University of Colorado's Outreach Council, my students and I assisted LWOG in prioritizing cleanups in the watershed. One of my students, Alice Wood, who hails from a farm town in Indiana, even served as LWOG's first coordinator while she obtained her master's degree. We looked for the major sources of zinc, copper, and lead using metal-loading tracer dilution tests.[23] LWOG received another grant for the EPA to extend this work, and the EPA provided laboratory analysis of the metal concentrations in the samples, which is the major expense of such fieldwork. The results of our tests were incorporated into LWOG's watershed plan, which has been used to guide remediation efforts.[24] To date, about $4 million has been spent to clean up mines in the watershed. In addition to the Captain Jack Mill Superfund site and the Burlington Mine cleanup by Honeywell, the U.S. Forest Service cleaned up the Golden Age and Fairday Mines; the EPA cleaned up the Bueno Mine tailings; Boulder County secured an EPA Brownfields grant to clean up the Evening Star and Argo Mines; and LWOG is cleaning up tailings along the Little James Creek in 2008 with Section 319 funding from the EPA through the Colorado Nonpoint Source Council. Kathy Hernandez, an EPA manager in Region 8, coordinated the cleanups, and she and the Lefthand Watershed Revitalization Team were given a national EPA award in 2006 for their efforts. As part of Kathy's team, I proudly and prominently hung the award plaque in my office in the Engineering Center at the University of Colorado.

Despite the laudable progress, more high-priority abandoned-mine sites remain in the watershed, and obtaining sufficient and sustained funding for the cleanup of these abandoned mines will be a daunting challenge.[25] Cleaning up abandoned mines is unquestionably expensive. For example, Honeywell spent about $1.5 million for the voluntary Burlington Mine cleanup in which waste rock was moved away from Balarat Gulch, an intermittent stream, and the waste rock was capped with soil and vegetation. Under the rules of Colorado's voluntary cleanup program, none of the $1.5 million addressed the contaminated water seeping from a remaining subsidence pit at the mine because water treatment may not be performed under the terms of voluntary cleanups.[26] Honeywell is still considering a course of action to end the discharge of acid mine drainage from the subsidence pit.

And beyond the lack of funding for cleanups is the question of liability.[27] Under the Clean Water Act, stakeholder groups that attempt cleanups at abandoned mines assume liability for the contamination in perpetuity. The East Bay Municipal Utility District, a water utility that supplies the metropolitan area on the east side of San Francisco Bay with drinking water, found out the hard way about Clean Water Act liability. In 1993, the Committee to Save the Mokelumne River, an environmental group, sued the East Bay Municipal Utility District for allowing acid mine drainage from the Penn Mine to enter the Camanche Reservoir in the Sierra Nevada foothills. The East Bay Municipal Utility District had bought the Penn Mine as part of land purchased to construct the reservoir. They had constructed detention ponds to curb the flow of the acid mine drainage into the reservoir, but this solution was not always effective; after heavy rains, contaminated water would spill over the detention pond dams and into the reservoir. The Ninth Circuit Court of Appeals held that the East Bay Municipal Utility District was responsible for the acid mine drainage even though it was never involved in mining operations at the Penn Mine. The utility district was ultimately required to complete a more extensive cleanup of the Penn Mine for $10 million.

This case, *Committee to Save Mokelumne River v. East Bay Municipal Utility District* (13 F.3d 305, 9th Cir. [1993]), caused many environmental "Good Samaritans" to call off their abandoned-mine cleanups both in progress and planned. In Colorado, the state's Division of Minerals and Geology had been constructing a passive treatment system to remove

FIGURE 8.4. The sign identifying the Pennsylvania Mine site in Summit County, Colorado, with the names of the project's sponsors removed.

metals and acidity in the discharge from the Pennsylvania Mine in Summit County. When the state heard about the East Bay Municipal Utility District case, it shut down the Pennsylvania Mine cleanup project. At the site, a sign identifying the project remains, but the names of all of the sponsors have been removed. Since 1993, states and stakeholder groups acting as Good Samaritans have proceeded with mine cleanups that focus on moving waste rock away from streams, like Honeywell's Burlington Mine project, but cleanups that address acid mine drainage from abandoned-mine adits have been completely halted in the western United States.

Over the past fifteen years, the Western Governors Association[28] and a handful of legislators have proposed a way around the Clean Water Act liability—a Good Samaritan amendment to the act. Bills have been introduced in the U.S. House and Senate that would afford states and stakeholder groups protection against Clean Water Act liability, and in 2007 even President George W. Bush's EPA pushed Good Samaritan legislation. Some of these bills also provided for funding of abandoned-mine cleanup by imposing a royalty on hard-rock mining profits, a contentious issue for mining companies, which pay no royalties on minerals under the 1872 General Mining Act.[29] Despite all these efforts, very little progress has been made in cleanup legislation. The EPA managed to streamline administrative agreements that provide limited Good Samaritan protection under CERCLA, but none of the bills has passed, and there's not much evidence that any of them has been seriously discussed in Washington.

The Commonwealth of Pennsylvania chose not to wait for federal legislation: it passed its own Environmental Good Samaritan Act in 1999 to help its citizens participate in the remediation of abandoned coal mines across the state.[30] Pennsylvania provides the funding, too. Some of the funds are generated by the federal Surface Mining Control and Reclamation Act of 1977, which funds reclamation of coal mines through a royalty on coal producers. In 1999, then-governor Tom Ridge initiated the "Growing Greener" program, which initially provided $550 million from the general funds—from taxpayers—for watershed restoration and protection and for abandoned-mine reclamation. Now a tax on municipal waste has augmented the Growing Greener fund to $1.3 billion. Pennsylvanians are clearly committed to healing their injured watersheds.

Citizen participation in the cleanup of Pennsylvania's waterways can be measured by the proliferation of stakeholder and community groups: more than three hundred alliances, associations, commissions, conservancies, councils, networks, partnerships, stewardships, and task forces are now in existence in the state. One project in Pennsylvania may be particularly inspiring to westerners—the AMD&ART Park in Vintondale, Pennsylvania.[31] Vintondale grew up on coal mining, but when the colliery closed in the 1940s, the town's growth and prosperity ended. About five hundred people now live in Vintondale, and the per capita income is about $12,000 per year. The legacy of the coal mining was thirty-five acres of abandoned coal-processing buildings, piles of waste rock, and fifty to four hundred gallons per minute of acid mine drainage into the south fork of the Blacklick Creek. Yet the people of Vintondale were still proud of the role their parents and grandparents had played in providing energy for a growing country. Enter AMD&ART, an organization founded by historian T. Allan Comp in 1994 with the mission of "artfully transforming environmental liabilities into community assets."[32]

Comp hypothesized that environmental remediation projects were not fully succeeding because the solutions were dominated by the technical aspects and not mindful of the importance of history and the arts. As a result, a vital connection to the communities affected by the cleanups was lost.

In Vintondale, the AMD&ART team engaged the community in designing an acid-mine-drainage treatment system under the guise of a new park and a remembrance of the town's history. The treatment system, in which reddish orange–tinged acid mine drainage flows through a series of trapezoidal pools to emerge cleansed of metals and neutralized to a healthy pH, is surrounded by the Litmus Garden, plantings of native trees and sand shrubs that will reflect the treatment process in their fall colors. The foundations of the colliery's coke ovens and other structures remain as landscape elements in the History Wetlands, which provide both final treatment to the water and habitat for waterfowl. The recreation area includes fields for team play and quiet areas for picnics and horseshoes. An education center has been established in the town to promote understanding and advocacy of the project. The main portal to the mine, through which hundreds of Vintondale's men passed as they began and ended their shifts, is marked by a slab of polished black granite etched with images of those men during a shift change.

A similar project was recently completed in England—the Seen and Unseen Project at Quaking Houses.[33] Quaking Houses is home to a community of senior citizens near Durham, England. They grew concerned about pollution in a small stream near the Quaking Houses, the Stanley Burn. Acid mine drainage from nearby coal-waste piles had long ago turned the Stanley Burn into a lifeless stream. The residents sensed that they needed both artistic and technical assistance to restore their stream, so they recruited Lucy Milton of the Artists' Agency and Professor Paul Younger at the University of Newcastle-upon-Tyne, and thus was the Seen and Unseen Project born. Professor Younger and his associates provided the design of a passive treatment system that removed the metals and acidity. Through the Artists' Agency, Helen Smith provided the design for a park that would help people see and understand the process by which the stream was being restored. A major feature of the park was a boardwalk that carried visitors over the treatment ponds. The boards of the boardwalk are replaced with glass in spots where signs explain the function of the treatment processes. The community of seniors, led by the late Terry Jeffrey, promoted the construction by educating school children and starting a radio program about environmental issues.

Can westerners follow these examples of abandoned-mine cleanup? The obstacles of liability and funding must still be overcome. It's clear that westerners need to look to the easterners, to Pennsylvanians in particular, for innovative approaches to cleaning up abandoned mines. The liability problem may someday be solved by amendments to the federal Clean Water Act, but many Good Samaritans will not want to wait for the federal government to act. Instead, action must occur on the state level, following Pennsylvania's lead, with the cooperation of the U.S. EPA. The EPA already allows for Good Samaritan remediations at Superfund sites,[34] and some argue that the precedent set by the *Committee to Save the Mokelumne River v. East Bay Municipal Utility District* case has made Good Samaritans "unnecessarily hesitant"—that the East Bay Municipal Utility District was actually not a good example of the kind of environmental Good Samaritan a stakeholder group should be.[35]

If state lawmakers prove no more interested than federal lawmakers in passing Good Samaritan legislation, one angle not yet explored is taking the issue to the people in a ballot initiative: Who would vote against improving water quality even if that improvement did not meet Clean Water Act standards? The main opposition to Good Samaritan legislation addressing Clean Water Act liability has been environmental organizations, which foresee one exception to the Clean Water Act leading to other exceptions. However, an argument can be made that abandoned mines must be considered differently from other generators of pollution in the Clean Water Act. A premise of the Clean Water Act is that regulators can stop pollution by fining or shutting down the offending polluter, but pollution from abandoned mines cannot be stopped simply by fining or shutting down a mining company. Even if a mining company folded in the face of environmental problems or some other pressure, its mines nevertheless have continued to release acid mine drainage.

To solve the funding shortage, we must first recognize that hard-rock mining happened because we, the people, created a demand for the metals. We must acknowledge the role that mining plays in our lives, as Professor Younger did in the opening of his book *Mine Water*. He surveyed his own office for mining-derived items and found clay and limestone in the bricks and mortar wall; slate, lead, and zinc in the roof; quartz in the window glass, light bulb glass, and computer microchips; tungsten in light bulb filaments; copper in electrical wires; and an assortment of metals in his computer.[36] Indeed, the electricity itself was supplied by the burning of coal and by uranium-based nuclear energy. The Mineral Information Institute in Golden, Colorado, reports that the average American uses 1,600 pounds of copper, 900 pounds of zinc, 42,000 pounds of iron, and 1.736 troy ounces of gold in his or her lifetime. Rather than look to the U.S. mining industry, which must compete in a worldwide market, to pay for century-old transgressions, we must admit our own responsibility for the abandoned-mine problem. Again, we can look to Pennsylvania, where the majority of the money used to reclaim abandoned mines and restore watersheds comes from the commonwealth's general funds as part of the Growing Greener program. Where the people are willing to make the cleanup of abandoned mines a priority, money will be made available

Various estimates of the costs to clean up abandoned mines in the United States range from $5 billion for mines on public lands to between $32 and $72 billion for the 557,000 mines throughout the entire United States.[37] The $1.5 million spent on the Burlington Mine, the $225 million needed to undo the environmental damage caused by the Summitville Mine abandonment in 1992, the $1.2 billion that will eventually be put into the cleanup of the Clark Fork River in Montana—these sums quickly add up.[38] Perhaps a less daunting way of bearing these costs would be to consider the fact that 290 million Americans create the demand for mining products, so the cost to clean up the abandoned mines is only $240 per American.

The liability and funding issues still exist for the Lefthand Creek watershed, and despite seeing paths to overcome these obstacles, the EPA expects the stakeholder group, LWOG, to make progress toward remediation of abandoned mines in the watershed in exchange for the EPA's leaving the mines around Jamestown off the Superfund list. Although LWOG has made progress toward this goal, funding is available only in small amounts and at a slow rate.

Perhaps an obstacle bigger than liability and funding is the community's commitment to cleaning up abandoned mines. The Vintondale AMD&ART project and the Quaking Houses Seen and Unseen Project would not have succeeded without the active participation of each village's residents. The champions of these projects were clearly talented in their ability to rally the populace around the projects by creating tangible benefits beyond the actual cleanups—the new parks. But it may not have been so hard to convince the residents of these former coal-mining communities that the projects were worthwhile. These eastern communities seem more closely connected to the past and more willing to deal with the legacy of abandoned mines. In contrast, current residents of many of the former hard-rock mining districts in the western United States seem less connected to the past and thus less willing to take responsibility for the abandoned mines.

The residents of Jamestown are well aware of mining's role in their history. Just a few years ago the Jamestown Area Musicians put on a well-attended musical production called *Hard Rock Fever,* an "original rock opera of historic proportions" that celebrated the town's mining roots. The show was sold out for two weekends. At the town's Fourth of July celebration, the residents celebrate (and dread) the hourly ritual of dynamiting a one-hundred-pound steel anvil a hundred feet into the sky. The approximately twenty students at the town's elementary school recently heard stories of the mining days from a third-grader's grandfather.

Jamestown's Fourth of July celebration is held on what was long ago dubbed "Elysian Park," a flat five-acre field that seems out of place in the mountainous terrain. Elysian Park offers a softball diamond, a volleyball court, a band pavilion, a playground, and a set of communal golf clubs for driving practice. The field is so flat because it was once a tailings pond—a repository for a slurry of silty refuse from the Governor Mill, which was operated on the site by the Ozark-Mahoning Mining Company until the 1950s. Some of the mines around Jamestown produced fluorospar, a mineral containing fluoride, which was processed at the Governor Mill. After Ozark-Mahoning closed the mill, Jamestown residents complained about incessant dust from the desiccated tailings pond. During the 1960s, the town struggled to get Ozark-Mahoning to fix the dust problem, but state health officials considered the dust to be just a nuisance, not a health problem. Finally, in the early 1970s, the town convinced Ozark-Mahoning to sell the property to the town for $2,000 and arranged for capping of the tailings with soil.

Elysian Park was the focus of the EPA's evaluation of the need for Superfund cleanup in Jamestown. In many spots, including second base of the softball diamond, the soil cap over the tailings had thinned. The EPA's 1999 sampling of Elysian Park's surface soil revealed an average lead concentration of about 1,500 milligrams of lead per kilogram of soil in five samples. The EPA's standard for soil in children's play areas is 400 milligrams per kilogram. The CAGE group lobbied the EPA to do more extensive sampling—it did not want a Superfund site decision based on so few samples. The EPA returned in 2002 to sample a full grid of about forty locations. The "hot spots" of high lead concentration were still present, but because the soil cap had not thinned everywhere, the average lead concentration of the surface soil was only about 350 milligrams per kilogram, just below the EPA "action level" of 400 milligrams per kilogram. In other words, children playing in the park would be safe from excessive exposure to lead as long as they were not playing second base.

At a meeting in the Jamestown town hall in 2003, an EPA official reported that these results would not trigger Superfund remediation of Elysian Park. Some of the Jamestown residents attending the meeting responded with cheers. They were relieved that their property values would be preserved and that dump trucks would not be going past their homes to carry clean soil to Elysian Park. Later surveys of the town's residents have revealed, however, that many families now do not use the park because of the lead contamination. The EPA qualified its finding that Elysian Park does not require remediation by noting that the lead concentrations in the soils were acceptable as long as use of the park did not increase. Now some residents are pushing for improvements to the recreational facilities at Elysian Park, but before this can happen, something needs to be done to prevent exposures to the hot spots. The town obtained some funding from the state last year, but not enough to do the whole job, and now I am assisting the town with the submission of a second proposal to the EPA for Brownfields cleanup money (the first proposal was not funded).

The unsuccessful Brownfields proposal introduced Jamestown residents to one of the frustrations of stakeholder-run initiatives. About seven hundred applications were made nationally for Brownfields funds, but only fifty applications were funded. Many of the Jamestown residents who cheered the decision that Elysian Park would not be designated a Superfund site were those who had pushed for blocking Superfund listing in favor of stakeholder initiatives. They were aware that stakeholder initiatives face serious obstacles to remediation—Clean Water Act and funding issues—and that these obstacles would impede cleanup of the abandoned mines presenting the greatest hazards. Their actions were guided more by short-term self-interest than by the sense of responsibility for future generations that we need to solve these problems. Their actions did not show promise for the kind of community involvement needed to drive stakeholder-run initiatives. The rejection of Superfund should have been followed by a community commitment to get the work of abandoned-mine remediation done.

Is this kind of denial of responsibility for the past unique to the West? Perhaps there is less connection between the present and the past for today's Jamestown residents than for those of Vintondale, Pennsylvania. For LWOG and similar stakeholder groups, this reluctance to take responsibility for the legacy of mining makes it imperative that remediation projects create new public spaces for recreating in the outdoors, understanding history, and appreciating art.[39] Without community benefits beyond restoration of aquatic habitat, community involvement may be difficult to recruit. Perhaps an Elysian Park remediation project that results in an improved public space will give rise to new rituals that, like the *matachines* dancing rituals described by Brenda M. Romero in chapter 7, will give Jamestown a renewed sense of community and accomplishment.

The founder of Pennsylvania's AMD&ART, Allan Comp, said about acid-mine-drainage cleanups: "It's not the water; it's us." He meant that if the cleanups are to be supported and promoted, they must benefit communities as much as the cleanups benefit the water quality. In the western United States, his words should remind us that we may have to heal faulty memories of the history and legacy of mining before attempting to enlist today's communities in the healing of the mine-contaminated waters. And if we bear up to our responsibility to clean up these wounded landscapes we have inherited, we stand a good chance of developing a sense of civic cooperation and foresight for future generations that might serve us well in tackling some of the West's other long-standing problems.

Part 3
Lessons from Conflict

9

The Klamath Basin as a Proving Ground for the Endangered Species Act

William M. Lewis Jr.

EVEN WHEN THE United States was struggling to wring economic gain from a great wilderness, it had outspoken admirers of pristine landscapes. As early as 1799, Daniel Boone pronounced the state of Kentucky overcrowded (Faragher 1992). Even so, the vast majority of Americans seem to have been committed utilitarians well into the twentieth century; they were content to see the landscape manipulated in all conceivable ways that might generate wealth or convenience (Limerick 2000, chap. 3A).

Although the tide of utilitarianism turned only gradually, the corresponding legal changes became tangible very suddenly in just a few years around 1970, through federal environmental legislation and regulation of great scope that for the first time treated the environment of the United States as a commons deserving of protection for the general welfare. In the aquatic realm, the federal government began in the 1960s to use its Commerce Clause authority, coupled with federal loans and grants, to force reductions in the discharge of pollutants to surface waters. This action was followed in 1972 by major revisions in the Federal Water Pollution Control Act, which subsequently became known as the Clean Water Act, whose breathtaking purpose, to be achieved in stages, is to eliminate pollution entirely from waters of the United States. The Clean Air Act of 1970 set similar goals for the quality of the atmosphere. The new environmental legislation was reinforced with executive authority through creation of the U.S. Environmental Protection Agency in 1970. Furthermore, through the National Environmental Policy Act of 1970, disclosure of construction plans was required of certain traditionally secretive and sometimes impetuous federal agencies. A fitting corollary to protection of the physical and chemical attributes of environment was the Endangered Species Act (ESA) of 1973, which directly protects imperiled species (NRC 1995).

Federal legislation of the 1970s intended to protect the quality of air and water initially faced strong resistance from industries, municipalities, and states as they contemplated the cost of compliance. In contrast, the public seems to have been generally pleased with the idea of correcting environmental damage, much of which was plainly visible to the untrained eye, and of preventing its further occurrence. Thus, federal politicians on the whole were comfortable in maintaining the new environmental legislation and in fending off most attempts to eliminate or weaken it. Over the ensuing decades, the notion of environmental protection under federal authority has been fully assimilated by American society, despite much continuing debate over its details and its mode of implementation.

The ESA

The ESA has had a more tenuous existence than any of the other major pieces of environmental legislation originating from the era of environmental reform. For reasons that are not immediately obvious, and despite its conceptual support from the American public, the ESA has never reached the more settled status of the other acts. It differs in some important respects from the Clean Water Act and the Clean Air Act, which focus on environmental media rather than on organisms per se. For this reason, the ESA's benefits are not so clearly visible to the average citizen, who can more easily imagine direct personal benefits from clean air and clean water than from avoidance of extinctions. Although the ESA sustains much momentum from iconic species such as the Bald Eagle (the "charismatic megafauna"), local ESA controversies more typically involve creatures that are either obscure (the snail darter) or, at least to the uninitiated, even repugnant (the rice rat). The government is a hero when it saves the acrobatic, intelligent sea otter, but resembles a relentless, unreasoning machine when it blocks hundreds of building permits to preserve habitat for a special kind of mouse or insect whose existence would be completely unknown to the average person were it not for the trouble that it has caused landowners and developers (see the full list of species now protected under the ESA on the U.S. Fish and Wildlife Service [USFWS] Web site).

In the long run, the ESA must survive primarily on the merits of its conceptual basis, which is the value of biological diversity, with all of its inherent emotional appeal and unrealized practical possibilities. In the meantime, the local nuisance of maintaining rare and often unfamiliar species weighs heavily against the national instinct that extinction of species is unjustifiable waste.

As would be expected, the ESA is applied through a series of formal actions, the purpose of which is illustrated in subsequent sections of this chapter (see also the USFWS Web site). From the average citizen's viewpoint, however, the essence of the ESA is that it restricts in three ways the interaction of humans with any species listed under it. The first way is that species classified by the appropriate federal agencies as either endangered (in imminent peril of extinction) or threatened (nearing the status of endangerment) cannot be harvested commercially or for sport except under some rare, narrowly defined circumstances expressly permitted by the relevant federal agency. This aspect of the ESA is not especially troublesome given that state or federal laws have long excluded from harvest many species not listed under the ESA (e.g., songbirds, nongame mammals, reptiles).

A second requirement is that listed species cannot be killed or impaired (stressed, restrained, blocked from completion of the life cycle). This provision of the ESA is a bit more inconvenient than prohibition of harvest in that it may reduce the efficiency or increase the cost of activities that are legal but happen to occur in proximity to species that are protected under the ESA. The ESA bans on harvesting and on inadvertent killing or impairment are referred to collectively as "prohibition of take."

The third restriction on human interaction with listed species is prohibition of damage to habitat that is essential for support of the species (and thus called "critical habitat"). To the extent that such habitat may be damaged by normal commercial or agricultural activities, this prohibition can be very disruptive on a local or regional basis and is probably the main cause of frustration with the ESA. Protection of habitat seems unfair in part because it is not customary under force of law. For example, although state fish and wildlife agencies are well aware of the essential nature of appropriate habitat for the many ordinary species under their protection, they typically have no legal tools with which they can require the maintenance of habitat by private parties, even though they can prevent or limit take under state law. Because legal protection of habitat is culturally unfamiliar, it seems to warrant resistance. Its inclusion in the ESA is essential, however, given that prohibition of take cannot compensate for loss of habitat in promoting the survival of species.

The listing of species under the ESA is conducted by executive-branch agencies that have the most relevant administrative responsibilities for the habitat where the species is found. For species that have no marine affiliations, the USFWS (Department of the Interior) is responsible for listings; species with marine affiliations are the responsibility of the National Marine Fisheries Service (NMFS, Department of Commerce). Candidates for listing may be identified by these agencies or may be nominated for listing by state agencies, other federal agencies, conservation groups, or private parties of any kind. The suitability of a species for listing is a matter of judgment based on information about the abundance and range of the species, particularly with reference to recent reduction in range or abundance coupled with loss of habitat.

Although it is common to think of environmental restoration as a by-product of the ESA, the ESA is not intended to be broadly used for environmental improvement. It is in essence an emergency act that is invoked only when a species is in its last phases of existence, and it has legal force for only as long as it takes to reverse the species' decline. The interface between the ESA and broader attempts at environmental restoration is an interesting topic to consider, but there should be no mistaking the ESA as a substitute for other laws or regulations that promote more general restoration and maintenance of environmental quality.

The Klamath Basin

The Klamath basin (twelve thousand square miles; see fig. 9.1) is one of numerous moderately large coastal drainages on the Pacific Coast. Like other drainages of this type, it contains mountains that give rise to cold streams and rivers of high gradient that are well suited for salmonid fishes (salmon, trout, and their allies). Unlike other Pacific Coast drainages, however, the Klamath basin also has three very large shallow lake basins (two of them, Tule Lake and Lower Klamath Lake, have largely been

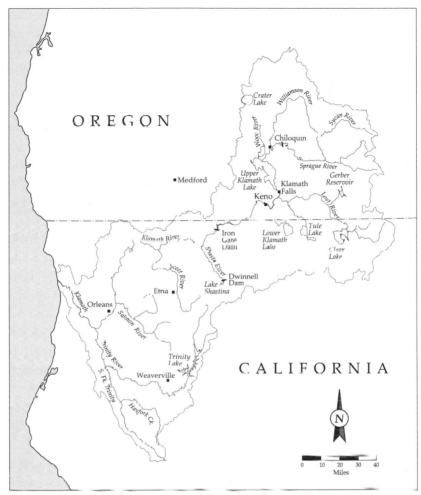

FIGURE 9.1. The Klamath basin. (Reprinted from NRC 2004; reprinted with permission from the National Academies Press, Copyright 2004, National Academy of Sciences)

drained) and very extensive marshlands both near the lake basins and separated from them. A substantial part of the basin is blanketed with volcanic debris. These volcanic deposits and a low degree of tectonic activity have given the basin's northeastern portion a gentle gradient, which in turn has led to the formation of its extensive marshes and shallow lakes. The rest of the basin has the rugged terrain that is more typical of coastal drainages in this region.

Because of its mix of geomorphic features, the Klamath basin supports not only salmonids and other fishes that are well suited for life in cold, fast-flowing waters, but also warm-water fishes that favor lakes or warm streams and rivers of lower gradient. Thus, among the basins of the Pacific Coast, the Klamath basin has exceptional aquatic biodiversity.

Marshes and shallow lakes also favor waterfowl and shore birds. In its original condition, the Klamath basin probably was the single most important waterfowl habitat in the western United States, as shown by the creation of seven separate national wildlife refuges within the basin (USFWS 2002). Although waterfowl populations are now reduced by anthropogenic environmental change, the basin, through its marshes and lakes, continues to provide a substantial amount of waterfowl habitat.

Waters of the upper basin include Upper Klamath Lake and its main tributaries, the Wood River and the Williamson River, along with the Sprague River, a large tributary of the Williamson (fig. 9.1). The Chiloquin Dam, which is small and now of limited use, is located on the Sprague River.

Below Upper Klamath Lake, but still within the upper basin, is the Lost River, which once had a diffuse connection with the Klamath main stem during floods. The Lost River now either receives or gives water to the main stem under control of irrigation works operated by the U.S. Bureau of Reclamation's (USBR) Klamath Project, which delivers water for irrigation east of the main-stem Klamath. Near the headwaters of the Lost River are two reservoirs, Clear Lake and Gerber, which were created by the Klamath Project as a means of capturing flows from the upper Lost River for water-management purposes. To the south of the main stem of the Lost River are remnants of two very large lakes (originally approximately equal in size to Upper Klamath Lake), Lower Klamath Lake and Tule Lake (fig. 9.1). These lakes were 80 to 90 percent drained in the early twentieth century to provide new agricultural lands.

On the main-stem Klamath, there are six dams (fig. 9.2), the first of which (Link River Dam) regulates the water level of Upper Klamath Lake for water-management purposes. The other dams were constructed for hydropower production. All dams are operated by PacifiCorp, with oversight by the USBR. The last dam in the series, Iron Gate Dam, regulates the flow of water to the Klamath River main stem in the lower basin.

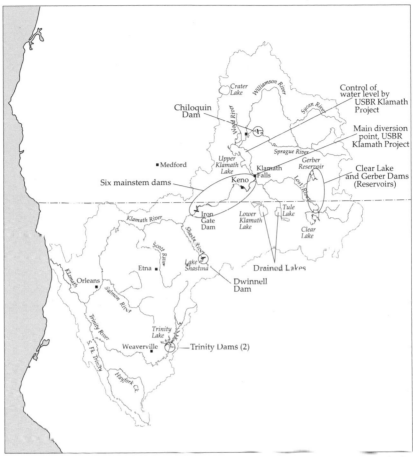

FIGURE 9.2. Major dams and diversions of the Klamath basin. (Modified from NRC 2004)

There are four main tributaries to the Klamath River main stem in the lower basin. The Shasta River is dammed in its upper reaches for irrigation and shows severe depletion of flow by irrigation over much of the year (figs. 9.2 and 9.3). The Scott River also supports irrigated agriculture and shows depleted flows. In contrast, the Salmon River is surrounded by federal lands and is not used for irrigation. The Trinity River is by far the largest tributary in the Klamath basin. It often is treated as a separate basin because it enters the Klamath main stem relatively near the estuary and because its water management revolves around large transfers of

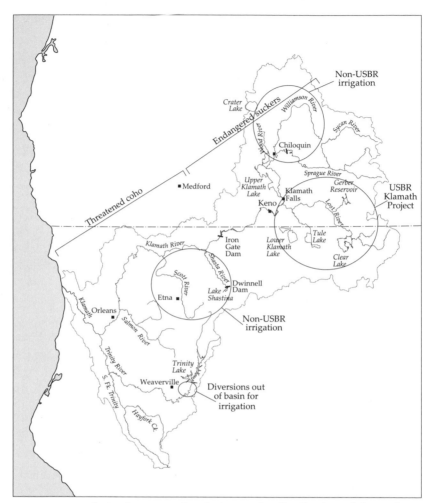

FIGURE 9.3. Irrigation zones in relation to the distribution of the endangered suckers and threatened coho salmon of the Klamath basin. (From NRC 2004; reprinted with permission from the National Academies Press, Copyright 2004, National Academy of Sciences)

water to California's Central Valley Project from the Trinity Diversion Project, which includes two USBR-operated dams and diversion facilities (fig. 9.2). Environmental controversy in the Trinity River basin has been largely separate from that of the rest of the Klamath basin, but the Trinity River is not truly separate in a biotic sense, given that it has migrations of coho and other fishes that are part of the same genetic stocks found in the rest of the basin. In addition to the major tributaries, the many minor tributaries of the Klamath main stem are collectively important to fish.

The Klamath basin was developed through resource extraction and agriculture, which led to large changes in the landscape and its natural resources, even though the population density of the basin has never been high (the approximate current population is 120,000 [NRC 2004]). Mining became important in the middle of the nineteenth century and ruined many miles of tributary stream channel in the lower basin. Timber harvest started about that same time and continues; it has damaged streams primarily through erosion. Fishing, both inland and on the coast, was a major source of food for the Indian tribes that occupied the basin, but it became excessive in the nineteenth century with colonization of the basin and depleted the abundance of many fishes in the basin.

The lands of the Klamath basin are not naturally well suited for agriculture, but portions of the upper basin as well as the Shasta and Scott watersheds, if irrigated, yield alfalfa and grains in considerable quantity and support grazing. Thus, one consistent pressure within the Klamath basin beginning even in the nineteenth century has been routing of water from rivers and streams to lands that are suitable for farming if irrigated (fig. 9.3).

Although irrigation has been important in the economic development of the Klamath basin, it involves diversion of less than 10 percent of the total flow of the Klamath River. The environmental effects of this diversion, however, have been disproportionately large in that it is concentrated within the upper basin and the uppermost portion of the lower basin (fig. 9.3), where the total amount of runoff is much lower than in the lowermost part of the basin. Apart from depletion of flow, which can be acute during the low-flow season, especially in dry years, the irrigation works themselves and the water-routing schemes that accompany irrigation have caused considerable environmental change, most of which has been detrimental to aquatic life. Diversions entrain fish or block their migrations, and dams that serve irrigation purposes reduce the frequency and intensity of flushing flows and prevent the recruitment of gravels, thus starving the streambed. Water that is impounded or returned from fields is undesirably warm for salmonids, and agricultural practice often involves the removal of riparian vegetation as well, which contributes to warming of the water. Thus, the by-products of agriculture, especially through irrigation, are numerous and go beyond reduction in mean flow.

The Klamath basin prior to colonization was exceptionally rich in ecological capital. Since that time, it has been substantially degraded by resource extraction and irrigated agriculture. Although considerable resource management for economic growth could have occurred with much less damage, neither the will nor the means to restrain management was available during the era of development between around 1850 and 1960. Despite damage, the basin remains impressive biotically and ecologically to this day.

Endangered Suckers and Threatened Coho Salmon in the Klamath Basin

The freshwater fishes of the Klamath basin are mostly endemic; in other words, they do not occur elsewhere (Moyle 2002). Thus, they are unique genetically and ecologically, and they present high risk of extinction because they are confined to the Klamath basin. Ocean-running fish that spend part of their life cycle in freshwater within the Klamath basin also show some degree of genetic specialization. Their genetic identity does not rise to the level of species, but rather is reflected in genetically distinctive stocks that are associated with the Klamath basin and adjoining basins. Under the ESA, genetically distinctive stocks can be recognized and protected as "evolutionarily significant units" of a species.

Listing Klamath Basin Fishes under the ESA

The USFWS listed the Lost River sucker and the shortnose sucker, both of which are endemic freshwater species, as endangered in 1988, and the NMFS listed the environmentally significant unit of coho salmon that occupies the Klamath basin and adjoining basins as threatened in 1997. Another species, the bull trout, is listed under the ESA as threatened, but because it is distributed extensively beyond the Klamath basin and occupies habitat that is minimally disturbed, it has not been the focus of much controversy in the basin.

The two listed suckers and the coho salmon occupy different parts of the Klamath basin and differ in their life cycles and habitat require-

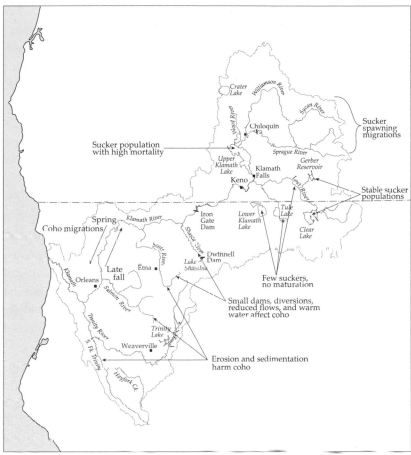

FIGURE 9.4. The status of endangered suckers and threatened coho salmon in various parts of the Klamath basin. (From NRC 2004; reprinted with permission from the National Academies Press, Copyright 2004, National Academy of Sciences)

ments. The two suckers are found only in the upper basin (see fig. 9.4). Although they spawn in rivers and streams, they live most of their lives in lakes and thus do not have suitable habitat in the lower basin, where there are no natural lakes. Coho salmon are confined to the lower basin. They originally occupied the upper basin as well, but dams on the main stem now block their upstream migration.

The endangered suckers were once among the most abundant fishes in the Klamath basin. They are quite large as compared with suckers in general. The Lost River sucker, which is the larger of the two, reaches a length as great as forty inches (more commonly twenty-five to thirty-five inches) and may live more than forty years (USFWS 2002). Because of their large size and their tendency to migrate for spawning either to lakeside springs or into tributaries of lakes, these large fish were easily captured by American Indians for subsistence and were quite vulnerable to mass exploitation by settlers. A cannery was established on the Lost River adjacent to Upper Klamath Lake during the late nineteenth century, and large numbers of fish were taken by crude means to feed hogs (USFWS 2002).

Commercial fishing for suckers became impractical in the early twentieth century after drainage of Tule Lake and Lower Klamath Lake and hydrologic alteration of the Lost River, but intensive sport fishing, which also focused on the adults during spawning, continued. The adults, which concentrate en route to or on spawning grounds, were snagged with large hooks attached to a weight (often a spark plug). Although the sport fishery ultimately was regulated, steady loss of large fish no doubt reduced the population's reproductive capacity even after commercial fishing had ceased.

Coho salmon, along with other salmon, are most vulnerable to capture during or just prior to spawning, as are the suckers. The life cycle of the coho salmon involves approximately a year and a half of development and growth from the egg to the migratory smolt stage in streams, about the same amount of time for maturation in the ocean, and finally a spawning run back to tributary streams, after which the fish die (Moyle 2002). Indians harvested the salmon for food. Colonization brought commercial fisheries, which conducted ocean harvest as well as river harvest and were essentially unregulated for decades. Salmon probably began to decline in the Klamath basin during the 1920s, in part because of overfishing (NRC 2004).

Causes for ESA Listing of Suckers and Coho

Wherever overfishing is the primary cause for depression of abundance of a fish species, appropriate regulations can restore that abundance or at least arrest a decline in abundance before the ESA is invoked. Where depression caused by overfishing is compounded by other factors, however, the removal or reduction of fishing pressure may fail to produce recovery of the species—as was the case for the two sucker species and the coho salmon in the Klamath basin.

The two ESA listing agencies were required at the time of listing and numerous times after the listing to describe factors likely to be causing decline in abundance of the two suckers and the coho salmon. For all three species, the agencies cited overfishing as one contributor to the original decline, but also identified a number of other factors that would explain these species' failure to respond more favorably to elimination of fishing (NMFS 2002; USFWS 2002). For the two sucker species, the USFWS named water-management practices, physical impairment of habitat, poor water quality, competition from nonnative species, and a number of other anthropogenically derived environmental changes that contributed to suppression of the species. For coho salmon, the NMFS produced a similar list of causes, except that the list applied to the lower basin rather than to the upper basin and was focused on flowing waters rather than on a combination of lakes and flowing waters, as was the case for the suckers.

Relevance of the USBR Klamath Project to ESA Listings

Although the factors influencing the listing of these three species covered a broad range of environmental change, the listing agencies focused sharply on changes caused by the USBR's management of water through its Klamath Project.

The Klamath Project began in 1904 with Oregon's and California's blessing and cooperation, and was funded by Congress in 1905. The USBR, true to its purpose, which today would more likely be called "water development" than "reclamation," identified the Klamath basin as one of numerous places in the West where water could be made to serve as a cornerstone of economic activity, primarily through the development of irrigation infrastructure. Between 1904 and 1960, the USBR developed extensive water rights that were superseded in seniority only by a few small private rights and the extensive but still unquantified rights of Indian tribes, which date from "time immemorial." A natural rock sill at the outflow of Upper Klamath Lake was removed, and Link River

Dam was installed a short distance downstream for regulation of lake level, thus allowing the storage capacity of Upper Klamath Lake to be used in support of irrigation and incidentally doubling the natural amplitude of annual water-level variations in the lake. Another part of the project involved construction of dams in the upper reaches of the Lost River, thus producing Clear Lake Reservoir and Gerber Reservoir. These reservoirs provided irrigation water to downstream reaches of the Lost River, but were equally important in preventing water from entering Lower Klamath Lake and Tule Lake, which were slated for drainage so that their lake beds (about 100,000 acres each) could be used for agricultural purposes. Between the headwaters of the Lost River and the Klamath main stem, an extensive system for routing water was installed for irrigation of about 220,000 acres. The project was essentially completed by around 1960. The USBR operates the Klamath Project under contract with irrigation districts, which in turn serve individual farms. The contracts are not immutable, but they make a firm, long-term commitment for delivery of water to private parties under all but the most unusual circumstances.

The use of Upper Klamath Lake for storage has affected not only water levels in the lake, but also the Klamath River's seasonal flow regime. Seasonal low flows in the Klamath main stem are lower than they were prior to water development.

Because the Klamath Project extended over most of the two endangered suckers' range, the project was bound to affect the suckers. Through reduction of flows in the Klamath main stem, the project potentially affected coho as well. Hindsight has verified that the project has harmed the endangered suckers, but also indicates that the degree of focus on the project in investigating the causes of endangerment was excessive (NRC 2002). Half of the irrigation-based water management in the upper basin occurs through private parties and not through the USBR (fig. 9.3). An additional amount of management approximately equal to that of USBR management occurs on the Scott and Shasta Rivers, beyond the Klamath Project, with known negative consequences for coho, and still more occurs on the Trinity River, which provides habitat for coho salmon (fig. 9.3). Furthermore, the USBR is not involved in some important types of environmental change that federal agencies cite as affecting the listed species (e.g., nonnative species competitive with suckers; warm tributary waters harmful to coho).

One might ask why the listing agencies tended to focus on the USBR as opposed to taking a broader approach. One reason is that the ESA specifically requires listing agencies to "consult" with (and thus to review and potentially limit operations of) any other federal agency that is managing environmental resources where listed species occur. The USBR's management of water through its irrigation project is both obvious and extensive, and thus requires scrutiny under the ESA.

In engaging the USBR, the listing agencies also engaged the parties served by the USBR (irrigation districts representing farmers who hold the rights to irrigation of lands served by the Klamath Project) and in this way entered into a heated political controversy that consumed progressively increasing amounts of effort, thus diverting attention away from other important targets of analysis and action.

Consequences of the ESA Listings

As required by the ESA, each round of consultation between the USBR and the two listing agencies for the endangered suckers and coho salmon involved the preparation of a report (a "biological assessment") by the USBR describing management actions that the USBR considered potentially harmful to the welfare of the listed species, a technical and scientific evaluation of the degree of harm caused by these actions, and a proposal for changes in project operations as necessary to reduce or eliminate harm to listed species (e.g., USBR 2002). The relevant listing agency then evaluated the validity of the biological assessment and, as required by the ESA, issued a "biological opinion." As is usual for large projects, the consultations and the issuance of assessments and opinions occurred multiple times and in fact were recurring on an annual basis prior to 2002 because of the agencies' inability to find a stable basis for a multiyear plan.

Biological opinions always must explain why the management agency's proposals will or will not present a continuing danger of extinction to the listed species. In ESA parlance, continued impairment of listed species that might be sufficient to push the species toward extinction is called *jeopardy*. When a listing agency judges a plan presented by the managing agency as inadequate, it finds jeopardy and presents what amounts to a rebuttal, which is called a *reasonable and prudent alternative* (RPA). The RPA consists of a list of requirements that are additive to the proposals already made by the management agency. Thus, if the management agency (in this case the USBR) proposes six actions intended to make its management less damaging to the listed species, the listing agency (in this case either the USFWS or the NMFS) may accept these six actions, but also find that additional actions, issued through an RPA, are necessary to avoid jeopardy.

In the Klamath basin, the listing agencies have consistently found USBR's proposals to be inadequate and have issued RPAs containing lists of additional requirements. Some of these requirements have involved quantitative restrictions in the latitude for water management, and some have involved other matters, such as screening water as it is removed from the Klamath River in order to avoid trapping fish behind irrigation structures.

Although a consultation process sounds like an evenhanded debate, it really is not in that the listing agencies have the final word. Management agencies that in the past have considered certain RPA requirements to be weak have challenged the RPAs through the courts or at the cabinet level of the executive branch (NRC 2004). Because the courts have been consistently supportive of listing agencies, and cabinet-level administrators have declined to participate in specific ESA actions, the listing agencies in effect hold final authority on management actions. Even so, the management agency does not always implement the listing agencies' requirements in a timely way. For example, the USFWS repeatedly over a decade or more required the installation of a fish screen on the largest canal diverting water into the Klamath Project from Upper Klamath Lake, but the screen was not actually funded or installed until 2004 (NRC 2004). Although it is possible for a management agency to say legitimately that its funding source (the U.S. Congress in the case of the USBR) has not given it money for a capital project pursuant to an RPA, it is less feasible for such an agency to refuse to make operational changes that are physically feasible without capital funds. Thus, the main way in which the listing agencies affected USBR prior to 2002 was with regard to daily and seasonal operations of the Klamath Project.

The Water Crisis of 2001

In 2001, the federal agencies went through their usual consultation and document-exchange procedure. The listing agencies, as usual finding the USBR proposals to be inadequate, issued RPAs. The RPA from the USFWS had a number of features (including the fish screen, which had not yet been installed as of 2001), but its only truly controversial component was to place new limits on drawdown of Upper Klamath Lake, which has the largest single population of endangered suckers within the Klamath basin. The USFWS reasoned that drawdown of the lake, as necessary for full use of the lake's storage capacity in support of agricultural supply, was harmful to the endangered suckers, and so it tightened its restrictions on drawdown, thus establishing a new limit on the availability of water from Upper Klamath Lake for the Klamath Project. Similarly, the NMFS required higher minimum flows downstream of the Klamath Project in the Klamath main stem, beginning at Iron Gate Dam. This requirement for higher flows in effect reduced the reserve of water available for irrigation.

The ESA requirements of 2001 for change in the USBR's water management would have produced deficiencies in water supply to the Klamath Project for years drier than average, which would have led to steady controversy between environmental interests on one side and water users on the other. Through an unlucky coincidence (which might in the long run be considered beneficial in the sense that it forced some beneficial actions that otherwise might not have occurred), however, the Klamath basin experienced a severe drought during 2001, just as the new water-management restrictions came into effect. The result was that the federal government closed the water supply to the 220,000 irrigated acres of the Klamath Project for the first time since the project was completed in the 1960s. Thus, contracts that had been honored for two or more generations of irrigated farming were not honored in 2001 because of the ESA's superseding authority.

The water restrictions' drastic economic consequences for irrigators and their economic dependents (suppliers of agricultural goods and services, for example), plus the symbolic significance of irrigation water being closed by federal authority through legislation adopted long after water contracts were first initiated, gave irrigators a profound sense of being mistreated. They reacted angrily when the gates were closed, hoping by this means for a quick reversal that would save their crops, but when that didn't happen, they settled into a more organized resistance spearheaded by the Klamath Water Users Association, which represents largely the private water users under contract with the USBR to receive water.

The water users and their consultants reviewed the biological opinions that had been prepared by the listing agencies. Not unexpectedly, they found weaknesses in these documents and questioned the cause-and-effect relationships cited as reasons for shutting off the water supply to their irrigated lands.

After the debate between the water users and the listing agencies (each side with many supporters) shifted to some degree from the political to the technical arena, the Department of the Interior and the Department of Commerce felt increasing pressure to get outside review of the technical and scientific content of the ESA documents. It was not intended that any such review supersede the established legal authority of the listing agencies to make judgments, but rather to find out whether the irrigators' vehement opposition had any scientific or technical merit.

Formation of the National Research Council's Klamath Committee

In 2001, the Interior and Commerce Departments approached the National Academy of Sciences (NAS) with a request that it create a committee to study the biological assessments, biological opinions, and underlying technical and scientific information on the Klamath Project and through this study to reach conclusions about the strength of scientific support for the opinions and decisions rendered by the three federal agencies involved in the consultations surrounding the project. The results of this study were to be given in an interim report. A second phase of study, which was to culminate in a final report, was to move beyond the agencies' actions to a consideration of the long-term future requirements for recovery of the three listed species.

The request to the NAS from the Interior and Commerce Departments followed a pattern that is relatively common within the federal government when issues involving scientific and technical matters under control of federal agencies become controversial. The NAS (now joined by the National Academy of Engineering and the National Institute of Medicine, and collectively known as the National Academies) was formed in 1863 by President Lincoln through a congressional charter as a means of facilitating the transfer of scientific and technical information from individual specialists to the federal government by some organized process that could be mobilized on short notice (see the NAS Web site for more details). In fact, President Lincoln had an abiding interest in the science and technology underlying ballistics, so the topics of interest have evolved since his time, but the academy's function remains essentially the same: to advise the government on matters of science and technology.

In its original form, the NAS was intended to conduct business through its members, each of whom is elected by the NAS membership on the basis of extraordinary levels of scientific achievement. With the growth of government and of science and technology, however, the NAS became overwhelmed with requests and formed a subsidiary organization, the National Research Council (NRC), through which it conducted much of its business. Today, the NRC, under supervision and oversight by the academies, employs a professional staff that forms numerous committees of voluntary consultants in response to government requests; one such committee was the NRC's Committee on Endangered and Threatened Fishes in the Klamath Basin.

Since its beginning, the NAS has been completely independent of government even though it serves the government. Independence means that it can reject requests from the government that it judges to be infeasible for study by scientific or technical means or inconsistent with the NAS policy of avoiding politics and the formulation of policy. Furthermore, the NAS and its sister organizations operate by a strict set of rules involving extensive use of closed sessions (to encourage formation of consensus among committee members through open exchange of ideas), committees whose members are diversely constituted with respect to background and perspective, extensive peer review and procedural oversight, and a requirement for group conclusions to be approved in written form by all members of a committee (minority reports are accepted, but are exceptional). Thus, the NAS has institutionalized through the NRC all reasonable practices that would minimize distortion of a committee's work by political agendas or personal biases. For this reason, and because the NAS is not under government control, observers and the government itself often take NRC reports quite seriously (but not always uncritically). Thus, although the NRC Klamath Committee's opinions were binding on no one, the committee's task was significant through its potential influence on ESA actions in the Klamath basin and beyond.

The NRC Klamath Committee's Interim Report

The NRC Klamath Committee released its interim report in 2002 (NRC 2002). In evaluating the USBR's 2001 biological assessments on endangered suckers and coho salmon, the committee concluded that the USBR, if allowed to proceed with the operating rules that it proposed for water management, might cause mean minimum water levels in Upper Klamath Lake and mean minimum flows in the Klamath River main stem below Iron Gate Dam to decline during dry years. This outcome may not have been the intent of the USBR proposals, but the NRC committee nevertheless concluded that the USBR had not given a justification for operating at lower mean water levels for Upper Klamath Lake or lower flows in the Klamath main stem, and therefore could not be credited with a scientific or technical justification for these proposals.

The NRC committee also identified some scientific weakness in the RPA of the biological opinion prepared by the USFWS for endangered suckers. The committee endorsed the USFWS requirements for fish screens, given the abundant and uncontested evidence that entrainment of the endangered suckers in the canals was causing mass mortality for all age classes of fish, and found strong scientific support for a number of other USFWS requirements. On one key requirement related to water levels in Upper Klamath Lake, however, the NRC committee found negligible scientific support. This conclusion came as a surprise to many of the highly qualified scientists who were working on environmental evaluations in the Klamath basin, and there were charges, delivered with varied degrees of emotion, that the NRC committee must either have done a sloppy job or did not have the appropriate expertise to understand the issues (Cooperman and Markle 2003).

Water level in Upper Klamath Lake is potentially linked to a number of environmental features that can affect the endangered suckers.

One of these features is water quality. Upper Klamath Lake's water quality is notoriously poor because the lake develops very dense blooms of suspended algae (phytoplankton). At the algae's peak abundance, as is characteristic of organisms that show development of very dense populations, mortality is triggered by some environmental event, and the algae die in large numbers. For Upper Klamath Lake, the key event appears to be a mixing of the water column after an extended period of calm. The mechanisms are not well understood, but deep mixing may deprive the dense algae populations of light exposure, thus inducing physiological stress and blocking photosynthetic oxygen output. The key result for the endangered suckers' welfare is loss of oxygen from the water column. Mass mortality occurs irregularly, but was evident in three consecutive years during the 1990s (1995, 1996, and 1997). Mortality selectively affects large fish, which is unfortunate in that large fish are extremely valuable to the population because of their high reproductive capacity. Excessive growth of suspended algae also is associated with other water-quality problems, but there seems to be general agreement that the worst problem is loss of oxygen leading to mass mortality (USFWS 2002).

Very early in its study of the environmental problems in Upper Klamath Lake, the USFWS concluded that manipulation of water levels in Upper Klamath Lake through the operation of the USBR's Klamath Project likely was a factor contributing to poor water quality, thus leading to mass mortality of fish. The USFWS did not place the blame for mass mortality exclusively on water-level manipulation, given that mass mortality was recorded even prior to 1900, when water-level manipulation did not occur, but it did conclude that water-level variations probably exacerbated the mass mortality. Because studies were conducted on water quality, fish, mass mortality, and related phenomena during the 1990s, the NRC committee members were able to examine the consistency of data on environment and fish with the hypothesis linking water-level manipulation and mortality of fish. Although the details require much explanation, as given in the NRC's reports (NRC 2002, 2004), the committee's general conclusion was that the data contradicted the water-level hypothesis. Experts still defending the hypothesis have argued that the hypothesis would be verified if only more data were available. The committee, however, considered this possibility and concluded that there almost certainly was something wrong with the hypothesis. Thus, it rendered its opinion of negligible scientific support for the RPA requirement that water levels be held higher on grounds of improved water quality. The committee also stated that this conclusion did not give license on a scientific or technical basis for water levels to be lower than levels in the 1990s, which would amount to experimentation with unfamiliar combinations of conditions that might be harmful to the fish.

There were other arguments as well for higher water levels, involving the young suckers' need for shallow-water environments containing emergent vegetation (USFWS 2002). Once again, the committee looked at the data. Although the data were less comprehensive in this case than for water quality, they showed no hint of a relationship between amount of inundated shoreline vegetation (which is positively related to water level) and the success of any particular year class of fish as determined by the sampling of young fish or by the strength of previous year classes that were entering the subadult or adult phases. Thus, once again, the committee concluded that the hypothesis, although surely reasonable at the outset, was contradicted by the data and therefore without significant scientific support.

Environmentally oriented observers interpreted the NRC committee's interim findings on the endangered suckers as insensitive to the need to protect the suckers, and water users interpreted them as a righteous vindication of the need to use water in quantity for irrigation. In fact, the committee's opinions as delivered in the interim report fell into neither of these categories. The committee accepted as an undebatable premise the ESA and its components, one of which is the necessity to reverse any human influences on the environment that compromise a listed species' ability to recover. Furthermore, however, the committee abided by its charge, which was to evaluate the strength of scientific support for any particular strategy contained in the federal documents. Without abandoning the notion that recovery strategies should be developed for the fish, the committee simply could not verify that the initially proposed strategies, which were quite reasonable in the absence of information, could be sustained in the presence of information to which they were contradictory. In essence, the committee concluded that the search for actions that would favor the sucker populations in Upper Klamath Lake must go on, and it devoted considerable attention to an analysis of strategies for this search over the near-term future.

The NRC committee took a similar approach in evaluating the welfare of coho salmon downstream of Iron Gate Dam on the Klamath River main stem. Once again, the committee found the USBR proposals, whether intentionally or not, to be essentially a request for permission to operate at lower minimum flows in the main stem than had been the case historically, and it noted that there was no scientific justification for this proposed change. The committee also concluded, however, that the NMFS had proposed higher minimum flows without giving convincing scientific evidence that these higher flows would benefit the coho. The committee's main objection was that computer modeling, which was used to link habitat availability to amount of flow, was based on the life-cycle requirements of Chinook salmon, which differ critically from coho salmon in that Chinook are capable of maturing through the freshwater phase of their life cycle by using the main stem exclusively, whereas coho are almost entirely tied to the tributary waters for development during their freshwater phase. Thus, more habitat for maturation in the main stem might benefit Chinook or other important salmonid fishes such as steelhead, but is much less likely to benefit coho. The one possible exception, which was speculative but not contradicted by available information, was the benefit to coho of higher flows over a brief interval in spring during the migration of the smolt phase from tributaries to the Klamath River estuary along the main stem. In all, however, the committee concluded that the scientific and technical basis for proposing higher minimum flows in the main stem was weak.

According to the committee, the greatest environmental crisis for coho lies in the poor condition of the tributaries, which suffer the effects of the full range of environmental changes that have occurred in the Klamath basin, including water management, loss of riparian zones, erosion and siltation, thermal overload, and channel degradation through mining, logging, and ranching. The tributaries in most instances have suffered greater degradation in all of these arenas than has the main stem because of their smaller size and their closer integration with land-use practices. Of key importance, however, is the long stay of young fish in these damaged environments (fourteen to sixteen months). Because the tributary waters are not part of the Klamath Project, no amount of consultation or regulation of USBR activities can relieve environmental pressures on coho in the tributaries.

After release of the NRC committee's interim report, the listing agencies and the USBR concluded an additional round of consultation, which was essential because the previous assessments and opinions covered only one year of Klamath Project operations. The three agencies produced new assessments and opinions (NMFS 2002; USBR 2002; USFWS 2002), but in this case the documents covered a ten-year rather than a one-year operating period. Extension of the operating plan over ten years represented considerable progress on the agencies' part, given that the one-year duration of previous plans was unstable and required large investments of energy in annual document preparation. The ten-year time course for the documents issued in 2002 does not preclude reopening of specific issues or of the entire consultation process at the listing agencies' discretion.

An examination of the 2002 biological assessment (which in 2002 was combined for the endangered suckers and the threatened coho salmon) and the two biological opinions shows that the agencies were influenced by the NRC committee's interim report and that they put new energy into innovative strategies for stabilizing operation of the Klamath Project. The USBR, perceiving the need to find ways of accommodating ESA demands on water, proposed (no doubt with encouragement from the listing agencies) creation of a water bank that would provide some reserve capacity in times of drought. The exact configuration of the water bank was not specified, leaving the validity of the USBR's proposal in legal trouble, but the general idea, which the two listing agencies accepted and reinforced with specific scheduling requirements, will be a step forward if it can be successfully implemented. It will probably mean that certain agricultural water rights will be made conditional on a voluntary basis in return for compensation. The USBR in 2002 also offered concessions in the operations arena that it had not previously offered.

In its biological opinion on the suckers, the USFWS in 2002 was more careful not to make firm requirements of the USBR for measures that could be considered scientifically questionable based on available data. Even so, it did not abandon its conceptual endorsement of higher water levels in Upper Klamath Lake. It required procedural changes in forecasting of water level to reduce the possibility of erroneously high water use in dry years in the event of faulty forecasting. It did not, however, add stringency to water-level controls already in place.

The NMFS, in rendering its 2002 biological opinion on coho salmon, recognized for the first time that the USBR Klamath Project consumed only a little more than half of the irrigation water used in the upper basin and for this reason should not be held 100 percent accountable for depression of low flows in the Klamath main stem. The NMFS required that the USBR develop measures, such as the water bank, to offset its own contribution to depletion of flows in the main stem. It also required that the USBR assist irrigators outside the Klamath Project in the development of measures to offset flow depletions caused by non-USBR irrigation. Despite the NRC committee's severe misgivings, the NMFS continued to use habitat modeling based on Chinook habitat requirements as the main basis for its requirement of higher water levels in the Klamath River main stem. The USBR suggested a spring flow pulse to improve conditions in the one situation for which minimum flows might be most important to coho—that is, the spring smolt migration. For other times of the year, the NMFS continues to require higher minimum flows for protection of coho. Ways of dealing with tributary conditions for coho are still uncertain, but are on record and presumably will be addressed in the coming years.

Scientific Validity in the ESA Context

Scientists are trained to think in terms of hypotheses being tested rigorously with observations (data). When valid observations are inconsistent with a hypothesis, the hypothesis must be discarded. The goal is to minimize the likelihood of anointing hypotheses as valid that later observations may show to be false, thus undermining collective confidence in scientific information. Because the statistical label for an error of affirmation (asserting a supposed truth that is actually false) is *alpha error,* one might say that scientists' general goal is to find the truth by using data to test ideas in such a way as to minimize alpha error. Minimizing the opposite type of error (*beta error:* failure to identify and validate a truth) has much lower priority with scientists under most circumstances because experience shows that the truth will be found later if not sooner.

Federal agencies with ESA responsibilities use scientific information and scientific methods. In fact, the ESA charges them to use the "best available scientific and commercial information." They use scientific methods under unusual constraints, however. Because the ESA sets its highest value on preserving a species and precludes any extended period of study on grounds that the species may disappear while being studied, the ESA agencies in fact must avoid overlooking a true cause of decline. In statistical terms, they cannot focus on alpha error selectively at the expense of beta error (error of omission) to the extent that scientists functioning in an unconstrained manner easily tolerate. Thus, it is not reasonable to hold the agencies administering the ESA to the same standards that would apply to straightforward scientific investigation.

Although ESA agencies should be expected to regard as potentially valid any hypotheses that have not been tested or that have been tested only weakly, there are limits to which retention of a hypothesis is defensible. For example, one might argue that the USFWS was being scientifically reasonable in postulating, without significant amounts of background information, that a reduction in drawdown of Upper Klamath Lake would be favorable to the endangered suckers, but observations contradictory to this initial presumption eventually should have moved the agency away from this concept. Practical difficulties in abandoning a hypothesis include the inertia of scientists who are doggedly persistent in testing an idea and the difficulty an agency will have in reversing itself after it has made much expenditure and public commitment to a particular idea. Failing to change ground in view of new information, however, is ultimately risky in that it diverts resources away from solutions that need to be discovered before recovery can occur. Thus, judgment based on experience without direct information must be respected, but the same judgment when retained in the face of contradictory relevant information is much less defensible. As would be expected, there are no hard and fast rules by which to proceed here, but the NRC committee brought out this often-hidden issue in its findings on the Klamath basin suckers in particular.

The NRC Committee's Final Report

As required by its charge, the NRC Klamath Committee took a much broader view as it moved from the interim report to the final report. In condensed form, the committee's conclusions and recommendations on the general state of affairs involving ESA actions in the basin centered on

(1) the excessive focus on the USBR Klamath Project, which precluded meaningful consideration of numerous other important factors; and (2) weaknesses in organization, planning, and communication regarding ESA matters within the basin. The committee concluded that no degree of manipulation of USBR operations would in and of itself produce recovery of any of the three listed species. Thus, although USBR operations must be scrutinized, substantial energy must be expended elsewhere as well. Weaknesses in organization and communication were in part caused by sporadic funding and strong partisanship within the basin. Collective, transparent efforts with cooperation at their base are essential, but will require reduction of partisanship through the creation of committees of interested parties or other mechanisms. In addition, speculation about certain management practices whose effects cannot be deduced reliably should be circumvented by experiments in management. This mode of study goes under the heading "adaptive management," which is more often endorsed than practiced, but would be an eminently suitable way of attacking some of the more complicated questions related to endangered species in the Klamath basin.

For the endangered suckers, restoration of the Upper Klamath Lake population seems most attractive because all age classes are still present in the lake, and reproduction is occurring annually. Further scrutiny shows, however, that any strategy based mainly on restoration of the Upper Klamath Lake populations would be risky. The NRC committee concluded that efforts to improve water quality by regulating water levels in Upper Klamath Lake or by intercepting nutrients in the watershed are unlikely to be successful in restoring the abundance of endangered suckers. Given the popular attention that these strategies have drawn and their intuitive appeal, this conclusion was unwelcome in some quarters, but it is based on the committee's analysis of existing information. With this conclusion in mind, the committee drew the corollary conclusions that (1) for Upper Klamath Lake, measures not involving water quality should be emphasized in an attempt to boost recruitment of young fish into the population sufficiently to offset mortality of larger fish caused by poor water quality, and trials should be conducted on artificial oxygenated refugia; and (2) much more attention to other sucker populations or potential populations is needed on grounds that restoration of the Upper Klamath Lake suckers may be infeasible. For stimulation of the production of young suckers in

Upper Klamath Lake, the NRC committee suggested actions (including removal of Chiloquin Dam) that might improve the success of tributary spawning, which appears to be the main source of new fish. Other actions with similar objectives might include reestablishing lost spawning populations in lakeside springs, restoring physical conditions of certain springs, and other similar measures intended to increase the number of young fish. It is uncertain, however, whether this approach, even if successful, would in fact offset mass mortality of large fish caused by poor water quality.

Beyond Upper Klamath Lake, it is important to ensure special protection for the two populations that seem to be stable (in Clear Lake and Gerber Reservoirs) and to explore possibilities for reestablishing suckers where they were extirpated intentionally before the suckers were listed (Lake of the Woods). Still another appealing possibility is to promote completion of the life cycle at locations where the suckers were once abundant but now are represented only by old fish (i.e., no successful life-cycle completion) or no fish. The merit of these efforts is that they will reduce the risk of losing the species if the Upper Klamath Lake populations do not respond to restoration efforts.

Work on tributary waters above Upper Klamath Lake on behalf of the suckers would involve direct interaction between the listing agencies or its contractors and private landowners. Although difficult, this interaction is probably unavoidable, given that spawning habitat in tributary waters is critical to population sustainability. In addition, the creation of new populations would involve listing agencies' interaction with management agencies other than USBR or with private parties. The strategy for working with these groups would be very different from the one that USFWS has followed with the USBR, its customary antagonist in ESA actions involving western fishes.

For coho salmon, the committee recommended study of the removal of two dams. Removal of Iron Gate Dam on the main stem would open tributary waters that are now closed to coho salmon, thus possibly offsetting damage to tributary habitat downstream. It is not a foregone conclusion that this action will be feasible or advisable, but it deserves careful consideration. Similarly, removal of Dwinnell Dam on the Shasta River, which was once among the most productive waters for salmon and now is greatly degraded, would be beneficial in opening new habitat and in reversing both the undesirable hydrologic changes and the changes in sediment transport downstream of the dam. The NRC committee also recommended intensive efforts to improve physical conditions in channels. Elimination of channel blockage by dozens of small, privately operated dams used for irrigation purposes is one high priority. Restoration of riparian vegetation, which would provide sufficient shade to lower water temperatures that are now critically high for coho salmon in tributaries, is also a priority, as is consultation with the U.S. Forest Service on federal lands where timber harvest continues to generate unacceptable erosion. In addition, the committee recommended closure of hatcheries for an interval of several years on grounds that it is the only way to determine with certainty whether the very abundant, more robust hatchery-produced fish (mostly not coho) are detrimental to the offspring of wild-spawning coho. Like several other proposals, this recommendation runs counter to traditional thinking, which holds that continuous introduction of hatchery-raised salmon reinforces salmon populations. Looking specifically at the welfare of coho, however, the NRC committee concluded that a great abundance of introduced steelhead and Chinook salmon might be directly contrary to the ESA's objectives. This is an example of a situation in which hypothetical reasoning is not much help and the very long and involved studies that would be required to reach a scientific conclusion would be impractical under the press of time. Therefore, hatchery closure as an adaptive management strategy is warranted.

In all, the NRC committee's recommendations call for a great expansion of the ESA's actions on behalf of the three listed fishes, but this expansion appears to be the only realistic way to work toward restoring sustainable populations of these three species. Obviously, increased financial support, much of which must go to remedial actions rather than to studies, is critical as well.

Responses to the Final Report

Given the storm of controversy that followed issuance of the interim report, the NRC committee was on notice to expect more of the same for its final report. The general response was quite different, however. The broader scope of the final report was beneficial to its reception in that it integrated some controversial conclusions into a comprehensive expansion and redirection of ESA programs and actions, substantially increased funding, emphasized cooperation and communication, and provided for much wider distribution of responsibility for adverse environmental conditions than had been inherent in previous ESA work in the basin. Although individuals and organizations continued to object to various points, their views typically were softened by the realization that spreading ESA responsibilities within the basin, coupled with increased cooperation, would be a more realistic and profitable mode of operation than the historical approach involving a rather narrow and fiercely contested focus on the USBR's Klamath Project. It is not clear as yet, however, whether the ESA goals are now achievable.

Lessons from the Klamath Basin

The Klamath basin presents most problems of ESA implementation in microcosm and therefore might provide some useful guidance for the future wherever the ESA is applied.

1. Excessive partisanship blocks recovery efforts. Individuals and organizations with interests in the costs and benefits of ESA actions have a certain amount of energy and money to expend. They can make this expenditure either in fighting each other through legal channels, mass media, and confrontations or in negotiating the mechanics of restoration. A shift in the latter direction is essential in the Klamath basin. A community that devotes itself entirely to partisan activities will probably paralyze most beneficial action that might come from federally initiated ESA actions and will deprive the ESA process of the encouragement and participation by private parties, which are not easily compelled by the federal government. Although in a sense it is an imposition to expect management agencies such as the USFWS to bring about cooperation in the private sectors, federal agencies have in fact been successful in doing so (generally more successful than the states have been, for example; see Getches 2003) and probably should regard establishing cooperation as part of their portfolio of responsibilities.

2. The most obvious actions may be insufficient. The USBR's Klamath Project is the largest single manipulator of the environment in the Klamath basin. For this reason, and because it is a sister agency of the USFWS, a listing agency, it is natural that it should fall first under ESA

scrutiny. From the perspective of total environmental manipulation in the basin, however, it should be clear from the outset that consultation with the USBR would be insufficient for protection of any species that is widely distributed. Although the USBR project has important effects directly at the center of distribution for the two endangered suckers, private water management has effects of about the same magnitude in the tributary waters where the suckers spawn. Downstream, tributary waters critical for the coho are managed by private parties (primarily on the Shasta and Scott Rivers, but also on small tributaries) in ways that are not related to USBR operations. In addition, many potentially important environmental manipulations do not involve water management. Physical impairment of streams, dams, blockages, and other such influences involve parties besides the USBR. No doubt the most obvious target often receives the most attention in any ESA action. The Klamath experience shows, however, that intense focus on one avenue of enforcement may be inadequate or even completely ineffective in moving species toward recovery.

3. Initial judgments of cause and effect are essential, but can be wrong. In the Klamath basin case, judgments made by the listing agencies about cause-and-effect relationships between endangered species and environmental factors were reasonable, but some proved to be ultimately untenable. This sequence of findings can be expected in any type of inquiry that is scientifically based. It is routine for scientists to have notions based on experience or intuition that they themselves or others subsequently prove wrong. Retention of an appealing idea when it begins to appear weak on the basis of credible evidence simply delays the derivation of an effective recovery plan. Critics, for their part, must be denied a false sense of vindication when an agency is wrong in its initial judgments. Ultimately, ESA actions must be evaluated just as the practice of medicine or engineering is evaluated. With little evidence, the physician makes a judgment based on experience. When the laboratory data come in, the physician is excused for adjusting the initial judgment to bring it into line with the new information. We must have the same forgiving attitude toward environmental medicine as we do toward human medicine.

4. Adaptive management is a critically valuable shortcut to understanding cause-and-effect relationships related to management. It is widely embraced as desirable, but it is not much practiced. For the ESA,

which operates under the pressure of time more than some other types of environmental analysis or study, adaptive management principles are especially important because they reduce the delay in establishing cause-and-effect relationships. Once again, the analogy with medicine is appropriate. The physician who suspects a cause but is uncertain of it may try one remedy and then another if the first one is ineffective. This avoids the necessity of a long research project on a sick patient.

5. ESA actions cannot always be consistent with other environmental objectives. The case of the Klamath basin provides a number of examples of ESA objectives interwoven with general objectives related to environmental improvement. For example, the desire to improve water quality in Upper Klamath Lake has been specifically motivated by the welfare of suckers, but also is driven by water-quality requirements through the Clean Water Act that are not specifically related to the ESA. Thus, when the NRC Klamath Committee concluded that pursuit of these strategies for ESA purposes related to the suckers offered virtually no hope of success in any reasonable amount of time, it was not saying that these actions are undesirable from other points of view. For example, capture of nutrients in the watershed might improve water-quality conditions in tributary streams, which might be considered beneficial to organisms that live in the streams or to the general ecological functions of the streams even without benefiting the suckers. It is unreasonable to expect that every environmentally beneficial action will be on a list of ESA objectives at a particular location or that measures designed to achieve environmental restoration will benefit listed species.

The Aftermath

Following release of the Klamath Committee's final report, a number of changes occurred that might be classified as "healing," the topic of this book. For either physical or sociopolitical wounds, healing requires contact. The NRC Klamath Committee diagnosed a chronic lack of direct contact between groups with different vested interests in the Klamath basin. Thus, although interest groups had formed, each was pursuing a different agenda, and their main interaction was through courts or through the media and not through direct contact. Following release of the NRC Klamath report, there has been more direct contact between parties with different interests. A diagnosis of the causes for this increased contact, which has led to some negotiation and adaptation, might be useful for other locations with similarly complex environmental problems.

The federal agencies played a key role in facilitating an increased degree of collaboration among stakeholders in the Klamath basin after 2004. Two factors were critical: new federal money and commitment to a broader scope of recovery efforts. The new money—which, according to the regional congressional delegation (U.S. House of Representatives n.d.), amounts to some $500 million—allowed the execution of projects that had been on a wish list for some time and were on the NRC's priority list for immediate action. For example, a fish screen was placed on the Link River at the major point of withdraw for irrigation water by the Klamath Project. In direct contradiction to ESA requirements, take (killing) of fishes at this location had occurred every year after the suckers were listed as endangered. Although the federal agencies recognized this take, no money was appropriated for the physical changes necessary to minimize it. A second example is commitment to the removal of Chiloquin Dam on the Sprague River, which is to occur in 2008. Other new commitments include an expanded fish ladder system in the upper basin, a water-banking system, and serious studies of the potential removal of major dams in the upper basin that block salmons' use of tributary waters. As compared with the static and unproductive pattern of controversy narrowly focused on management of water deliveries to the Klamath Project, this more realistic breadth of action is refreshing and has injected a new sense of optimism within the basin. Along with the optimism, parties previously estranged have been able to exchange views and attempt to find compromises that seemed impossible before. Money has given life to expensive proposals that seemed infeasible earlier, and a broadening of the recovery effort has shifted recovery to a greater degree of realism and away from an unrealistically simple focus of blame specifically on use of water for irrigation.

It is not yet clear how far the healing will go in the Klamath basin, but there is no question that it is now under way and that the change from intractable conflict to constructive collaborations has occurred over a very short time. Recovery efforts still need to be prioritized and require scientific evaluation, guidance, and stakeholder participation. Even so, tangible new commitments to environmental improvements that will raise the likelihood of recovery for the endangered fishes have fostered a healing process that has changed the mindset in the basin.

Conclusions

The first phase of ESA actions in the Klamath basin, which can be dated from the listing of the endangered suckers in 1988, came to a close with the NRC Klamath Committee's final report. No meaningful recovery of the listed species occurred over this interval, but a great deal of valuable information was collected, and numerous ideas were explored and debated. To be true to the ESA's purpose, the federal agencies were still faced in 2004 with a need to prioritize and pursue remedial actions that would produce recovery in the basin and to capture the societal energies attached to environmental issues in some way that would be beneficial to the recovery effort. Since 2004, gridlock affecting both the agencies and the stakeholders has seemed to soften through new federal money and a new breadth of action intended to achieve the ESA's goals.

Acknowledgments

I thank the members of the NRC Klamath Committee for the considerable amount I learned from them in my position as committee chair. I also thank the NRC staff for facilitating the analysis leading to the committee's two reports, upon which this chapter is primarily based. Finally, I thank the scientists and others in the Klamath basin and in Washington, D.C., who provided me with information while I was a member of the NRC Klamath Committee.

Literature Cited

Cooperman, M. S., and D. F. Markle. 2003. The Endangered Species Act and the National Research Council's Interim Judgment in Klamath basin. *Fisheries* 28:10–19.
Faragher, J. M. 1992. *Daniel Boone: The Life and Legend of an American Pioneer.* New York: Henry Holt.
Getches, D. H. 2003. Constraints of Law and Policy on the Management of Western Water. In *Water and Climate in the Western United States,* edited by W. M. Lewis, 183–234. Boulder: University of Colorado Press.
Limerick, P. N. 2000. *Something in the Soil: Legacies and Reckonings in the New West.* New York: W. W. Norton.

Moyle, P. B. 2002. *Inland Fishes of California*. Rev. and exp. ed. Berkeley and Los Angeles: University of California Press.

National Marine Fisheries Service (NMFS). 2002. *Biological Opinion: Klamath Project Operations*. Long Beach, Calif.: NMFS, Southwest Region, National Oceanic and Atmospheric Administration, May 31. Available at http://swr.ucsd.edu/psd/kbo .pdf; also available through the National Research Council's Public Access File.

National Research Council (NRC). 1995. *Science and the Endangered Species Act*. Washington, D.C.: National Academies Press.

———. 2002. *Interim Report from the Committee on Endangered and Threatened Fishes in the Klamath River Basin: Scientific Evaluation of Biological Opinions on Endangered and Threatened Fishes in the Klamath River Basin*. Washington, D.C.: National Academies Press, February.

———. 2004. *Endangered and Threatened Fishes in the Klamath River Basin: Causes of Decline and Strategies for Recovery*. Washington, D.C.: National Academies Press.

U.S. Bureau of Reclamation (USBR). 2002. *Final Biological Assessment: The Effects of Proposed Actions Related to Klamath Project Operation (April 1, 2002–March 31, 2012) on Federally-Listed Threatened and Endangered Species*. Mid-Pacific Region. Klamath Falls, Ore.: Klamath Basin Area Office, USBR, Department of the Interior.

U.S. Fish and Wildlife Service (USFWS). 2002. *Biological/Conference Opinion Regarding the Effects of Operation of the U.S. Bureau of Reclamation's Proposed 10-Year Operation Plan for the Klamath Project and Its Effect on the Endangered Lost River Sucker* (Deltistes luxatus), *Endangered Shortnose Sucker* (Chasmistes brevirostris), *Threatened Bald Eagle* (Haliaeetus leucocephalus), *and Proposed Critical Habitat for the Lost River and Shortnose Suckers*. Klamath Falls, Ore.: Klamath Falls Fish and Wildlife Office.

U.S. House of Representatives Committee on Natural Resources. n.d. Web site, http:// resourcescommittee.house.gov/index.php?option=com_content&task=vi.

10

Hope in a World of Wounds

SUSTAINABLE STEWARDSHIP IN COLORADO

David M. Armstrong

A LONG GENERATION ago Aldo Leopold observed that "one of the penalties of an ecological education is that one lives alone in a world of wounds" (1953, 165). Times have changed. Ecologists are no longer alone; we live and labor with increasing numbers of people who sense the hurt and promote the healing. At least the rudiments of ecological education are widespread. But what about the "world of wounds"? Is that a useful metaphor or mere hyperbole? I believe it is useful.

Newly arrived in the American West, Paleolithic folk were merely superpredators. Today we are a geologic force imposed in a geologic instant. The wounds of the West are mostly inadvertent, the unintended consequences of economic and political decisions. They are wounds nonetheless, and wounds need healing. Time heals, the adage says, and that is as true in ecological systems as in human relationships. But recognizing a wound and intervening in a timely manner may speed healing and reduce permanent scarring.

Like all politics, all conservations are local. Local is where individual homeostatic organisms are recruited to populations, develop, mature, and perhaps achieve fitness. Local is where human impacts, direct or indirect, impinge on the lives of nonhuman organisms. Local is where land-use decisions are made, and (perhaps most important) local is the scale at which the land is experienced, partially understood, used, and perhaps even loved. Local individual and community decisions add up to regional trends and eventually to global impacts, positive or negative.

In this chapter, I briefly review the global biodiversity "crisis" and highlight some global responses to it, a macroscopic view. I then turn to the situation in the United States. Finally, I focus at the fine scale on Colorado as a conservation microcosm and a productive nursery of exportable ideas.

Biodiversity is the global inventory of species and much more; it is "the variety of life on Earth and the natural patterns it forms" (UNEP 2000, 2). Biodiversity is the sum of the kinds of organisms, complicated by their genetic variability, their historical relationships, and their symbiotic inter-actions. At any particular moment, biodiversity is a progress report on the cosmic process of evolution, to paraphrase Julian Huxley (1943), or "the evolutionary play in the ecological theater," to use G. E. Hutchinson's (1965) pithy title. Biodiversity is not something to count or memorize, but a "happening" to appreciate deeply. Study of biodiversity forces us to integrate concepts, to look hard at human impacts on the ecosphere, and to raise concern for the future of ecological and evolutionary processes.

Humans have been noticing and naming organisms for a million years or more (depending on how we choose to define humans). In the quar-ter millennium since Linnaeus set the official standard, something in the range of 1.5 to 1.8 million species have been named (Wilson 2002). How many species actually exist we cannot say. We do not know whether the inventory is one-half or one-tenth finished. The answer we get depends on the group of organisms and where on Earth we ask the question. Our ignorance of microbial diversity is perhaps greater than 99 percent. However, birds and butterflies in Europe and temperate North America surely are almost completely known, except for an occasional cryptic spe-cies. D. L. Hawksworth and M. T. Kailin-Arroyo (1995) estimate the eventual total at 13.6 million, and Dirzo and Raven (2003, 137) make a "best guess" of around 7 million, so the catalog, the basic accounting, is perhaps 10 to 25 percent complete.

Extinction is the rule; in the history of the biosphere, most species that ever have been are now extinct. How many species there have been we do not know and we cannot know, if only because of the imperfection of the geological record. Surely some untold (but certainly large) number of species originated, persisted for a time, and then vanished, all without a trace. Nonetheless, caution aside, let us guess. Suppose that there really was a "Cambrian Explosion" and that the number of species was rather low prior to about 550 million years ago. Then suppose that the average lifetime of a species is 1 to 10 million years (a reasonable enough number based on the biota of the past 100 million years). Therefore, since the Cambrian Explosion there has been time for from 55 to 550 "turnovers" of the biota. That number suggests that the biota at any point in time—such as the present time—is no more than about 1 percent of total biodiversity over evolutionary time and may be some modest fraction of 1 percent.

Extinction happens. Appropriate concern is not about extinction per se, but about current rates and causes of extinction. Current extinction rates are apparently high relative to average rates over most of biological history, and current causes of extinction are certainly unique in the history of the biosphere.

Even a crude estimate shows that present rates are high. There are roughly 15,000 species of warm-blooded vertebrates—birds and mammals. If species last on average 1 to 10 million years, one would predict extinction rates of 1 percent to 0.1 percent—that is, one extinction in both these groups together every 150 to 1,500 years. However, from 1600 to 1990 CE some 42 species of mammals and 94 species of birds became extinct (Caughley and Gunn 1996). That is about 0.4 species per year, forty to four hundred times the predicted rate of 0.1 to 1 percent. What does it mean to increase a rate by fortyfold? The speed limit is 65 miles per hour. Exceed that fortyfold, and you are moving at 2,600 mph. The difference between natural rates of extinction and culturally influenced rates is the difference between a legal drive from Boulder to Denver and Mach 4. Is that a matter for concern? Certainly it is a matter for discussion. Concern, however, is a moral construct, not a scientific fact; concern, like hope, is a choice.

Extinction is a natural process with a fundamental cause: failure to adapt. To persist over evolutionary time, species have had to cope with climatic change, the effects of mountain building, volcanism, drifting continents, and the origins and activities of other species—competitors, predators, parasites, pathogens.

Failure to adapt to change is still the fundamental cause of extinction. What is unique in the past few millennia and especially in the past two centuries? Over the 3.8-billion-year history of the biosphere, successful species merely had to adapt to cosmic, physical, and biological challenges. Today, species face cultural challenges as well. Causes of population declines among threatened or endangered vertebrates in the United States are estimated as follows: habitat degradation and loss, 85 percent; introduction of exotic species, 49 percent; pollution, 24 percent; direct exploitation, 17 percent; and disease, 3 percent (categories are not mutually exclusive, so sum to more than 100 percent) (Stein, Kutner, and Adams 2000, 243).

Extinction rates have not been constant over evolutionary time. The fossil record documents at least five mass-extinction events in the history of the biosphere. These events define several major breaks in the geologic column. A "mass extinction" is global, extends across many taxonomic groups, and is rapid relative to background rates (Jablonski 1995).

Assuming that contemporary extinctions represent (or soon will represent) a certifiable mass-extinction event, the question remains: Is the current extinction "crisis" unique? As with many "simple" questions in evolutionary ecology, the answer is complex—a resounding "yes" and "no." The quantitative answer clearly is "no"; the biosphere is on the verge (or in the midst) of simply yet another mass-extinction event. Qualitatively, however, the current extinction is unique; it is the first mass extinction in the history of the biosphere that is a choice—cultural rather than geological or cosmic.

Is this event a crisis? What is a "crisis"? In the popular sense, a crisis is a "catastrophe." In another sense, however, the "crisis" in the course of a disease is the point at which the physician can guess whether the patient will live or die—when healing or death will occur. Perhaps the present extinction event meets both definitions of the term *crisis*.

The root of the cultural extinction process is clear: the spectacular increase in the human population in the past two centuries multiplied by increasing demand per capita. It took the million or more years from the origin of *Homo sapiens* until roughly the year 1800 to reach a net global human population of 1 billion; it took just two hundred years to add the next 5 billion. Human population (about 6.6 billion and increasing at 1.2 percent annually, meaning it will take only fifty-eight years to double [Population Reference Bureau 2007]) multiplied times our demand for resources and times the inefficiency of meeting that demand renders our individual and global ecological "footprints" (see Chambers, Simmons, and Wackernagel 2000), footprints left as temporary or permanent scars on the biosphere.

Global Conservation

Where do we stand as global stewards of biodiversity? That question can be explored "retail," at the level of individual species or communities (as in the chapters by William Lewis Jr. and Sharon Collinge in this volume), or it can be explored "wholesale," at the level of the whole evolving biota. We cannot really know extinction rates, so let us emphasize preservation rates. This focus allows greater certainty and helps us to choose hope. A first approximation of the extent of protection for biodiversity is the United Nations' List of Protected Areas (Chape et al. 2003), which names more than 102,000 "protected areas," totaling some 18.1 million square kilometers (an area about equal to that of South America).

The most preserved habitable regions are Central and South America (including the Caribbean) and Australasia/New Zealand. The least preserved continent is Europe. Tropical rain forest and islands are the most protected biomes, whereas temperate grasslands (which for the most part have been converted to "breadbaskets") and lakes are the least.

Moreover, not all protection is equal. Earth has some unknown number of "paper parks" that amount, at best, to good intentions. The International Union for the Conservation of Nature (IUCN) categorizes protected areas by the degree of protection for intrinsic natural values. Of the twenty largest protected areas of Earth (Chape et al. 2003), none is in IUCN Category Ia (Strict Nature Preserve) or Category Ib (Wilderness Area), and only one (Greenland) is in Category II (National Parks); all others are in categories IV to VI, which are to some variable extent "multiple-use" areas. (Of course, even the highest levels of protection may be inadequate in some cases. For an eloquent exposition of this topic, see the special edition of *National Geographic* titled *Hallowed Ground*, October 2006).

In addition to conservation by governments, a number of nongovernmental organizations (NGOs) are making a major difference in protection of landscapes and biodiversity. I mention just one of these, The Nature Conservancy (TNC), because it is the international NGO most active on the ground locally, at home in the West. TNC was established in 1951 (although its roots in the Ecological Society of America date back to the 1920s; see Shelford 1926 and Goodwin 2002). To date, TNC has protected approximately 117 million acres—mostly in the Americas and the tropical and subtropical Asia-Pacific region.

In December 2003, the TNC Board of Governors adopted a resolution committing the organization to an ambitious new goal: "By 2015, The Nature Conservancy will work with others to ensure the effective conservation of places that represent at least 10 percent of every Major Habitat Type [biome] on Earth" (TNC 2004b, 1).

That 10 percent goal is aligned with the goal of the 188 nations that have signed the Convention on Biological Diversity (Convention on Biological Diversity 2002). The seventh Conference of the Parties to the Convention, meeting in Kuala Lumpur, Malaysia, in 2004, agreed to a global network of ecologically representative protected areas on land by 2010 and at sea by 2012. Signatory nations (a list that does not yet include the United States) committed to establish measurable, timely targets and a comprehensive monitoring program to assess effectiveness (TNC 2006).

I do not know where the 10 percent goal originated. As a "tithe," it may seem a lofty goal to some; as a "tax" on development, however, it might seem onerous to others. In biological terms, it may be inadequate to the task at hand. We really do not know how much is enough. However, a species-to-area relationship is well known. The larger the area, the greater the number of species that can be supported. As a patch of habitat shrinks, the number of species that can be supported shrinks as well, but this relationship is not linear. Specifically, a 90 percent reduction in habitat causes the biota to decline by about one-half (Wilson 2002). That is, saving 10 percent of Earth's functioning natural habitats might save 50 percent of Earth's biota. That may not be enough species to run the ecosphere.

Within biomes, according to TNC's protocol of "conservation by design" (see Groves 2003), planning and conservation on the ground must take place at the level of portfolios of sites in each of Earth's ecoregions, which number more than one thousand in a recent analysis (World Wildlife Fund 2003). The importance of the ecoregional scale cannot be overstated. Ecoregions are the distinctive patches in the tapestry of the ecosphere as seen from space—the Great Plains, the Southern Rockies, the Chihuahuan Desert. A cursory glance at the "Red List of Threatened Species" (IUCN 2003) suggests that most threatened and endangered species are local or regional endemics. Ecoregions are the scale of most endemism, so they are the scale within which extinction occurs. They are also the scale at which regional "ecosystem services" are delivered, and ecosystem services are delivered to "cold spots" as well as to hot spots (Kareiva and Marvier 2003).

Land Protection in the United States

All extinction is local. The locality of extinction is the locality of the last viable population of reproducing individuals. Global conservation is necessarily a local activity. With that in mind, let us shift toward home and the regional context of this book, the American West.

The United States pioneered some concepts of biodiversity protection, including national parks, wilderness areas, and conservation easements, perhaps because destruction of natural landscapes has been so prominent a feature of our national history and our personal experience. By 2001, total developed area in the conterminous forty-eight states was 105 million acres, roughly the area of California (Vesterby and Krupa 2001).

Federal lands protected for biodiversity (if only as a consequence of legislative mandates for "ecosystem management" [see Christiansen et al. 1996]) compose 29 percent of the United States (22 percent of the lower forty-eight states), but 43.7 percent of the land in eleven western states (without Alaska) (Riebsame, Gosnell, and Theobald 1997). These lands are managed by the Bureau of Land Management (41 percent), the Forest Service (31 percent), the Fish and Wildlife Service (15 percent), and the National Park Service (13 percent). Each of these agencies has its own legislative mandate, and those mandates differ in their focus on biodiversity. Most federal lands are dedicated to some degree of multiple use, so biodiversity values are a few among many competing values.

The National Wilderness Preservation System was established in 1964 "for the permanent good of the whole people, and for other purposes" (Wilderness.net 2004). Wilderness is thus intended for people, not for the planet, although biodiversity can be inferred among the "other purposes," and protection of biodiversity is a goal of management on the ground. Designated Wilderness Areas compose about 4.6 percent of the United States (about 5.6 percent of the lower forty-eight states). Total area of designated wilderness is some 105.7 million acres, somewhat larger than California. That is an encouraging number, but still it is roughly the same area as is occupied in the United States by highways or by land developed for residential, commercial, and industrial purposes (Vesterby and Krupa 2001).

The strongest protection for private land is often a perpetual conservation easement, a binding restriction on use of a tract of land deeded to a qualified land trust or governmental entity (see Diehl and Barrett 1988). Growth of the land-trust movement in recent years has been remarkable (Brewer 2003). Land protected by land trusts grew more than threefold in the United States in the 1990s, to a total of some 35 million acres (1.7 percent of the land area of the lower forty-eight states), of which 6.2 million acres were held by local and regional land trusts (Land Trust Alliance 2001), 13 million by the American Farmland Trust, and 15 million by TNC. The total growth of protection in the Southwest (Arizona, Colorado, New Mexico, Utah) was more than five times the national average (Land Trust Alliance 2001). Rapid growth continues; private land conservation showed a 54 percent increase from 2000 to 2005 (Land Trust Alliance 2006).

Of course, emphasis on number of acres protected may be misplaced. We do not know how much is enough; we do not even know whether our present efforts are having their intended impacts. Protocols and standards for an accounting of protection are evolving. The general idea is to have an explicit model of ecosystem processes and threats to their integrity; to make interventions that are monitored, evaluated, and revised on an ongoing basis using new information; to communicate what is learned; and to iterate the cycle of planning, action, monitoring, and learning—in short, to practice adaptive stewardship (Christiansen 2003).

Colorado: A Case Study

With this sketch of protection of biodiversity on global and national scales as background, I turn to a case study in the American West: Colorado. Emphasis on Colorado is not justifiable quantitatively. Colorado is just 2.7 percent of the area of the United States (3.3 percent of the lower forty-eight), and a mere 0.2 percent of Earth's land surface. From the standpoint of biodiversity, Colorado is quantitatively trivial, with less than 1 percent of species of most taxonomic groups. Nonetheless, consideration of Colorado may be justifiable qualitatively. Colorado is disproportionately visible because of its natural values: dramatic mountain landscapes and abundant wildlife, for example. Five major rivers of the western interior originate in Colorado: the Colorado, the Rio Grande, the Arkansas, the North Platte, and the South Platte. What happens at the headwaters influences much of the rest of the West.

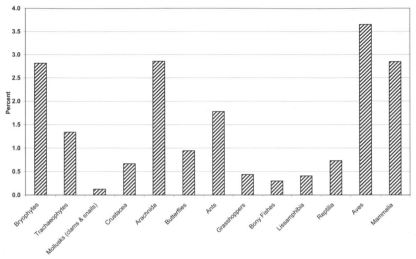

FIGURE 10.1. The percentage of Earth's species of various groups present in Colorado. (After Armstrong 1992)

Colorado not only deserves attention; it needs attention. Some 275 acres of open land are developed daily, more than 150 square miles per year (Colorado Conservation Trust 2004), equal to a strip of land a mile wide from Fort Collins to Pueblo. The Colorado human population in 2003 was 4.6 million and growing at about 1.2 percent per annum, a rate roughly twice the U.S. average; in the 1990s, Colorado grew at roughly four times the national average (Colorado Demography Office 2004). Allen Wallis and Gene Bressler's contribution to this volume reviews the wounds of growth and sprawl in Colorado's "wide-open spaces" and suggests some antidotes.

And finally, Colorado is home, and "home" is central to the thesis that all conservation is local. Home is a place where each of us can make a difference, and many are making a difference, a difference that offers a telling and even inspiring case study.

By 2003, the total area of conservation lands (roughly IUCN Categories I through III) in Colorado was about 6.8 million acres, approximately 10 percent of the state. These lands are protected as wilderness areas (49 percent); state parks and wildlife areas (25 percent); national parks (8 percent); private lands (owned by individuals, corporations, or

NGOs); lands under conservation easement (16 percent); and county and municipal open lands (2 percent). Land under the latter two kinds of protection increased by about 10 percent in 2005 alone (Colorado Conservation Trust 2004).

Lands under conservation easement are not the only private lands protected for biodiversity, but lands under easement are protected by law. An unknown area of private land is protected by family traditions and personal stewardship ethics, by landowners who recognize that property rights imply property responsibilities. Unfortunately, however, these traditional commitments do not necessarily pass from one generation to the next (and sometimes they simply cannot persist due to the unintended consequences of inheritance law on biodiversity). High-minded commitment to stewardship does not "travel with the deed" when land is sold, but conservation easements do. The use of conservation easements is growing, and that growth is being encouraged by both governments (in the form of generous tax incentives, for example; see Colorado Department of Revenue 2007) and NGOs.

The centerpiece of state governmental efforts in land conservation is Great Outdoors Colorado (GOCO), funded by lottery proceeds "to preserve, protect, enhance and manage the state's wildlife, park, river, trail and open space heritage" (Colorado Constitution, Article XXVII). To date, GOCO has funded forty Legacy Projects of regional importance and hundreds of individual open-space projects, protecting in perpetuity about 1 percent of the state (GOCO 2007). Nonetheless, our reach exceeds our grasp, annual demand for GOCO funds exceeds supply by 300 to 400 percent (GOCO 2004).

At local levels, the generosity of Colorado's taxpayers for the future continues to expand. In the past two decades, there have been 151 local, county, and state ballot measures intended to raise funds for conservation lands; about three-quarters of those measures have passed, generating some 80 percent of the dollars at stake, a total of $3.9 billion (Trust for Public Lands 2006, 2007), but unmet needs and unseized opportunities remain. The Colorado Conservation Trust (2004) estimated the price of the unmet needs for conservation lands (as identified by local governments and NGOs) at $1.2 billion. That is about $260 per capita in Colorado, a steep bill to pay all at once, but spread over a decade it might be practicable, a modest price to pay now for posterity—a perpetual endowment of functioning land for future generations of people and other native species.

TNC exists "to preserve the plants, animals, and natural communities that represent the diversity of life on Earth by protecting the lands and waters they need to survive" (TNC 2004a). It formerly focused mostly on threatened and endangered species and biotic communities. In the past two decades, however, its vision has broadened, and its commitment has deepened to preserve not only "the last of the least" but also—moving "beyond the Ark" (Weeks 1997)—to preserve "the best of the rest," the remaining intact functioning landscapes. Planning and goal setting are strategic and at the scale of ecoregions (Redford et al. 1997; Groves 2003).

TNC Colorado accepted its first conservation easement in 1966 (the Mexican Cut Preserve in the West Elk Mountains above Gothic). By 2003, it had achieved direct protection, in perpetuity, of about 245,000 acres (0.4 percent of the state) (N. Fishbein, TNC Colorado, personal communication, February 2004). In addition, the chapter funded the research that led to designation of more than 147,000 acres of federal land in Colorado as Research Natural Areas (Forest Service) or Areas of Critical Environmental Concern (U.S. Bureau of Land Management).

Cooperative projects involve TNC with private and governmental entities, sometimes in the form of "bridge" funding to preserve threatened lands of high conservation value when they become available but before a public agency has funding to close a particular deal. Such cooperative projects total some 150,000 acres. The largest such transaction was completed in September 2004: purchase of the Baca Ranch in the San Luis Valley in a complex arrangement that doubled the size of Great Sand Dunes National Monument (TNC Colorado 2004), transforming it into a national park, and protecting a significant sample of the full spectrum of ecosystems from the valley floor to the lofty crest of the Sangre de Cristo Range.

Impressive as the data may be, such "bucks and acres" accounting does not capture TNC's fundamental contribution to sustainable land stewardship in Colorado: community-based conservation. This concept did not originate in Colorado, but the Colorado experience has been a national and international model and inspiration. Let us focus on one such project to get a sense of what can be accomplished where there is a common vision so compelling that nobody much cares who gets the credit.

TNC's work in the Yampa Valley began in 1985, with establishment of a 99-acre preserve below Steamboat Springs. Studies of dynamics of the river and its riparian vegetation (Richter 1999) revealed the importance of natural flooding and channel migration to the maintenance of the multistoried, riparian cottonwood-dogwood forests unique to the region. TNC soon realized the need to protect not simply species or even biotic communities, but the underlying hydrologic processes that drive the biotic communities, and that it could not achieve this goal alone. In 1992, TNC opened the Northwestern Colorado Office in Steamboat Springs, a "storefront presence" on Main Street from which it could reach out to involve the community in long-term conservation of the legacy of its productive landscapes. E. J. Pike (2001) analyzed the early evolution of the program.

The Yampa Valley was a likely place for conservation action to take root because the area combines a long ranching tradition with a major ski area that is a magnet for amenity migrants. Both old-timers and newcomers value the open lands associated with the ranching heritage (Walsh, McKean, and Mucklow 1993). Conservation easements provided a tool to accomplish a common goal—keeping open lands open, or, as the green bumper stickers urged, "Cows Not Condos." Some landowners drawn to the power of conservation easements were wary of a large national organization such as TNC, even in the guise of a local office. Enter in 1994 the Yampa Valley Land Trust. By 2003, this trust had protected some 25,000 acres in forty-eight conservation easements in Routt and adjacent counties.

Nevertheless, some ranchers were hesitant to deal with "city folks." Enter the Colorado Cattlemen's Association (CCA). In 1995, CCA, led by Yampa Valley producers, founded the Colorado Cattlemen's Agricultural Land Trust (CCALT) "to help Colorado's ranchers and farmers protect their agricultural lands and encourage continuing agricultural production for the benefit of themselves, their families, and all of Colorado's citizens" (CCALT 2007). CCALT has expanded well beyond the Yampa Valley. By January 2007, it had worked with ranchers across the state to protect nearly one-quarter of a million producing acres (CCALT 2007). Further, there have been impacts beyond Colorado. CCALT's success has catalyzed sister organizations in states as diverse as Wyoming, Kansas, California, Oregon, and Nevada.

In 1996, TNC acquired about 900 acres of the historic Carpenter Ranch on the Yampa between Steamboat Springs and Hayden. The ranch continues in the cattle business, for which it was already nationally famous (due to the renown of Hereford breeder Farrington "Ferry" Carpenter, who ran the ranch from 1926 to 1980 and who was in the 1930s the first director of the Federal Grazing Service, now the Bureau of Land Management). As a significant landowner, TNC had a seat at the table in local land-use deliberations. The organization continues to build common cause with ranchers, townspeople, and even second homeowners. In addition to its direct conservation, TNC Colorado has inspired sustainable stewardship of unknown thousands of acres simply by being a good neighbor, ready with ideas and contacts, scientific data, a cup of coffee, and the fence posts and wire needed to enforce a right relationship between cattle and native biodiversity.

The exportable lesson from the Yampa Valley is that community-based conservation is hard work, but it does work. Community-based conservation is founded in part on the notion that conservation of species and natural communities can coexist with productive landscapes (Knight 2002). From 1990 to 2003, more than 42,000 acres in Routt County were protected by conservation easements held by seven different land trusts (C. J. Mucklow, personal communication, February 2004), and the community process continues.

Closing Thoughts

Several chapters in this book address broad issues in conservation science with local case studies. Sharon Collinge's contribution reviews her painstaking work on California's vernal pools, involving research and restoration at the level of biotic communities and their peculiar (and patchy) physical habitats. William Lewis Jr. recounts his work on the endangered fishes and hydrology of the Klamath basin, focusing on the high monetary and social costs of remediation. Joseph Ryan's chapter on restoration of human habitats adjacent to mined lands is also significant in the context of natural habitats. From this range of local stories, a general take-home lesson emerges: rescue, remediation, and restoration are expensive

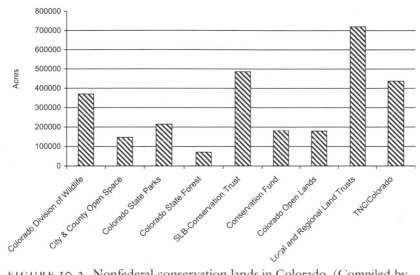

FIGURE 10.2. Nonfederal conservation lands in Colorado. (Compiled by the author from information gathered by various agencies and from NGO Web sites)

in many ways and rife with both practical and political uncertainties. As Hannah Gosnell suggests in her chapter on "rewilding" the West, it takes an expansive vision to capture patterns and processes at appropriate scale, and political and ethical trade-offs are imperative.

Encouraged by these examples of therapeutic intervention, I conclude that proactive, preventative land conservation holds the promise of being both efficient and effective. Not that it is without challenges. The "blind progress" of business as usual remains the default scenario over much of the American West (see the chapter by Alan Wallis and Gene Bressler). But there are inspiring examples of alternatives that preserve the quality of life for human communities and for the nonhuman biota as well.

Nonfederal conservation lands in Colorado total about 4.2 percent of the state. These lands and designated wilderness areas add up to about 10 percent of the state. That feels like a good start; in commerce, 10 percent is a reasonable down payment. But how much really is enough?

I have been privileged to be a member of the TNC Colorado Board of Trustees for much of the past two decades. Early in my tenure on the board, a senior board member, a self-styled "hard-headed businessman" who was also a deeply committed conservationist, approached me and asked simply, "How much land do you need? When will we be finished?" I fell reflexively into the standard, scientific answer and defense: "I don't know . . . but nether does anyone else," and then made some vague assertions about the importance of scale and process and redundancy.

In hindsight, I realize that I missed an opportunity. I might have dropped the role of biologist and assumed the role of the Lorax (Geisel 1971), presuming "to speak for the trees." I might have said, "We need it all, and we'll never be finished . . . at least not finished with the steward-ship." Or, more fundamentally and more precisely, everyone concerned (as TNC is concerned) about the ecosphere for the long-haul needs to influence the stewardship of all of it, forever. Or I might have turned the question around. "How much do *you* need, I mean really *need*? How much is enough? Enough for what purpose? Enough for how many people?"

I am optimistic about the future of Coloradan landscapes because I am involved daily with the good people who are making the choices that are preserving the land. I would not be as optimistic without that involvement. In fact, those who are not involved in such a process have not really earned the right to be optimistic about its outcome. As the say-ing goes, if we are not part of the solution, we are part of the problem; or, as Garrett Hardin noted so eloquently, "we can never do nothing" (1972, 262). Not to choose is a very strong choice.

Acknowledgments

For unpublished information, I thank Lynne Sherrod, former CCALT executive director; Nancy Fishbein, Ann Davidson, Mike Tetreault, and Heidi Sherk of TNC Colorado; and C. J. Mucklow, Routt County Coop-erative Extension, Colorado State University.

Literature Cited

Armstrong, D. M. 1992. Hard Data for Conservation of Colorado's Biodiversity—Where Do We Stand? Unpublished report, Colorado Division of Wildlife.

Brewer, R. 2003. *Conservancy: The Land Trust Movement in America.* Hanover, N.H.: University Press of New England.

Caughley, G., and A. Gunn. 1996. *Conservation Biology in Theory and Practice.* Cambridge, Mass.: Blackwell Science.

Chambers, N., C. Simmons, and M. Wackernagel. 2000. *Sharing Nature's Interest: Ecological Footprints as an Indicator of Sustainability*. London: Earthscan.

Chape, S., S. Blyth, L. Fish, P. Fox, and M. Spalding. 2003. *2003 United Nations List of Protected Areas*. Gland, Switzerland: International Union for the Conservation of Nature.

Christensen, N. L., A. M. Bartuska, J. H. Brown, S. Carpenter, C. D'Antonio, R. Francis, J. F. Franklin, et al. 1996. The Report of the Ecological Society of America Committee on the Scientific Basis for Ecosystem Management. *Ecological Applications* 6, no. 3: 665 91.

Christiansen, J. 2003. Auditing Conservation in an Age of Accountability. *Conservation in Practice* 4, no. 3: 12–19.

Colorado Cattlemen's Agricultural Land Trust (CCALT). 2007. Colorado Cattlemen's Association Agricultural Land Trust. Available at http://www.ccalt.org/

Colorado Conservation Trust. 2004. *Colorado Conservation at a Crossroads*. Interim Report. Boulder: Colorado Conservation Trust.

Colorado Demography Office. 2004. Historical Census Population. Available at http://www.dola.state.co.us/domog-webapps/population_census

Colorado Department of Revenue. 2007. Gross Conservation Easement Credit. Available at http://www.revenue.state.co.us/fyi/html/income39.html

Convention on Biological Diversity. 2002. *Sustaining Life on Earth: How the Convention of Biological Diversity Promotes Nature and Human Well-Being*. Available at http://www.biodiv.org/doc/publications/guide.asp

Diehl, J., and T. S. Barrett. 1988. *Conservation Easement Handbook*. Washington, D.C.: Land Trust Alliance.

Dirzo, R., and P. H. Raven. 2003. Global State of Biodiversity and Loss. *Annual Review of Environment and Resources* 28:137–67.

Geisel, T. [Dr. Seuss]. 1971. *The Lorax*. New York: Random House.

Goodwin, R. H. 2002. *A Botanist's Window on the Twentieth Century*. Petersham, Mass.: Harvard Forest.

Great Outdoors Colorado (GOCO. 2004. Open Space Grants. Available at http://www.goco.org/

———. 2007. Accomplishments. Available at http://www.goco.org/GrantPrograms/Openspace/tabid/119/default.aspx

Groves, C. R. 2003. *Drafting a Conservation Blueprint: A Practitioner's Guide to Planning for Biodiversity*. Washington, D.C.: The Nature Conservancy and Island Press.

Hardin, G. 1972. *Exploring New Ethics for Survival: The Voyage of the Spaceship Beagle*. New York: Viking.

Hawksworth, D. L., and M. T. Kailin-Arroyo. 1995. Magnitude and Distribution of Biodiversity. In *Global Biodiversity Assessment*, edited by V. H. Heywood, 107–91. London: Cambridge University Press.

Hutchinson, G. E. 1965. *The Ecological Theater and the Evolutionary Play*. New Haven, Conn.: Yale University Press.

Huxley, J. S. 1943. *Evolutionary Ethics.* London: Oxford University Press.

International Union for the Conservation of Nature (IUCN). 2003. 2002 IUCN Red List of Threatened Species. Available at http://www.iucnredlist.org

Jablonski, D. 1995. Extinction in the Fossil Record. In *Extinction Rates,* edited by J. H. Lawton and R. M. May, 25–44. New York: Oxford University Press.

Kareiva, P., and M. Marvier. 2003. Conserving Biodiversity Coldspots. *American Scientist* 91:344–51.

Knight, R. L. 2002. The Ecology of Ranching. In *Ranching West of the 100th Meridian,* edited by R. L. Knight, W. C. Gilgert, and E. Marston, 123–44. Washington, D.C.: Island Press.

Land Trust Alliance. 2001. National Land Trust Census. Available at http://www.landtrustalliance.org/about-us/land-trust-census/census

———. 2006. *2005 National Land Trust Census Report.* Washington, D.C.: Land Trust Alliance.

Leopold, A. 1953. *Round River.* New York: Oxford University Press.

The Nature Conservancy (TNC). 2004a. About Us. Available at http://nature.org/aboutus/

———. 2004b. *Conservation by Design: A Framework for Mission Success.* Arlington, Va.: The Nature Conservancy.

———. 2006. More Than 185 Countries Unite to Protect the World's Critical Ecosystems under Historic New Commitment. Press release, February 20. Available at http://nature.org/pressroom/press/press1346.html

The Nature Conservancy (TNC), Colorado. 2004. San Luis Valley—Baca Ranch. Available at http://nature.org/wherewework/northamerica/states/colorado/preserves/

Pike, E. J. 2001. Community, Cows, and Conservation: The Nature Conservancy in Colorado's Yampa Valley. PhD diss., University of Colorado, Boulder.

Population Reference Bureau. 2007. 2007 World Population Data Sheet. Available at http://www.prb.org/Publications/Datasheets/2007/2007WorldPopulationDataSheet.aspx

Redford, K., M. Andrews, D. Braun, S. Buttrick, S. Chaplin, M. Coon, R. Cox, et al. 1997. *Designing a Geography of Hope: Guidelines for Ecoregion-Based Conservation in The Nature Conservancy.* Arlington, Va.: The Nature Conservancy.

Richter, H. E. 1999. Alteration of Forest Structure and Ecosystem Function along the Yampa River, Colorado. PhD diss., Colorado State University, Fort Collins.

Riebsame, W. E., H. Gosnell, and D. Theobald, eds. 1997. *Atlas of the New West: Portrait of a Changing Region.* New York: W. W. Norton.

Shelford, V. E. 1926. *Naturalist's Guide to the Americas.* Baltimore: Williams and Wilkins.

Stein, B. A., L. S. Kutner, and J. S. Adams. 2000. *Precious Heritage: The Status of Biodiversity in the United States.* New York: Oxford University Press.

Trust for Public Lands. 2006. *LandVote 2006.* Boston and Washington, D.C.: Trust for Public Lands and Land Trust Alliance.

————. 2007. TPL LandVote Database. Available at http://www.conservationalmanac
    .org/landvote/

United Nations Environmental Program (UNEP). 2000. *Sustaining Life on Earth:
    How the Convention on Biological Diversity Promotes Nature and Human Well-Be-
    ing.* Montreal: Secretariat of the Convention on Biological Diversity.

Vesterby, M., and K. S. Krupa. 2001. *Major Uses of Land in the United States, 1997.*
    Statistical Bulletin. Washington, D.C.: Resource Economics Division, Economic
    Resource Service, U.S. Department of Agriculture.

Walsh, R. G., J. R. McKean, and C. J. Mucklow. 1993. *Recreation Value of Ranch
    Open Space.* Report to the Routt County, Colorado, Board of Commissioners.
    Ft. Collins: Department of Agricultural and Resource Economics, Colorado State
    University.

Weeks, W. W. 1997. *Beyond the Ark: Tools for an Ecosystem Approach to Conservation.*
    Washington, D.C.: Island Press.

Wilderness.net. 2004. The National Wilderness Preservation System. Available at
    http://www.wilderness.net/

Wilson, E. O. 2002. *The Future of Life.* New York: Knopf.

World Wildlife Fund. 2003. Global 200: Blueprint for a Living Planet. http//www
    .panda.org/

11

Open Wound from a Tough Nuclear History

FORGETTING HOW WE MADE OURSELVES AN ENDANGERED SPECIES

Len Ackland

THE ROCKY FLATS nuclear weapons complex produced tens of thousands of plutonium bombs for the U.S. nuclear arsenal from 1952 to 1989, poisoned hundreds of workers, and contaminated the environment with radioactive and toxic substances. Now, however, most of the grassy mesa near Denver, Colorado, where the controversial bomb plant was located has been turned into a national wildlife refuge.[1] And if the U.S. Department of Interior's Fish and Wildlife Service gets its way, this eight-square-mile refuge will even offer restricted public use such as bicycle trails and hunting. A "normalized" Rocky Flats will become just another piece of open space along Colorado's Front Range.

The makeover of Rocky Flats from a site producing some of the world's most deadly weapons to a relatively benign, if still contaminated, plot of land has been an impressive feat to watch. This transformation began after the Cold War when the federal government announced an end to the plant's weapons-production mission in 1992, following its shutdown of plutonium production three years earlier for safety and environmental reasons. Several years later government contractors began a serious soil cleanup and the decontamination and demolition of more than eight hundred production and auxiliary buildings. The U.S. Department of Energy (DOE), which is in charge of U.S. nuclear weapons production, is now touting Rocky Flats as a model for other cleanups. Although many of the specific technical features of this cleanup model are laudable, it is profoundly flawed in one crucial aspect.

According to this model, DOE's new Office of Legacy Management would assume long-term responsibility for so-called legacy liabilities once the cleanup was officially completed.[2] At Rocky Flats, such environmental liabilities exist primarily in the 1,300 acres for which DOE retains ownership and responsibility. This DOE acreage amounts to 21 percent of the original 6,240-acre site. After the $7.2 billion cleanup was completed in 2006, the designated refuge land was turned over to the U.S. Fish and Wildlife Service the following year.[3] DOE officials adamantly deny that the retained land—which plant employees have suggestively labeled the "DOE blob"—was too contaminated to hand over to Fish and Wildlife. The officials argue that the land was retained only for the monitoring and "management of ongoing remedies."[4] At the least, such jargon suggests that the cleanup involved uncertainty, a point made by activist LeRoy Moore in an article advocating that the refuge not be opened for public use.[5]

Although the questions about contamination uncertainty and the public use of the future Rocky Flats refuge are not trivial, they do not reflect the major flaw in the DOE's cleanup model. That flaw is one of omission. The DOE describes its Office of Legacy Management as "a significant step to ensuring the long-term protection of human health and environment."[6] This narrow description ignores the fact that the U.S. National Park Service added Rocky Flats to the National Register of Historic Places in 1998 for "making a significant contribution to the broad patterns of U.S. history."[7] It dismisses the provision in the Rocky Flats National Wildlife Refuge Act of 2001 that supports a site museum. Indeed, in seeking to "manage" the site's legacies, the DOE is discouraging the public from remembering and considering the broad historical legacies of Rocky Flats.

The legacies are both physical and perceptual. In addition to the contaminated environment, one legacy is physical illness. Hundreds of the more than twenty thousand production workers employed at Rocky Flats over the years have been afflicted by chronic beryllium disease or its precursor. The disease, similar to black lung disease and asbestosis, is fatal. Other workers have suffered from brain tumors, lung cancer, and other cancers that may have been caused by radiation exposure. The numbers are elusive due to factors that confound the identification of a disease's exact cause, exemplified by workers with lung cancer who also smoked. Offsite illnesses reputedly caused by plant operations and accidents are virtually impossible to pin down. Some area residents suspect that cancers, in particular, resulted from the plant's toxic releases. The lack of validated scientific studies to support the latter claims hasn't ended the argument.

The legacies of Rocky Flats reside beyond the local environment and people as well. During the plant's thirty-seven years of weapons production, it manufactured plutonium bombs for most of the total 70,000 nuclear weapons produced by the United States. The Rocky Flats bombs—modern descendents of the plutonium bomb that destroyed Nagasaki, Japan, in 1945—serve primarily as detonators for much more powerful thermonuclear, or hydrogen, bombs (H-bombs). Today, plutonium bombs manufactured at Rocky Flats remain in the cores of the approximately 10,300 nuclear weapons composing the U.S. arsenal.[8]

These weapons of mass destruction are the most important tangible legacy of Rocky Flats. If used, they would cause catastrophic death and destruction. They also signify a bitter, unresolved controversy about this bomb plant and the whole nuclear weapons enterprise: Do nuclear weapons ensure U.S. national security or pose an unacceptable risk to humanity? "If humans are so smart, why have we built huge arsenals of weapons capable of destroying ourselves?" was the question I asked myself even before starting to do work on my Rocky Flats book in 1990. Why, to use the language of the 1973 Endangered Species Act, have we made ourselves an endangered species? The answer, I found, is a complicated blend of factors including short-term thinking, desire for jobs and contracts, denial and justification, faith in experts, and blind trust in authority.[9]

In the aftermath of the Cold War, signaled by the fall of the Berlin Wall in 1989, I had hoped that diminished tensions between the United States and the Soviet Union (Russia after the Soviet disintegration in 1991) and the end of inflammatory Cold War rhetoric would enable humans to recognize that nuclear weapons of mass destruction have put the world at risk. We had a chance to make real progress toward abolishing them. Yet since 1989 three more countries (India, Pakistan, and North Korea) have joined the so-called nuclear club (the United States, Russia, the United Kingdom, China, France, and Israel); weapons proliferation continues; and approximately 30,000 nuclear weapons exist, with more than 95 percent in U.S. and Russian hands.[10] And the United States, the world's sole superpower, rather than taking the lead in outlawing nuclear weapons, again started producing plutonium bombs at the Los Alamos National Laboratory in New Mexico in 2003 and has plans for a new version of

Rocky Flats on one of five DOE sites.[11] The U.S. government behaves as if the only dangerous nuclear weapons are those not possessed by the United States and its allies.

In my end-of-the-Cold-War optimism, I underestimated the powerful symbolism that nuclear weapons have come to possess for many Americans. Many are unwilling to accept or even discuss either the consequences of their use—at Hiroshima and Nagasaki—or the potential global risk they pose. Nor did I anticipate how Cold War anger, dogma, and disputes would carry over into the present by means of a dominant narrative, or storyline, about the past. This storyline, which I call the "Cold War Heroes" narrative, has been promoted intensely at Rocky Flats, perhaps because it is the first major nuclear weapons plant in the nation to be fully dismantled.

Owing largely to the site's proximity to Denver and its suburbs, Rocky Flats became the focus of angry demonstrations and counterdemonstrations at the height of the Cold War during the 1970s and early 1980s. The epithet *war criminals* was sometimes hurled at managers and workers for manufacturing nuclear weapons, and protesters were labeled "unpatriotic" and worse for questioning the requirements of U.S. national security. Tensions ran deep, and few have evaporated.

"Everybody involved in Rocky Flats blames somebody for something," observed Dorothy Ciarlo, a retired psychologist who has completed dozens of oral histories for Boulder's Carnegie Library, about 75 percent from workers and 25 percent from activists.[12] Some of that blame stems from old animosities about the plant's deadly products. Some of it comes from mistrust of the DOE and its contractors. Still more comes from aggrieved families and individuals such as sick workers who are seeking compensation from the government for occupational diseases they blame on the plant. In 2007, the federal government was still refusing to recognize many of those claims.[13]

But even when former employees criticize the DOE or contractors or both for poor waste practices or dangerous working conditions at Rocky Flats, they usually don't question the need for nuclear weapons, as I discovered when interviewing dozens of workers. Most seem to want to believe that they are "Cold War Heroes," as they are called in the celebratory narrative promoted by the DOE, its bomb-building contractors, the George W. Bush administration, and both Democratic and Republican politicians, among others. This narrative portrays plant managers and workers as having "won" the Cold War by building nuclear weapons crucial to defending the nation against the Soviet Union, which then collapsed. Historians will debate for a long time the actual impact the arms race had in the Soviet demise, but whatever they conclude, the irrefutable fact is that these weapons constituted and continue to constitute a terminal risk to humanity.

In watching the Cold War Heroes narrative develop, I have been reminded of the Party slogan in George Orwell's *1984:* "Who controls the past controls the future: who controls the present controls the past."[14] Adherents to the heroes' narrative minimize the risks posed by nuclear weapons, but the risks are staggering, as historian Donald Worster notes. "The Age of Ecology began on the desert outside Alamogordo, New Mexico on July 16, 1945, with a dazzling fireball of light and a swelling mushroom cloud of radioactive gases," he writes about the first nuclear bomb test, code-named "Trinity." "For the first time in some two million years of human history, there existed a force capable of destroying the entire fabric of life on the planet."[15]

Such a force came frighteningly close to being launched by U.S. and Russian leaders during the Cuban Missile Crisis of 1962, as we now know from the accounts of both American and Soviet participants. For example, former secretary of defense Robert McNamara has said that the world came even closer to nuclear war than Hollywood vividly depicted in the movie *Thirteen Days.*

A more localized, different level of risk to Denver residents occurred on Mother's Day in May 1969 when a raging fire in a Rocky Flats production building holding more than seven thousand pounds of plutonium almost burned through the roof and dispersed plutonium into the atmosphere. A year later, U.S. Air Force general Edward Giller, a top official in the Atomic Energy Commission (AEC), testified before Congress that if the fire "had been a little bigger it is questionable whether it could have been contained." If it had gone out of control, he said, "hundreds of square miles" could have been contaminated.[16]

The worst didn't occur in either case. And that fortuitous fact, based on narrow escapes, emboldens those who dismiss the argument that nuclear weapons constitute an unacceptable risk to humanity. A top Dow Chemical Company official, for example, denied the significance

of enormous risks exposed during the Rocky Flats fire: "the possibility that [the fire] might have resulted in a significant off-site release of
plutonium was countered by the [official's] observation that it did not
happen."[17] In the case of the missile crisis, of course, if things had turned
out differently, nobody would be around to point fingers.

Risk denial is a powerful force fueled by the Cold War Heroes narrative. Replacing this narrative won't happen unless both its proponents
and its opponents make compromises and take responsibility for their
respective roles in the nuclear arms race. The possible payoff is that by
confronting the fact that we made ourselves an endangered species, we
can find a way to resolve the dilemma. Although I believe it is possible
to create a new narrative, perhaps "Unacceptable Risk," the challenge is
daunting. That becomes clear in examining the roots of the Cold War
Heroes narrative, by looking first at the 1994 *Enola Gay* incident and
then at the history of Rocky Flats itself.

The Good War

Thinking about the Cold War Heroes narrative reminded me of a talk
I gave in May 2000 at the Lafayette Historical Society titled, "Can We
Learn from the History of Rocky Flats? or Why Do Good People Build
Weapons of Mass Destruction?" During the question-and-answer period
afterwards, I was surprised that the first question came from an older
gentleman, who asked me what I thought about the U.S. bombing of
Hiroshima. I don't remember if he said that he was on a ship waiting to
invade Japan on August 6, 1945, or that he had a close relative on a ship.
In either case, the questioner contended that the American soldier's life
was saved by the atomic bomb. And he may have been correct.

I didn't realize at the time just how central the man's question was
to the developing triumphal narrative about Rocky Flats. My answer to
him, by the way, was along the lines of what I wrote in my book, that
historians had unearthed information that Japan was exploring surrender
options and that the U.S. government's announced numbers of potential American casualties in an invasion of Japan had been inflated. In my
opinion, "With American soldiers dying daily in summer 1945, it would
have taken a president possessing extraordinary understanding and foresight not to order the use of a powerful weapon that promised to save

American lives, regardless of how many. And in the modern age of total war, civilians were no longer off-limits."[18]

In terms of narrative, however, the man's question contained two key elements. First, he was speaking from personal experience, from *memories*, and those memories included strong feelings and attitudes. Second, his question reflected the official, widely accepted U.S. government interpretation that the atomic bomb quickly ended the war and saved lives—American lives. What later became known as "collateral damage," civilian deaths, is ignored in this storyline. Robert J. Lifton and Greg Mitchell analyze the storyline this way: "By thus rendering the weapon a *preserver* rather than a *destroyer* of life, celebratory emotions have been sustained to this moment."[19]

The two nuclear weapons that destroyed Hiroshima and Nagasaki, killing some 210,000 people in an instant and in the short-term aftermath, are depicted in two contradictory narratives. Since 1945, these two storylines—"of a weapon that brought peace and victory, and of a weapon that brought destruction and fear to the world—rested uneasily in American consciousness," the editors of *History Wars* note.[20] Just how uneasily became clear in 1994 when the Smithsonian Institution's National Air and Space Museum was planning a fiftieth anniversary World War II exhibit. The exhibit was to feature the *Enola Gay*, the B-29 that dropped the atomic bomb code-named "Little Boy" on Hiroshima. The exhibit was to contain displays and explanations about events leading up to the bombing and its consequences, including the Japanese casualties.

The Smithsonian's plans unleashed a vitriolic dispute that essentially boiled down to an argument involving an analysis of the historical record versus "feelings," particularly of veterans who wanted to celebrate the World War II victory without complication. Historian Paul Boyer observes, "One reason Americans have had so much trouble coming to terms with Hiroshima and Nagasaki surely lies in the fact that what our atomic bombs did to those cities has never been easily assimilable to the prevailing public view of World War II as the 'Good War'—a noble struggle against forces that threatened not only western values but the survival of civilization itself."[21]

In the end, the Smithsonian exhibit was cancelled and replaced with a virtually stand-alone display of the plane. Historian Marilyn Young describes it as follows: "The Smithsonian has now presented the shiny fuselage of the *Enola Gay,* without context, without death, without reference to any meaning outside of itself." In this way, she writes, it simply says that "[t]here was a Good War: it ended when Good Men flew a Good Plane and dropped a New Bomb on Bad People. What those bombs did had nothing to do with Us, only with Them: their atrocities, their aggressive war, the horror their resistance would have posed to an invading force. To question this is to bring the meaning of the bomb home to us, where it belongs."[22]

After World War II, the New Bombs—nuclear weapons—existed in a world atmosphere dominated by U.S. economic and military power, but permeated with fear of the Soviet Union's dictatorship and international communism. President Harry Truman and Congress decided that these nuclear instruments of mass destruction were "weapons" and thus necessary to national security. Some concerned scientists, clergy, and others protested the building of U.S. "national security" on a nuclear murder-suicide pact. The public, however, was initially distracted by the recovery from World War II and was soon manipulated by the anti-Communist hysteria of Senator Joseph McCarthy and friends. In the absence of informed public debate, the federal government was able to sanctify nuclear weapons of mass destruction and order more and more of them. The U.S. military, particularly the air force, kept finding more targets in the Soviet Union that required more nuclear bombs, which in turn required the AEC to seek funding to build more plants to manufacture them and to develop a domestic site to test them.

Rocky Flats

The AEC expanded the U.S. nuclear weapons complex in the early 1950s. The agency again looked west for sites. Although the American East contained some key nuclear weapons facilities, such as at Oak Ridge, Tennessee, the West offered even more benefits to the complex. It possessed uranium deposits and vast spaces—which along with the Columbia River water supply and hydroelectric power had sent the 586-square-mile Hanford complex to Washington State and a laboratory to Los Alamos, New Mexico, during World War II. With pork-barrel politics added in, the West became the obvious choice for many new facilities and programs. Advances in nuclear weapons designs and the need to test them provided the main rationale for a test site within the United States to complement the Pacific Ocean testing. The seemingly isolated Nevada desert was picked, and the first weapon in this period was tested in January 1951.[23]

At the same time, the AEC chose Rocky Flats in nearby Colorado for an industrial-scale facility to process plutonium and manufacture bombs that were being produced on a smaller scale in Los Alamos. Pure politics provided the main impetus for selecting Rocky Flats: the state's two senators, a Democrat and a Republican, sat on the small congressional committee that had budgetary power over the AEC. A secondary reason for the selection was that the AEC wanted to avoid the problems presented by "company towns" such as isolated Richland, Washington, and Oak Ridge. The metro Denver area population then topped half a million.[24]

In March 1951, the AEC announced the selection of Rocky Flats at a Denver news conference, but provided few specifics other than the dollar commitment. "There's Good News Today: U.S. to Build $45 Million A-Plant Near Denver" read the enthusiastic headline in the March 23 *Denver Post*. The day after the announcement, even without government details, both Denver papers speculated correctly about three out of four of the plant's possible nuclear bomb products.

The news media reinforced the generally accepted notion that the federal government should be trusted and allowed to operate in secret. For example, a January 28, 1952, story in the *Rocky Mountain News* began, "The forty-one-million-dollar Rocky Flats plant will start producing— whatever it will produce—shortly after it is completed—whenever that is." A photograph showed a guard shack and temporary wooden buildings in the distance. The caption ended with a dare: "There are also a couple of fences and a row of guards in between—care to investigate?" Journalists didn't. Indeed, Rocky Flats became a "public secret" ignored by developers as they built up the Front Range during the next decades (see the chapter by Alan Wallis and Gene Bressler).

Later the same year, in October 1952, the United States successfully tested a New and Improved Good Bomb—an H-bomb with explosive power on the order of a thousand times larger than the Hiroshima or Nagasaki bombs. The plutonium bombs subsequently manufactured at Rocky Flats were to be used primarily to detonate or "trigger" the H-bombs. That connection suggests why—to this day—local papers often refer to Rocky Flats as a "nuclear trigger factory." What a mar-velous euphemism, a way to conceal the reality about a plant that built weapons of mass destruction.

For a long time, the public didn't question the existence or value of U.S. nuclear weapons, which could have made globally tangible such popular slogans as "Better Dead Than Red." During the 1950s, Ameri-cans accepted nuclear weapons as required for national security and didn't think about the consequences of their use. Gallup polls, for example, found that "a majority supported using the atomic bomb in Korea in 1951 after China entered the conflict; in Vietnam in 1954 when the French were surrounded; and against China in 1955 during the first Quemoy-Matsu crisis."[25]

Any risks that nuclear weapons production might entail were hidden behind the thick wall of national-security secrecy. The people of Denver barely heard about the first big plutonium fire at Rocky Flats. In Sep-tember 1957, a fire burst out in a production room holding 137.5 pounds of plutonium.[26] The day after the fire, the September 12, 1957, *Denver Post* carried a front-page story under the headline "Atomic Fire Causes $50,000 Loss." The story quoted a plant spokesman as attributing the fire to "spontaneous combustion" in a processing line. "The AEC spokesman declined to describe further the 'processing line,'" the unbylined story continued. Local papers didn't follow up on the story.

Most journalists didn't veer from society's acceptance of the national-security state's dependence on nuclear weapons. The general public gave at least tacit approval to the federal government's nuclear policies. The men and women who worked at Rocky Flats did the nation's bidding. They did the "dirty work" of building nuclear weapons, sometimes at great personal cost to their health, as many later discovered. But the jobs at the plant paid well, and the plant was modern by 1950s standards. By and large, the managers and workers at Rocky Flats were honest, hardworking, caring people. The record shows that a few officials took advantage of the secrecy-shrouded unaccountability by lying and com-mitting crimes, but probably no more or less than occurs in American society at large.

The Rocky Flats workers, unlike the citizens in nearby communities benefiting from the workers' spending their salaries, had to confront their deadly handiwork on a daily basis. They were well aware of what they were producing. Some had witnessed nuclear bomb tests in the Pacific or in Nevada and described their experiences to coworkers. As the late union leader Jim Kelly said, "To have a guy telling you what it was like, how unimaginable one of those [bombs] was, made you go home and not even talk to your family about it."[27]

Kelly and his coworkers found various ways to justify or deny what they were doing, or both. During the Cuban Missile Crisis, Kelly leaned heavily on his faith that President John F. Kennedy, a fellow Catholic, would make the right choice about the use of nuclear weapons. And, he explained later, "I always hid behind the fact that I was not the guy who would make that decision. Somebody out there had to be pulling the trigger, but that would never be me."[28] Kelly and his coworkers also used minimizing language for their deadly products, referring to "units" or "devices" instead of to bombs.

The public began hearing more about the costs and risks of nuclear bomb production after the nearly catastrophic 1969 Rocky Flats fire. Independent scientists discovered off-site plutonium contamination. Activists organized opposition. After the Vietnam War ended in the mid-1970s, peace activists focused on militarism and the need for nuclear disarmament. Environmentalists decried the damage to the site and its surroundings. Under the slogan "Local Hazard, Global Threat," activists organized many demonstrations and received considerable press coverage. Some of the harsh rhetoric referred to Rocky Flats as equivalent to the Nazi death camp at Auschwitz. Plant workers understandably were shocked and angered when their jobs and their mission came under attack.

The national public consensus that nuclear weapons were crucial to national security unraveled more in the 1980s. Long-standing antinuclear challenges earlier bolstered by the Cuban Missile Crisis spread more widely among the general public during the Nuclear Freeze Campaign of the early 1980s. The freeze prompted, ironically, the first widespread debate about nuclear weapons in this representative democracy. President Ronald Reagan dampened the debate with his Strategic Defense Initiative, better known as Star Wars, which was theoretically aimed at defending the country from nuclear weapons. Soon, however, the Chernobyl accident in 1986, revelations about problems in the U.S. nuclear weapons complex, and warming U.S.-Soviet relations stimulated more journalistic coverage and public discussion about nuclear weapons.

Then came a startling event at Rocky Flats—the federal government raided itself. On June 6, 1989, Federal Bureau of Investigation (FBI)and Environmental Protection Agency (EPA) investigators in a convoy of thirty vehicles, including two EPA mobile environmental crime labs, entered the plant and began gathering evidence to back up allegations that Rocky Flats was committing environmental crimes. During the next seven months, local newspapers published hundreds of articles about the plant, including stories about previous spills, contamination, and accidents. Amid repeated charges of safety violations, DOE secretary James Watkins "temporarily" suspended plutonium operations at Rocky Flats in November 1989. That same month the Berlin Wall fell.

Plutonium production at Rocky Flats never resumed. President George H. W. Bush declared in January 1992 that the plant's weapons mission was finished. Two months later plant operator Rockwell International pleaded guilty to environmental crimes in a settlement with the federal government and paid an $18.5 million fine. The debate continues to this day about that settlement, the lack of individual prosecutions, and the secrecy imposed on the grand jury.[29]

Even with the Cold War ended, animosity hovered over Rocky Flats. For example, when seven Russian scientists toured the plant's plutonium processing and manufacturing buildings in July 1994, many workers were shocked. "I have spent my life so that Russians would see the bottom side of bombs," said a worker in his early forties. "And now they get brought here to see them from the top. I don't like it."[30] The many workers holding similar views have undoubtedly been susceptible to the Cold War Heroes storyline, which enables them to forget about the risks to which they contributed. As psychologist Dorothy Ciarlo told me, "When you have so much ego and self-esteem invested, you can only go so far."[31]

If society is to learn anything from Rocky Flats, workers must disavow the Cold War Heroes talk and create a new narrative. Much of that new dialogue has been pushed by people outside the workers' ranks—for example, the employee for government contractor Kaiser-Hill Inc. who declared a few years ago that "the Cold War Heroes need to be turned into Cleanup Heroes."[32] Former Rocky Flats workers and managers should acknowledge and take responsibility for manufacturing weapons of mass destruction—not "devices" or "units" or "triggers"—that put the world at risk.

A new storyline about Rocky Flats also demands an admission from citizens who were outside the plant's security fences. Activists, neighbors, journalists, and others must acknowledge that we as the citizens of a democracy bear responsibility for the fact that U.S. "national security" ironically rested and still rests on nuclear weapons of mass destruction. When Rocky Flats produced weapons, the men and women at the plant functioned under the same national policy as everyone else. They weren't morally deficient. They were the public's surrogates.

Competing perspectives about Rocky Flats currently confront each other—but in a civil, respectful way—among a diverse group of activists, community members, Rocky Flats workers, DOE and Kaiser-Hill employees, academics, and others who have been working for the past few years to build the Rocky Flats Cold War Museum. The people volunteering in the nonprofit museum group—of which I was a founding board member, but in which I am no longer active—agree that the history of Rocky Flats is important and should not be lost to future generations. They agree that artifacts should be collected and displayed. And they agree that different versions of the past, or *histories,* and different accounts of personal experience, or *memories,* should be acknowledged. If this museum gains public support and funding and, in fact, presents the conflicting narratives of Rocky Flats, it will have achieved a rare success—one that didn't occur in the case of the Smithsonian's *Enola Gay* exhibit.

Unfortunately, DOE's Office of Legacy Management sought to undermine the museum in a draft report in December 2004, stating that "it is DOE's opinion that a Rocky Flats Museum should only be established if it can be viable without federal funding."[33] Backers of the museum weren't surprised by this announcement. Other government-supported museums, such as the Bradbury Museum at Los Alamos and the National Atomic Museum in Albuquerque, present the uncomplicated triumphal story of the nuclear age, the one I have referred to as the Cold War Heroes narrative.[34] By mid-2007, the Rocky Flats Cold War Museum had a presence on the Internet, but still lacked the major funding needed for a building.[35]

If, despite the odds, the museum were to be built, it might help the community achieve a shared narrative—perhaps the "Unacceptable Risk" narrative—that would replace the dead-end Cold War Heroes storyline. A new narrative would be an important start toward helping us think seriously about removing humanity from the endangered species list. Rocky Flats can serve as a real model for healing the nuclear weapons malady: a cleanup of its mess without a cover-up of its past.

Epilogue

HEALING THE WEST OVER TIME

Patricia Nelson Limerick

ALTHOUGH THE FOCUS of this book is, of course, the American West, still it must be said that the project of applying remedies to past injuries is national and international, not the property of any region. This movement, moreover, has picked up speed and participation in recent years. As William Throop points out, "Most of the key U.S. environmental acts of the 1960s and 1970s cited restoration as an explicit goal. As a result, the volume of restoration projects in the United States increased dramatically."[1] The Society for Conservation Biology was founded in 1985, and the Society for Ecological Restoration was founded in 1989. This professionalization of the field has been an important trend, but restoration remains an activity in which the work of volunteers, amateurs, and "regular citizens" matters a great deal.

Although it would be difficult to quantify and compare the manifestations of this trend in different regions, the West seems to be a hotbed of restoration, with multiple efforts under way to move beyond regret, resentment, and blame, and to find and apply remedies for earlier damage and loss. These efforts range from the replanting of native grasses to the reclamation of mining sites, the readmission of fire to forests and grasslands, the reintroduction of eliminated species, the restoration of wildlife habitat, the plans to remove dams in order to restore free-flowing rivers and help aquatic life recover, and the cleaning up of sites of industrial pollution and nuclear contamination. In the words of former secretary of the interior Bruce Babbitt, we are entering "an entirely new era of conservation history, moving beyond preservation or protection toward a deeper, more complex movement, the affirmative act of restoration."[2]

At this point, critical and alert readers might be asking just how "entirely new" this movement actually is. When did this enthusiasm we call "healing the West" actually begin? As Lee Clark Mitchell has shown in his book *Witnesses to a Vanishing America,* regret over the injuries of westward expansion has a long history. White Americans held a spectrum of opinions on the conquest of the West, and dismay and sorrow were far from rare in those opinions. Mitchell sees "a strain of misgiving" at work early in the nineteenth century. As he puts it, "the prospect loomed large but insistent that American expansion might destroy those aspects of frontier life that first attracted pioneers; that material progress would introduce serious new social and psychological pressures; that America was developing according to a cyclic pattern of rise and fall characteristic of other celebrated empires." To people who had these anxieties, "change seemed far too rapid."[3]

And if regret over the damage done by conquest has a surprisingly long history, then the search for remedies and antidotes to the injuries of conquest must also extend back into time. An earnest, but questionable effort to divide environmental concerns and activism into three separate categories—preservation, conservation, and restoration—makes it difficult to figure out the origins and chronology of this larger search. Environmental historians, philosophers, and analysts of policy have put considerable effort into drawing distinctions among these three activities. If we steer by the usual definitions, *preservation* means setting pristine nature apart from further human intervention or intrusion and is exemplified in the crusades of the Sierra Club's founder John Muir. *Conservation* entails balancing forms of use of natural resources (including mining, grazing, farming, logging, generating hydroelectric power, recreation, and aesthetic appreciation) with a commitment to make sure that those resources are available for the use of future generations, either by allowing the resources to replenish themselves or by restricting the intensity of their use; Gifford Pinchot, first head of the U.S. Forest Service, is the symbolic figure representing this approach. *Restoration,* still in search of its iconic figure, differs from both preservation and conservation; it means trying to bring disturbed, degraded, and diminished landscapes back to a state of well-being, often through the restoration of native species and a recapturing of biodiversity.[4]

These distinctions are, to a degree, useful, but it takes considerable effort to maintain them and to hold them in place. Unless the definitions are carefully policed, they will, in a manner that is at first intellectually annoying and then liberating, cross into each other's territories.

Preservation, after all, can rarely be a pure, "hands-off" procedure in which human intervention and intrusion cease or never occur at all; preserved lands in the West are, to take one example, also lands subject to the intrusion of weeds and other invasive species, and keeping them "natural" by controlling those invaders requires considerable human manipulation. In the same way, wildlife is rarely attentive to the borders surrounding preserved areas, making human exertion of control once again unavoidable. The categories become most difficult to keep separate when we think critically about the long-lived attempt to quarantine the campaign for preservation from more utilitarian (i.e., conservation or even restoration) programs. Despite this effort at separation, nearly all of the most dedicated of preservationists in our times live in constructed houses or condos or apartments; they light and heat—and sometimes air-condition—those houses, drive fossil-fueled vehicles (sometimes quite sizable ones, the better to transport outdoor recreational equipment!), and buy fruits, vegetables, and other healthful foods often grown in distant locations and transported with significant expenditure of energy resources. Their voting records and philanthropic habits may say "preservation," but their everyday habits make a "utilitarian" counterstatement. With the recognition that recreational users of natural places are material beings who change the turf they drive to, walk upon, and camp at, the line between "pure preservation" and "utilitarian conservation" has become unexpectedly shifty. In thinking that hiking, camping, and other forms of outdoor recreation can be removed from the category of environment-altering "use," the preservationists of earlier times enjoyed an innocent faith that the aesthetic appreciation of natural landscapes was entirely different from extraction; parades of walkers and hikers were to move through space as if a few inches off the ground, having no negative impact on the environment they passed through. In a commonly used phrase, it is now evident that preserved landscapes can be "loved to death" by those enthusiasts for nature who may still see themselves as an entirely different breed from those extractors and developers who put nature to use for their own profit and material comfort.

The distinctions between preservation and utilitarian conservation have become blurred. In truth, they began blurred. With this recognition, it becomes viable to declare that these two activities, along with the later-arriving restoration, can be reunited and relocated into the category of "healing the West." Even with different diagnoses and prescriptions, both programs respond to a reckoning with the injuries done to landscapes by full-speed-ahead, short-term development of resources. Noting this common ground, the two approaches can seem more parallel and complementary than opposed. If we give up the struggle to cast preservation and conservation in opposition, the search for remedies for the injuries of conquest emerges as the biggest story in the American West of the twentieth century and shows every sign of becoming an even bigger story in the twenty-first. Making this declaration allows us to recognize the conservation and preservation movements of a hundred years ago (especially the creation of the forest reserves and the national parks, as well as the creation of new agencies for the management of fish and game) as the first round of healing the West—that is, the first step toward meaningful action arising from regret over the injuries inflicted by conquest. Restoration, or the recognition that some damaged areas can be cleaned up and redeemed, is a logical second step. By this act of recategorization and reconnection, the movement on behalf of healing the West ceases to be a recent, untried infant of a trend. Instead, it picks up a century and is reconstituted as a venerable and time-tested elder!

Of course, big differences distinguish the searches for remedy in the early twentieth century from those of the early twenty-first. The biggest difference rests on the conception of nature as stable or dynamic. Making hay of older ideas of nature as a balanced, self-regulating, reliable system, biologists and ecologists now begin with a model of natural systems as dynamic, changeable, and ever evolving. Closely tied into this rejection of a static and stable nature is a recognition of the enormous complexity of the operations of any given ecosystem. One lesson drawn from that complexity is the necessity to apply sizable amounts of skepticism to any "one size-fits-all" policy because slight variations in slope, elevation, soil, and rainfall will produce different structures and processes. A century ago the Progressive Era reformers of national policy on natural resources could make their plans and design their actions while working in an intellectual world that must strike us as restful and simple when we compare it to the enormous complexity and change with which we must now constantly reckon.

A recognition of the complexity, uncertainty, variation, and unpredictability in natural (as well as cultural) systems inspires various writers in this volume, especially Sharon Collinge, William Lewis Jr., and David Armstrong, to call for more use of the strategy known as "adaptive management" (or "adaptive stewardship") in projects of restoration. The practitioners of adaptive management don't imagine they have figured things out for all time and prepare themselves to make permanent changes, but instead prepare the best possible plan, put the plan into operation, and then observe the results carefully, watching to see if the plan is delivering the desired outcomes or a different set of outcomes entirely. Based on those observations, the adaptive manager can then, if needed, shift course, redesign the plan, and generally manifest agility and nimbleness in trying to match nature in its merciless dynamism. A historian listening in as scientists call for adaptive management might be forgiven for an episode or two of thinking, "Isn't 'adaptive management' another phrase for that familiar old concept 'learning the lessons of history'?" Admittedly, the time frame is tighter, with the lessons arising out of the very recent past, but the basic operation seems clear: begin with humility, then look at what people (including yourself!) have tried to do, look at what their efforts actually produced, and adjust your conduct according to whatever you can derive in the way of lessons from comparing the intentions to the outcomes.

For the West's officials and experts, adaptive management offers a beneficial retraining program. Instead of having to be surprised and caught off guard by unexpected and unintended outcomes and results, managers can instead anticipate such reversals and, once they have occurred, instantly set to work on drawing lessons from them. Adaptive management is in other words a treatment program aimed at recovery from arrogance and a prime opportunity to experiment with the ways in which humility and a peaceful recognition of the limits of our expertise can make us at once more effective and much less burdened.

In the final section of the book, our attention is almost entirely on the subject of healing as it applies to natural systems, and yet one of the principal virtues of this collection is the combination of enterprises in healing that involve human communities and natural systems. In the most positive way, many of those writing on restoration make the point that the healing of landscapes is a project that has given new life and purpose to human communities, repairing divisions and uniting groups in common enterprise. Every chapter in this volume reinforces the introduction's declaration that all of these issues, including the ones that seem most focused on nature, are finally about people. The chapters by Sarah Krakoff, Andrew Cowell, John-Michael Rivera, Brenda M. Romero, Len Ackland, and Alan Wallis and Gene Bressler are explicitly about the restoration and recovery of human cultural practices and political powers, but each of those cases has unmistakable connections to land and nature. Meanwhile, the more "nature-centered" articles by Joseph Ryan, Sharon Collinge, Hannah Gosnell, William Lewis, and David Armstrong are well supplied with human actors because all these matters regarding the management of land and natural resources involve an intense process of debate and decision making among human groups. As Andrew Cowell argues, the most important target of healing the West may well be the repair of tattered and strained human relationships.

One of the rewards of reviewing the literature on restoration is finding repeated statements on the inseparability of this cause from the well-being of human beings. As James A. MacMahon and Karen D. Holl write, "Human needs and the ecological goals of restoration have a positive, reciprocal relationship."[5] Eric Higgs takes a similarly unifying tack: "In some ways I find the cultural dimensions of restoration as exciting as the ecological ones. By restoring ecosystems we regenerate old ways or create new ones that bring us closer to natural processes and to one another."[6] "Human influences," two authors sum up the orthodoxy in restoration circles, "ranging from the subtle and the benign to the overtly destructive, are pervasive throughout the earth's ecosystems."[7] Declarations that American nature loving went too far in the cause of separating "nature" from "human" have proliferated in the past two decades. Anyone attending to those declarations might wonder, "Let's say that the case for treating 'human' and 'natural' as if they were opposite categories is no longer convincing since in fact they overlap. Now what?"

Restoration is a logical answer to that question. As Peter Friederici remarks, "Restoration is a bridge between what has come to be viewed as the disparate realms of humans and of nature." That bridging quality explains its growing significance: restoration "is becoming a powerful social movement, precisely because it offers a chance to use human energies in ways" that are "deeply satisfying. It perfectly links individual action with the needs of something greater, both in human society and in nature." In Friederici's judgment, some restorationists who work in ecological restoration are "motivated as much by the desire to improve human welfare—economic, aesthetic, or spiritual—by repairing broken relationships between people and their surroundings." And in a memorable phrase bringing his argument to its peak, he says: "Restoration can also be a profoundly democratic act" because people who care about particular places must engage with each other in a direct and open discussion of the best approaches for taking care of those places.[8] And that proposition brings us to one of restoration's most important contributions to western American society: it gives us something to talk about, a stimulating topic that we can use to strengthen our now somewhat weak capacity for productive public discourse.

Restoring the Art of Democratic Conversation

For reasons I would not want to try to re-create, when we started the "Healing the West" lecture series, I believed that restoration was a cause that carried universal support. Of course, I was solidly wrong. No cause, however much it may appear to be on the side of the angels, is beyond reach of criticism and opposition. But when I realized that restoration had staunch and articulate opponents, I was at first crestfallen, wondering if any good cause on the earth had skated around potential opposition so nimbly that it had never been lamented and condemned.

But then, pondering the objections raised to restoration, I came to a different judgment. These debates, it became clear, provide good exercise for the mind. If the western public can be successfully invited to pay attention, explorations of the case for and against restoration can provide occasions for very interesting and worthwhile discussions. We live in a time when many lament the deficiencies, especially the crabbiness and polarization, of public political discourse. We live in a world in which specialists and experts lament the limited degree of knowledge that general citizens can boast in topics ranging from biological science to history, from the interpretation of statistics to the precise and clear use of the English language. But we also live in a society with a seeming insatiable enthusiasm for book discussion groups, indicating a considerable desire to talk with friends about topics of substance. Wouldn't even more people flock to such discussions if they were billed as "Paragraph

Discussion Groups" instead of as the more daunting "Book Discussion Groups"? And, at that point, the debates over restoration came to seem to me very valuable indeed, really something of a godsend to the double cause of finding routes to "redistribute the wealth" of expertise to regular citizens, while also rescuing and restoring productive and civil public conversation. In the rest of this epilogue, I do my best to present the debates over restoration as a kind of Kit of Western Conversational Opportunities for use by groups of westerners who may not always have the time to read entire books, but who would like to have the fun and satisfaction delivered to so many by the widespread book-discussion-group phenomenon and who might thereby be better enlisted into "page or paragraph discussion groups."

Friends Don't Let Friends Take Things for Granted: Allies Who Double as Critics and Thereby Give the Gift of Humility

The most severe and strenuous criticisms of and objections to restoration surprisingly come from environmental advocates. As Higgs describes the situation, "What caught restoration advocates off guard was that the detractors were the very people from whom one would most expect support."[9] Wouldn't those who consider the cause of environmental well-being their priority be predictable and automatic enthusiastic supporters of the cause of restoration?

Not necessarily.

Western Conversational Opportunity Number 1

Does this situation strike you as unusual? Is it more the rule than the exception for the most intense disagreements to occur between individuals and groups who would seem, from an outsider's point of view, to be on the same side? When this sort of split occurs, does it weaken both of the contesting groups, making them susceptible to the strategy of "divide and conquer"? Or is this disagreement a sign of vitality and a welcome proof that people care very much about these issues?

So what are the criticisms of restoration?

First, people who are enthusiasts for natural preservation object to the undisguised and unconcealed centrality of human preference and activity in restoration. Restoration means an active deployment of human design and intervention. As Throop puts it, "restoration often involves invasive human alteration and control, which seems the antithesis of the natural."[10] Thus, loyalists to the ideal of untouched nature operating without the taint of human meddling are not going to find much to like in a restored site. "Critics worry," writes Higgs, "that restoration will dilute our efforts at preservation and conservation and lead to an even deeper technological attitude toward nature."[11]

To people who prefer the pristine, a restored landscape will never match a landscape emerging from the process of evolution over centuries and millennia. It will always bear the mark of human manipulation and intervention. In an influential essay first published in 1982, Robert Elliot made an energetic case for the similarity between a restored landscape and a forged work of art, titling his essay "Faking Nature." One essential component for which we assign value in an object, he argues, is its origin. If he had been told that he owned an original work of art, and he then learned that what he had was just an exact replica, the value he placed on his possession would plummet. "Any attempt to allay my disappointment by insisting that there just is no difference between the replica and the original misses the mark completely. . . . The difference, of course, lies in the painting's genesis." Compared to a natural landscape brought into being by the processes of evolution, a restored landscape would be by comparison a fake, unavoidably diminished in value.[12]

Western Conversational Opportunity Number 2

There is no question that restoration is far from a simple matter of putting nature back into its original state; the roles of human will, preference, and action are unmistakable. Just for the exercise, whether you agree with this interpretation or not, practice making the argument that this central role for human beings discredits restoration. How much meaning is left in the ideal of a pristine world of nature uncontaminated by human interference? Given that every part of the planet, except Antarctica, had a significant degree of human habitation long before the era of European imperialism, how workable is the concept of a natural site unchanged by human activity? Does the comparison between a forged work of art and a restored landscape strike you as convincing?

To some critics, the project of restoration reaffirms and reinforces the anthropocentric overconfidence that got us into the soup in the first place. Many of the injuries and wounds addressed in this book originated in actions undertaken with the arrogant conviction that experts and specialists exercise the most justified and decisive power over nature and other people. Inevitably associated with white-coated authorities who know what's best for their patients, the metaphor of healing seems to embrace and defer to exactly that same arrogant belief that human beings are totally in charge and perfectly equipped to redesign and reengineer both natural and human communities. And yet Higgs makes the case for the power of restoration to counteract arrogance: "Acknowledging our role as designers of ecological and social processes lends humility to the already-daunting challenge of restoration. In the end it would be a failure if we did not recognize that the reality of nature and society are [sic] greater than our capacity to understand and manipulate them."[13] Rather than an affirmation and reconfirmation of anthropocentric arrogance, restoration might well be the treatment program and the cure as it reacquaints practitioners with the extraordinary complexity and sometimes intractability of the material and cultural world.

Western Conversational Opportunity Number 3

Is arrogance an incurable human condition? Will it submit to treatment and even to immunization? Is there any better antidote to arrogance or any better producer of humility than trying to match wits with an ecosystem in which so much complexity and so many elements work together to make a mockery of simple solutions and easy answers? And if there is a better way of producing humility, might it be the experience of having your most intense critics be those whom you expected to be your allies?

And now the argument gets very gritty. People who are already dismayed by the extent of the disturbance of natural systems by development feel that restoration offers aid and comfort to those who would take development even further. The better we get at restoration, this argument runs, the more license and support we will give to those who want to make messes in the present. Those who want to preserve intact nature believe that restorationists are undermining the rationale for preservation and for restraint on development. "Get out of our way, and let us go ahead and mine, drill, log, or graze," the advocates of development will be able to say. "Thanks to restoration, we know that you can always clean it up after we're through."[14]

Western Conversational Opportunity Number 4

Does the fear of opportunism *through* restoration seem justified? Is there a way of recognizing inadvertent implications in restoration's promises and guarding against them? Are there actually cases in which development would simply be stopped if reclamation didn't make it seem permissible and tolerable? Or might there be an advantage of beginning enterprises in the extraction of resources or the development of land with long-term plans for repair, remediation, and restoration already in place?

And now we attempt reconciliation. Would it be possible to scale down the struggle between preservationists and restorationists? Are they necessarily rival enterprises? As Higgs declares, "we are clearly running out of places for which preservation is a viable option."[15] Very few landscapes are free of human impact and influence; if preservation can operate only in certifiably pristine circumstances, it does not have much of a future. Consigning landscapes to a state beyond redemption because they have been affected by human use is in its own odd way emotionally kin to other practices of a "throw-away" society: buying a new car because the old one has acquired dents and a stain or two on the upholstery; building a new house because the old one has settled and developed a few cracks in the walls and tilts in the floor; tossing out a wardrobe because the fabrics have lost their crispness and the styles have surrendered their freshness of fashion. A more deliberate process of deciding when something is so "used" that it is beyond toleration and retention might well benefit us all.

Are preservation and restoration necessarily positioned at opposite sides of the boxing ring?[16] Asking the opponents of preservation to read and contemplate Joseph Ryan's chapter on the cleaning up of acid mine drainage from abandoned mines might provide a foundation for peace negotiations; it would be difficult to cast these well-intentioned efforts at healing the West as weakening or posing trouble for the cause of preservation. Meanwhile, McMahon and Holl have made an exemplary effort at bridge building by acknowledging restoration's flaws and deferring to the superior virtues of preservation: "Because restoration is difficult and often unsuccessful in restoring native ecosystem structure and functioning, restoration ecologists should stress the unparalleled value of preservation"; restoration should remain "a second choice to preserving more intact habitats and should not serve as an alternative to preservation." And then, in archetypal demonstration of the restorationist's commitment to making lemonade out of lemons, McMahon and Hall note that there are not many intact lands left for preservation, whereas "abandoned and degraded lands are increasing and may become some of the only lands available for conservation."[17]

Western Conversational Opportunity Number 5

Can the causes of preservation and restoration make peace and work together? Imagine yourself as a shuttle diplomat and negotiator. What peace terms would you propose to reduce the conflict and build a foundation for cooperation? Or is there a benefit to having the two constituencies challenging each other and thus keeping each other sharp?

Taxation and the Commitment to Community

In a world of limited funding, preservation and restoration must be pitted against each other. They are also, together and separately, pitted against projects in education, wars, infrastructure building and maintenance, emergency relief, and somewhat ironically, given our governing metaphor here—health care. As McMahon and Hall declare, "the primary factor limiting restoration efforts is typically funding."[18] When land managers are operating "with a finite set of resources and financial constraints, where should habitat be protected from destruction, and where should it be restored?" another group of authors ask.[19]

This matter of setting priorities and then allocating funding in line with those priorities is the toughest part of this whole enterprise. Therefore, reading over the chapters in this book, I came to feel a particular appreciation for Sarah Krakoff's discussion of the powers of the Navajo Nation to tax non-Indians. Taxation is a very prosaic matter, as Krakoff acknowledges, providing very little in the way of romance or drama.

It is most unlikely, as she writes, that Kevin Costner and his Hollywood colleagues are going to make a stirring movie about the tribal power to tax. And yet it is difficult to think of a power with greater consequence because the availability or unavailability of revenue (a.k.a. money!) will make or break the best-conceived undertakings of any community of people.

By focusing on the power to tax, Krakoff directs us to a crucial theme running through discussions of all the various undertakings in repair. Because these projects do not happen without funding, the exercise of the power of taxation is a crucial determinant of the viability of any and all projects that fall under the rubric of "healing." A willingness to be taxed is the most concrete way in which human beings declare their commitment to civil society and to common well-being. As Oliver Wendell Holmes said, "Taxes are the price we pay for a civilized society."[20] And yet the United States in the twenty-first century appears to be populated with citizens who do not see taxation in any such positive terms. The West may have a disproportionately high share of people whose attitude can essentially be characterized by the adjective *antitax.*

As the introduction to this book notes, restoration projects in the American West are very much intertwined with the federal government's land-management and regulatory agencies. With so much territory defined as public land under federal management, any question involving the repair of injury to nature or the correction of injustice done to Indian people will of necessity involve legislative, judicial, and executive branches of the federal government, especially the Department of the Interior in the latter. It will also lead us straight to the seemingly bland, but always highly charged term *federal funding.* Thus, American citizens' attitude toward taxation will always be an "independent variable" of great consequence as we try to imagine the role of restoration in the West's future. But here again we encounter the promise of restoration: these projects are intensely local, involving local communities and proximate forms of government; thus, nearly every restoration project provides an opportunity to experiment in the design of more productive relations between local authority and federal authority. One of the strongest features of this collection of essays is the recognition that the time is ripe for a redesign of the relationships between federal regulatory and land-management agencies, on the one hand, and private-property owners, on the other, as well as of the relationships among local, state, tribal, and federal governments. Wallis and Bressler make this point with particular sharpness, but in some form it figures in nearly every chapter.

Western Conversational Opportunity Number 6

What do we care about enough to fund collectively? Can we find ways of supporting restoration projects that bring federal, state, county, and municipal governments into an alliance with philanthropists, foundations, environmental groups, and stakeholder alliances? Or have we become, both regionally and internationally, an "antitax" people? Are there ways of recognizing American citizens' accumulated distrust toward governmental spending of tax revenue in ways that seem wasteful and inefficient or directed far from their own priorities, and then of creating trust?

Back to the Baseline

Setting the goal for an enterprise in healing would seem like an easy task. To repair the injury; to restore lost vigor, robustness, and resilience; to transform a bad situation into a good situation or at least a better situation: the goals should be easy to identify. Of all conditions that offer a dramatic and clear contrast, the state of being sick and the state of being healthy should be among the easiest to identify and distinguish.

Or so it seems until you try it.

The challenge comes packed into the term *reference condition*, the state of affairs at some point in the past in which things were better than they are now. As two conservation biologists put it, "What all of these activities have in common is an attempt to reestablish some ecological state and functioning believed to have characterized a site at some time in the past." These enterprises thus require their practitioners to "decide which time in the past should serve as the reference period."[21] The fading of the concept of a stable balance of nature and a parallel fading of the notion of pristine, place-based indigenous communities living in stable harmony with nature have made choosing a reference period into an enormously complicated exercise. "Ecosystems are dynamic," Throop puts it bluntly, "and the attempt to return to an earlier structure can appear as a naïve attempt to stop history or as mere nostalgia for a more innocent past."[22]

The Historical Ecology Handbook: A Restorationist's Guide for Reference Ecosystems, edited by Dave Egan and Evelyn A. Howell, addresses this problem directly, recognizing that every restorationist must ask the question, "To what period or time should I restore the site?" Egan and Howell make a useful modification to that question, recasting it to ask not which particular historical moment represents the goal to be recaptured, but "What was the historic range of variation in which the ecosystem or some sub-set of it operated when it was biologically diverse and ecologically healthful?" "Restorationists," Egan and Howell recognize, "are working with dynamic systems that are constantly changing over time and space, which makes the problem of developing and applying a reference model difficult and infuses it with a level of uncertainty."[23]

The selection of a reference period, for all its difficulty and uncertainty, may well be the most promising of the various topics restoration presents for public discourse. Asking ourselves what conditions in the past we would like to re-create offers a very fine opportunity to bring together the perspectives and knowledge of scientists and historians, Native peoples and the descendants of settlers, long-term residents and relative newcomers. The topic provides us with a great opportunity to be alert to and cautious about the ways in which nostalgia and a romanticized version of the past can get a grip on our minds and imaginations. In other words, choosing a reference period presents a fine opportunity to think—and to think expansively.

How far back in time will restorationists travel in their quest for a reference period? One group of conservation biologists has put forward a plan to import megafauna from Africa and Asia into North America, allowing these carnivores and herbivores "to repopulate the area where they lived until about 13,000 years ago." Reintroducing Bactrian camels and Old World cheetahs to areas in Arizona and the Great Plains, this plan for "Pleistocene rewilding" surely represents the most temporally ambitious vision of restoration currently in play.[24] Of course, climate change may pose the greatest challenge for this plan, as well as for many others involving smaller reaches in time: even if it were possible to restore and reintroduce departed species, transformed climate conditions make it unlikely that the populations of plants and animals of a past time can be replicated.[25] Nevertheless, some of the critics of the proposal for Pleistocene rewilding acknowledge the value of the proposal for enlivening public discussion. "It's not the usual scientific debate," wrote one such critic. "It's about a future direction of conservation biology; so you take it in the spirit of trying to figure out what's the best direction, and you go forward from there."[26]

Western Conversational Opportunity Number 7

Staying on high alert for the distortions of nostalgia, explore the desirability of recapturing some dimensions of the past. When were the good old days in the American West? What aspects of those days might deserve and reward our collective efforts at restoration? What standards—both of desire and of practicality—should govern our choice of "reference conditions"?

Borrowing the Doctor's Troubles: Metaphor, Heal Thyself

With the phrase "healing the West," we have picked (in some moments, "saddled ourselves with" seems more appropriate) an analogy that presents complications. The idea of healing initially presents itself as a wonderful metaphor—positive, illuminating, and heartening. But then, when you start to work through its implications, the medical analogy can transform itself into more of an irritant than a remedy. If we take as our model the practices that characterize much of twenty-first-century medical healing, are we going to recommend a battery of expensive, minimally revealing X rays, scans, and lab tests before we take any action? Are we going to prescribe for the region's troubles some equivalent to the cascade of high-priced pharmaceuticals that characterize much of today's actual health care? Will we put restoration and remediation projects in the West through the same process of wrangling that is often required to get payment for a needed procedure? Should the aspiring healers of the West seek out the equivalent of malpractice insurance and prepare for an onslaught of lawsuits?

In the minds of many articulate and audible policy analysts, the American health-care system in the early twenty-first century is a big mess. The system absorbs vast amounts of the nation's money; millions of people remain uninsured, heading toward the brink of financial calamity if stricken with serious illness; doctors flub now and then with failures in diagnosis; operations are sometimes performed on the wrong side of the body; physicians lament their vulnerability to charges of malpractice and to the distractions of mountains of paperwork; the nation faces an alarming shortage of nurses; and a societal inclination toward the denial of death keeps doctors captive to a point of view by which death represents their defeat rather than an unavoidable dimension of the human condition. In this context, the early twenty-first century might strike thoughtful readers as an ironic time to choose a medical metaphor for the work described in these chapters.

Western Conversational Opportunity Number 8

To what degree does the word *healing* make sense when applied to the West? Does the heavy baggage carried by the current American health-care system gum up the works when we try to think clearly about doing the right thing by the West's ecosystems and communities? Despite all the lamentation over the state of the health-care system, are there not plenty of current examples of medical care that work and that improve the quality of people's lives in astonishing ways?

Fortunately, we are not the first to puzzle over the advantages and disadvantages presented by this metaphor. In the most striking way, some writers have given this analogy a real workout, comparing what health means in organisms and what health means in ecosystems, and even exploring the ways in which medical practices such as triage or palliative care might guide and illuminate the management of landscapes and ecosystems.[27] Used as a metaphor, the term *health* in fact invites collaboration and communication between and among traditional disciplines and specializations: "Plainly, this concept cannot be defined or understood simply in biological or ethical or aesthetic or historical terms."[28] And perhaps most important, others have noted that pinning a precise definition on the word *health* has a particular capacity to surprise novices with its difficulty: "Health is one of those difficult concepts that everyone thinks they can define, until they come to try."[29]

Where did this complicated metaphor get launched? As is often the case in matters of conservation, the main road leads back to Aldo Leopold. Writing of his aspirations for better human relationships with nature and land, Leopold contrasted "land health" with "land sickness." As a definition of land health, he offered the still useful and thought-provoking concept of a capacity for "self-renewal." But other dimensions of Leopold's thinking on the matter have come in for challenge. He thought of wilderness as representing the "base-datum for land health"; in the years since he wrote this description, however, the idea of wilderness as an unchanging zone of natural balance untouched by humans has come in for hearty critique. And he sometimes cast natural systems as organisms, drawing an exact equivalence between the healing of a person and the healing of an ecosystem.[30]

Mainstream scientific opinion now rejects the idea that ecosystems are or resemble organisms. Because healing the human body means treating a defined, bounded organism, proponents of the metaphor must first assert that it does not require its users to think of an ecosystem as an organism. Those who support the use of the metaphor thus go to considerable trouble to "reject the concepts of ecosystems as superorganisms and as homeostatic [stable and unchanging] systems."[31]

Similarly, some critics of the metaphor assert that the meaning of human health is much clearer—and much more easily defined by norms, which makes possible the acquisition of objective, measurable evidence—than the meaning of ecosystem health. Those responding to this criticism make a telling point, though: "It is a much misunderstood aspect of the health sciences," writes David Rapport, who has become one of the most committed champions of the medical analogy, "that one often has the impression that human health determinations are wholly objective—a simple matter of clinical test results." But biomedicine involves matters of subjectivity, just as restoration ecology does: "While critics point to the non-scientific aspects (i.e., the value judgments that go into defining 'health'), this is part of the reality of both human medicine and ecosystem medicine, and in this sense is a strength rather than a weakness of the metaphor."[32] In other words, one benefit of the medical metaphor is its valuable service in reminding us that questions of values run through scientific inquiries, whether in biomedicine or ecology, once we take up the project of identifying the lessons we are to learn from the findings.

Those who support the use of the metaphor often rest their case on a claim of its power in public communication. "We all have personal knowledge about health and illness," one group of authors notes, "and this makes the ecosystem analogy so potentially powerful."[33] "The health metaphor is ideally suited to foster communication between scientists, the public and politicians and administrators," writes Rapport. "Therefore, the power of the metaphor rests on its capacity to convey the notion of ecosystem integrity and threats to ecosystem sustainability owing to easily made associations with the human condition."[34] In another article, he declares, "[The metaphor] has provided a powerful language by which to convey major environmental concerns in a focused, action-oriented way."[35] Another commentator observes, "People seem to relate to the analogy" between conservation practices and "restoring the human body and are intrigued by the similarities between the two processes."[36] Or, as J. A. Harris and R. J. Hobbs, two long-time endorsers of the metaphor, put it, "The ecosystem health concept is one way in which humanity can be conceptually 'corralled' into the consideration of the system as a whole, in a language that politicians can understand."[37]

Of course, the metaphor presents complications by the very fact of its familiarity, but as Rapport puts it, "Adoption of ecosystem health as a societal goal and as a basis for a new approach to environmental management does not equate to acceptance of all aspects of human medicine."[38] We can, in other words, select and put to work the pieces and parts of the healing metaphor that work, and discard the pieces and parts that don't. And, as a recent experience helped me realize, we can recognize that current medical practice gives us much to choose from in building this analogy.

A year ago my right ankle took to looking puffy, though it didn't hurt. I decided to have the swelling checked out to forestall any greater problem. My primary care physician referred me to a rheumatologist, a pleasant young man who examined my ankle and agreed with me that it was swollen. He soon had me out the door, off to a round of tests: a blood test for arthritis ("But," I said, "isn't arthritis supposed to hurt?"); an X ray to see if there were any problems with the bones and their alignment; and then an MRI. My insurance company paid most of the cost of the MRI, but I was impressed to see that the charge for it was more than $3,000.

I then returned to the rheumatologist, who said that he had received all the test results. The blood test showed no indication of arthritis; the

X ray was normal; and the MRI showed . . . ready for this? . . . that there was swelling in the soft tissue of the ankle, a discovery that I had been able to make with an untrained eye.

The doctor said I could consider steroid shots and other such options. Inspiration hit me, and I asked for a referral to a physical therapist. And that is when both I and the metaphor of healing the West got our footing restored. The physical therapist asked questions about how my walking and the alignment of my feet might have changed in recent times. She examined not just the right ankle, but also the left ankle and the related knees, hips, and back. She pointed out problems of alignment and uneven muscle strength; she put pressure here and there; she sent me home with a series of exercises to correct—over time!—my dysfunctions; she engaged in "adaptive management," having me return for inspection and modifying her instructions accordingly

The ankle stopped swelling, and with a price tag that never approached the cost of the time spent with the MRI machine.

So the physical therapist gave me a pepped-up, positive, and cost-effective way of thinking about healing.[39] The chapters in this volume propose actions that are, thank heavens, much more closely matched to the methods of the physical therapist than to the methods of the rheumatologist (though it is important to say that many physicians are closer to the physical therapist than to the rheumatologist in their approaches to patients!). The physical therapist's approach—asking questions about history, observing in an unhurried way, noting the distinctiveness of the organism under examination, looking at how the parts of that organism fit together (or didn't), and designing exercises that built strength and corrected unfortunate old habits—comes much closer to the concept of healing celebrated in this volume than does high-tech, high-expense medicine.

Western Conversational Opportunity Number 9

What would you keep and what would you discard in the project of using medicine as an analogy or metaphor for the project of repairing historical injuries? In our preoccupation with the metaphor of healing, have we failed to notice and seize on better and more productive metaphors for these undertakings?

First, Do No Harm

Sometimes presented as a creative and innovative new strategy for a new millennium, the practice called "restoration"—in many ways, the central activity driving the "healing of the West"—actually has the most pedestrian, terrestrial, commonsense meaning: cleaning up, repairing, correcting old wrongs, making amends. Rather than a very original approach showing smart people's extreme cleverness, restoration's best justifications and explications have registered in the form of literature known as platitudes, aphorisms, and popular sayings. "No use crying over spilled milk" provides the foundational ideology for the enterprise: no use crying, but every good reason to grab a rag and get to work cleaning up the spill. And Reinhold Niebuhr's ultrapopularized prayer, sold on greeting cards and wall plaques in hundreds of gift shops, does a spectacular job of summing up the guiding principle of restoration work: "Grant me the serenity to accept the things I cannot change, the courage to change the things I can, and the wisdom to know the difference." As cutting-edge undertakings go, restoration is curiously old hat and clichéd in its conceptual underpinnings, and it may thereby be comfortable and easy to accept. Unlike some social causes that seem to rub the public's fur the wrong way, restoration grows in the same direction as some of our most venerable and moss-laden old sayings.

And this brings us to the most relevant platitudes of all: "Look before you leap," "Act in haste, repent at leisure," and "An ounce of prevention is worth a pound of cure." We have declared repeatedly in this book that we will not waste our time blaming the historical figures who created the troubles at which we now direct our efforts at healing. The fact that we make this declaration repeatedly offers its own testimony that the blaming of those departed and out of our reach remains, nonetheless, a real temptation! This realization should, at the least, help us think that it would be nice if our successors on the planet were to feel less of that temptation when they look back at us. Why not do all we can to conduct ourselves in a manner that will produce fewer lesions that our successors in the region need to heal? Why not give posterity fewer temptations to condemn us? Why not court the good opinion of those who follow us? As other commentators have observed, the most important use of the metaphor of health, applied to ecosystems or to human communities, may well be to direct our efforts to the equivalent of preventative health care, looking for early warning signs and taking action before things get serious.

Over thirty years of teaching, I have told hundreds of students to avoid using long quotations, assuring them that every normal reader impatiently skips over those long indented blocks in order to get back to the main action of the text. But over those same thirty years, I myself have reread and admired one particular long quotation from Lord James Bryce's *American Commonwealth* (1888), a book drawn from his impressions on visiting the United States on several occasions. In this passage, Lord Bryce conveys his impression of the West as a region stocked with people in a hurry. He then sketches the speech he found himself wanting to give to these racing and rushing westerners:

> This constant reaching forward to and grasping at the future [expresses itself] in the air of ceaseless haste and stress which pervades the West. . . . Time seems too short for what [westerners] have to do, and [the] result always to come short of their desire. One feels as if caught and whirled along in a foaming stream, chafing against its banks, such is the passion of these men to accomplish in their own life-times what in the past it took centuries to effect. Sometimes in a moment of pause, for even the visitor finds himself infected by the all-pervading eagerness, one is inclined to ask them: "Gentlemen, why in heaven's name this haste? You have time enough. No enemy threatens you. No volcano will arise beneath you. Ages and ages lie before you. Why sacrifice the present to the future, fancying that you will be happier when your fields teem with wealth and your cities with people? In Europe, we have cities wealthier and more populous than yours, and we are not happy. You dream of your posterity, but your posterity will look back to yours as the golden age. . . . Why, then, seek to complete in a few decades what the other nations of the world took thousands of years over in the older continents? Why do things rudely and ill which need to be done well, seeing that the welfare of your dependents may turn upon them? Why, in your hurry to subdue and utilize Nature, squander her splendid gifts? . . . You have opportunities such as mankind has never had before and may never have again. Your work is great and noble; it is done for a future longer and

vaster than our conceptions can embrace. Why not make its outlines and beginnings worthy of these destinies the thought of which gilds your hopes and elevates your purposes?[40]

Bryce's language certainly echoes with the rhetorical preferences of another era, but the relevance of his remarks seems little diminished. Each time I encounter the quotation, I wish I could persuade westerners to open their various public meetings—of legislatures, county commissioners, regulatory boards, and so on—by reading this passage aloud. I wish I could persuade westerners to keep a photocopy on hand to share with family, friends, and coworkers on some regular and repeating schedule. Bryce's plea invites us to moderate our pace, to think about our actions in a longer framework of time, to restrain ourselves when it comes to the creation of lesions that will be in need of healing in the future. His invitation is a fine complement to the invitation presented by this whole volume: to learn lessons from the past and to apply those lessons concretely and pragmatically to our decisions every day. Of all the chapters in this volume, the one most directed to "preventative medicine" is Allan Wallis and Gene Bressler's "'Oh Give Me Land, Lots of Land,'" a prescription for conducting suburban development in the manner least likely to leave messes for our descendants to clean up. It is time, as Friederici writes, to "fix what's broken, even if it's badly broken; time to clean up our mess and learn how to live so that we don't make too many new ones."[41] Lord Bryce might be expected to respond, "It's about time."

Scale and Duration of the Healing

Projects in healing the West often require practitioners to put a great deal of work into relatively small-scale projects that end up with seemingly small-scale results. Thus, the projects described in this book may provoke the cold-hearted but legitimate question, "Are these undertakings worthwhile? What do they add up to? Does the size of the improvement achieved justify the expenditure of effort?"

This question sends us back for another examination of the metaphor of healing. Let's say a sick or injured person goes to a doctor who has worked closely with a first-rate physical therapist and seen the wisdom of adopting her methods. The doctor reaches a diagnosis, prescribes treatment, and offers a prognosis. The sick or injured person follows the doctor's orders and then (we will make this a best-case scenario) gets well and lives for a while longer.

Even if the healing episode goes well, the doctor's success can never be more than temporary. Healed or cured of one affliction (or even of many), the patient remains under a death sentence. Healing, when it comes, if it comes, carries a stern expiration date. The ever-quotable rock singer Little Richard, seventy-four years old and confronting his own mortality, made this same point: "Never put a question mark where God has put a period."[42]

Applied to the projects featured in this book, this line of thought delivers us to a positive conclusion. When attempts at healing are applied to the afflictions of the human body, they are certain to fail in the long run. In comparison to that transitory success, when attempts at healing are applied to the costs and injuries left over from westward expansion, they stand a far better chance of success. As the stories told in this volume show, people are making meaningful progress at correcting the injuries of the past, and the zones and arenas of progress register in many dimensions of the West. All these projects are inspiring, moving, spirit lifting, faith restoring, and very interesting. They begin in regret. They can even begin in despair and grief. But they move on to positive action.

Transforming grief to positive action is an exercise that tests every part of the soul and mind. This is a matter on which I have acquired an unwelcome expertise. When we began this lecture series and when I wrote the first draft of this conclusion, I was married. When we finished this book, Jeff Limerick had died at age fifty-six from a stroke. The limitations of medical healing will never be far from my mind. With its utter irreversibility, death defeats us. But it also reminds us that being alive, endowed with the power to choose, is a great privilege that should never be taken for granted. Choosing restoration, repair, remedy, and reconciliation over drift, despair, and fatalism is one of the greatest ways to exercise and celebrate that power of choice.

Regret can curdle into bitterness and despair. Or regret can be transmuted into hope. As the "Healing the West" lectures and chapters have shown me, regret provides the foundation for hope. Having had the good fortune to work with the professors who have told their stories here, I am the holder of a visa that permits me to visit a territory where hope has found its habitat.

Notes

Foreword

1. Preamble to the Constitution of the World Health Organization as adopted by the International Health Conference, New York, June 19–22, 1946; signed on July 22, 1946, by the representatives of sixty-one states (*Official Records of the World Health Organization*, no. 2, p. 100) and entered into force on April 7, 1948

2. Francis W. Peabody, "The Care of the Patient," *Journal of the American Medical Association* 88 (1927): 877–82.

Prologue

1. Peter Friederici, *Nature's Restoration: People and Places on the Front Lines of Conservation* (Washington, D.C.: Island Press, 2006), 41.

2. Gregg Mitman, "Geographies of Hope: Mining the Frontiers of Health in Denver and Beyond, 1870–1965," *Osiris* 19 (2004), 94–95.

3. Dave Egan and Evelyn A. Howell, "Introduction," in *The Historical Ecology Handbook: A Restorationist's Guide to Reference Ecosystems,* edited by Dave Egan and Evelyn A. Howell (Washington, D.C.: Island Press, 2005), 3.

4. A common saying, but specifically attributed to Voltaire, *Dictionnaire philosophique* (1764).

5. Friederici, *Nature's Restoration,* 41

6. Egan and Howell, "Foreword," in Egan and Howell, eds., *Historical Ecology Handbook,* xxv.

Introduction

1. Leonard A. Brennan and William P. Kuvlesky Jr., "North American Grassland Birds: An Unfolding Conservation Crisis?" *Journal of Wildlife Management* 69, no. 1 (2005): 1–13.

2. William Cronon, *Uncommon Ground: Rethinking the Human Place in Nature* (New York: W. W. Norton, 1996).

3. J. Belnap and S. Warren, "Patton's Tracks in the Mojave Desert, USA: An Ecological Legacy," *Arid Land Research and Management* 16 (2001): 245–59.

4. D. P. Coffin, W. K. Lauenroth, and I. C. Burke, "Recovery of Vegetation in a Semi-arid Grassland 53 Years after Disturbance," *Ecological Applications* 6 (1996): 538–55.

5. D. R. Foster, "Thoreau's Country: A Historical-Ecological Perspective on Conservation in the New England Landscape," *Journal of Biogeography* 29 (2002): 1537–55.

6. D. F. Foster, F. Swanson, J. Aber, I. Burke, N. Brokaw, D. Tilman, and A. Knapp, "The Importance of Land-Use Legacies to Ecology and Conservation," *BioScience* 53 (1987): 77–88.

7. F. Gerhardt and D. R. Foster, "Physiographical and Historical Effects on Forest Vegetation in Central New England, USA," *Journal of Biogeography* 29 (2002): 1421–37.

8. Theodore G. Schurr, "The Peopling of the New World: Perspectives from Molecular Anthropology," *Annual Review of Anthropology* 33 (2004): 551–83.

9. Dave Foreman, *The Big Outside* (New York: Three Rivers Press, 1992).

Chapter 1. Healing the West with Taxes

1. For the larger study, see Sarah Krakoff, "A Narrative of Sovereignty: Illuminating the Paradox of the Domestic Dependent Nation," *Oregon Law Review* 89 (2004): 1109–38.

2. Peter Iverson, *Dine: A History of the Navajos* (Albuquerque: University of New Mexico Press, 2002), 33.

3. Ibid., 48–57.

4. Charles Wilkinson coined the helpful term *measured separatism* to describe the unique political status of American Indian tribes in the postcolonial United States. See Charles Wilkinson, *American Indians, Time, and the Law* (New Haven, Conn.: Yale University Press, 1982).

5. *Worcester v. Georgia,* 31 U.S. (6 Pet.) 515 (1832); *Cherokee Nation v. Georgia,* 30 U.S. (5 Pet.) 1 (1831); *Johnson v. M'Intosh,* 21 U.S. (8 Wheat.) 543 (1823).

6. *Worcester v. Georgia,* at 515.

7. *Ex Parte Crow Dog,* 109 U.S. 566 (1883); *Talton v. Mayes,* 163 U.S. 376 (1896).

8. *Lone Wolf v. Hitchcock,* 187 U.S. 553 (1903).

9. Felix S. Cohen, *Handbook of Federal Indian Law,* edited by Nell Jessup Newton (Charlottesville, Va.: Michie, 2005), 78.

10. Tom Tso, "1992 Navajo Nation Code of Judicial Conduct: Moral Principles, Traditions, and Fairness in the Navajo," *Judicature* 76 (1992), 15, 16.

11. See in general Institute for Government Research, *The Problem of Indian Administration* (1928; reprint, New York: Johnson Reprint Corp., 1971), 1–55.

12. See Vine Deloria Jr. and Clifford M. Lytle, *American Indians, American Justice* (Austin: University of Texas Press, 1983), 15–20, discussing termination-era policies.

13. See Sarah Krakoff, "Undoing Indian Law One Case at a Time: Judicial Minimalism and Tribal Sovereignty," *American University Law Review* 50 (2001), 1204–5, summarizing laws and policies encouraging tribal self-governance.

14. *Washington v. Confederated Tribes of Colville Indian Reservation*, 447 U.S. 134, 152–53 (1980).

15. *Merrion v. Jicarilla Apache Tribe*, 455 U.S. 130, 137 (1982).

16. *Kerr-McGee Corp. v. Navajo Tribe of Indians*, 471 U.S. 195, 200–201 (1985) (citations omitted).

17. *Establishing a Navajo Tax Commission and Amending Approved FY 1974 Budget*, Navajo Tribal Council Resolution CJA-6–74 (1974).

18. See Office of the Navajo Tax Commission, *History of the Navajo Tax Commission and Office of the Navajo Tax Commission*, available at http://www.navajotax.org

19. *Enacting the Navajo Possessory Interest Tax*, Navajo Tribal Council Resolution CJA-13–78 (1978); *Enacting the Navajo Business Activity Tax and Clarifying the Question of Compensation of Commission Members*, Navajo Tribal Council Resolution CM-36–78 (1978).

20. Navajo Tribal Council Resolution CMY-35–85 (1985).

21. See Navajo Tribal Council Resolutions CO-79–85 (1985), CJY-27–92 (1992), CO-107–95 (1995), CAU-85–99 (1999), and CO 84–01 (2001). The sales tax went into effect on April 1, 2002.

22. Amy Alderman, Legal Department, Navajo Nation Tax Commission, interviewed by the author, Window Rock, Ariz., December 10, 2003 (notes on file with the author).

23. Amy Alderman, Legal Department, Navajo Nation Tax Commission, interviewed by the author, Window Rock, Ariz., July 8, 2003 (notes on file with the author).

24. See Navajo Tribal Council Resolution CJY-53–85 (1985).

25. *United States v. McBratney*, 104 U.S. 621 (1881), recognizing state criminal jurisdiction over white-on-white crime in Indian country; *Maricopa & P.R.R. v Arizona*, 156 U.S. 347 (1895), allowing Arizona territory to tax railroads running through Indian country; *Wagoner v. Evans*, 170 U.S. 588 (1898), upholding county taxes on nontribal member cattle grazed in Indian country.

26. *Moe v. Confederated Salish & Kootenai Tribes*, 425 U.S. 463 (1976); *Washington v. Confederated Tribes of Colville Indian Reservation*.

27. *Washington v. Confederated Tribes of Colville Indian Reservation*, at 155, 157. The Court held that "principles of federal Indian law . . . [do not] authorize Indian tribes thus to market an exemption from state taxation to persons who would normally do their business elsewhere" (155).

28. See *White Mountain Apache Tribe v. Bracker*, 448 U.S. 136 (1980); *Central Machinery Co. v. Arizona State Tax Comm'n*, 448 U.S. 160 (1980); *Ramah Navajo School Bd., Inc. v. Bureau of Revenue of New Mexico*, 458 U.S. 832 (1982).

29. *Cotton Petroleum Corp. v. New Mexico*, 490 U.S. 163, 176 (1989).

30. Ibid., quoting *Ramah Navajo School Bd.*, at 838.

31. *Cotton Petroleum*, at 176–77.

32. Ibid., at 185. "[T]he District Court found that 'no economic burden falls on the tribe by virtue of the state taxes,' . . . and that the Tribe could, in fact, increase its taxes without adversely affecting on-reservation oil and gas development."

33. *Navajo Nation Sales Tax,* §605, "Rate of Tax"; Alderman, interview, July 8, 2003.

34. See Office of the Navajo Tax Commission, *FY 2004 Revenue Projection,* and actual revenue figures from fiscal years 2002 and 2003, October 13, 2003, on file with the author.

35. Alderman, interview, December 10, 2003.

36. Alderman, interview, July 8, 2003.

37. See H.R. 293, 2001 Leg., First Reg. Sess. (N.M. 2001), codified at *N.M. Stat. Ann.* §7-9-88.2, §7-29C-2, §11-12.2.

38. See Navajo Tribal Council Resolution CAU-67–01 (2001), approving amendments to the BAT to offset dual taxation of coal-extraction activities in the New Mexico portion of the Navajo Nation and acknowledging parallel state laws passed by New Mexico.

39. See *Ariz. Rev. Stat.* §42-3302 (tobacco tax credit provisions).

40. See ibid.; see also *Utah Code Ann.* §59-13-201 (2003), §59-13-204 (2003), §59-13-301.5 (2003).

41. *Oliphant v. Suquamish Indian Tribe,* 435 U.S. 191 (1978).

42. *Atkinson Trading Co. v. Shirley,* 532 U.S. 645 (2001).

43. *Merrion,* at 137, 139.

44. See *Buster v. Wright,* 135 F. 947, 957 (8th Cir. 1905), cert. denied, 203 U.S. 599 (1906).

45. See Brief for Respondents at 3, 14–15, *Atkinson Trading Co. v. Shirley.*

46. Ibid., 3–4.

47. Ibid., 7, citing *Merrion,* at 137–38.

48. From the Historic Cameron Trading Post Web site at http://www.cameron tradingpost.com/giftshop.html (March 2, 2004)

49. See 24 Nation Code §§101–42 (1995).

50. Alderman, interview, July 8, 2003.

51. See Navajo Nation Tax Commission, *Taxes Collected,* at http://www.navajotax .org

52. See Navajo Nation Tax Commission, *FY 2004 Tax Revenue Projection,* Attachment B, on file with the author.

53. Allan Sloan and T. J. Holgate, Navajo Nation District Court judges, interviewed by the author, Window Rock, Ariz., July 9, 2003 (notes on file with the author).

54. Marcelino Gomez, Navajo Nation Department of Justice, interviewed by the author, Window Rock, Ariz., December 11, 2003 (notes on file with the author).

55. Unlike natural-resource extraction, a tourist-based economy has no natural limitation. Tourism is therefore a renewable source of income and one that can be practiced in ways that do not harm the natural or cultural environment, particularly if the Navajo Nation itself is in control of the enterprise. But see Hal K. Rothman, "Pokey's Paradox," in *Reopening the American West,* edited by Hal K. Rothman, 90–121 (Tucson: University of Arizona Press, 1998), for an exploration of cultural challenges presented by fostering a tourism economy.

56. *Strate v. A-1 Contractors,* 520 U.S. 438 (1997).

57. Amy Alderman, Legal Department, Navajo Nation Tax Commission, interviewed by the author, Window Rock, Ariz., July 7, 2003 (notes on file with the author).

58. Luralene Tapahe, Navajo Nation Department of Justice, interviewed by the author, Window Rock, Ariz., December 11, 2003 (notes on file with the author).

Chapter 2. Indigenous Languages of the West

1. Algonquian (Arapaho, Cheyenne), Siouan (Lakota), Uto-Aztecan (Ute, Comanche, Eastern Shoshone), Athabaskan (Plains Apache, Jicarilla Apache), Kiowa-Tanoan (Kiowa), and Caddoan (Pawnee). Some of these tribes (the Pawnee, for example) used Colorado more as a hunting territory than as a place of regular residence, camping there for extended periods during these hunts, but then returning to areas in neighboring states. Of course, for nomadic tribes with overlapping use areas, the model of six language families in six separate areas is primarily suggestive rather than a hard and-fast statement of the situation "on the ground" at any given historical moment.

2. See Marianne Mithun, *The Languages of the Native North America* (Cambridge: Cambridge University Press, 1999); and Ives Goddard, ed., *Handbook of North American Indians,* vol. 17: *Languages* (Washington, D.C.: Smithsonian Institution Press, 1996).

3. Figures taken from Mithun, *The Languages of Native North America,* various pages.

4. The names and dates for these individuals are taken from ibid., various pages.

5. Goddard, *Languages,* 3.

6. See Deborah House, *Language Shift among the Navajo: Identity Politics and Cultural Continuity* (Tucson: University of Arizona Press, 2002).

7. This shift began as early as 1887 with the General Allotment Act, which broke up communal lands into individual holdings.

8. House Concurrent Resolution 108, passed in 1953, officially established a congressional policy of seeking to terminate federal responsibility for Indian tribes. The policy was pursued throughout the 1950s.

9. For more details on the history of Arapaho language shift, see Jeffrey Anderson, "Ethnographic Dimensions of Northern Arapaho Language Shift," *Anthropological Linguistics* 40 (1998): 1–64.

10. The linguist was Zdenek Salzmann, who has published numerous works on the Arapaho language, including a dissertation on the grammar (Indiana University, anthropology, 1963), and *Dictionary of Contemporary Arapaho Usage* (Riverton, Wyo.: Wind River Reservation, 1983).

11. President George H. W. Bush signed the Native American Language Act (P.L. 101–477) in October 1990.

12. Studies on native-language preservation are numerous and varied. A good place to start is with two books by Leanne Hinton, *Flutes of Fire: Essays on California Indian*

Languages (Berkeley, Calif.: Heyday Books, 1994), and (coedited with Ken Hale) *The Green Book of Language Revitalization in Practice* (Burlington, Mass.: Academic Press and Elsevier, 2001). Major organizations include the Society for the Study of Indigenous Languages of the Americas; the National Indian Education Association; the American Indian Higher Education Consortium, with the associated tribal colleges; and numerous smaller groups.

13. On some interesting Arapaho projects, including an Arapaho-language version of the Walt Disney film *Bambi* and a preschool immersion project, see Stephen Greymorning, "Reflections on the Arapaho Language Project" in Hinton and Hale, eds., *The Green Book of Language Revitalization*, 287–98.

14. On the Hawaiian experience, see Lois A. Yamauchi, Andrea K. Ceppi, and Jo-Anne Lau-Smith, *A Socio-historical Analysis of the Hawaiian Language Immersion Program* (Washington, D.C.: U.S. Department of Education, Office of Educational Research and Improvement, 1998). See also the 'Aha Pūnana Leo Web site at http://www.ahapunanaleo.org

15. See Hinton, *Flutes of Fire*, and Leanne Hinton, "The Master-Apprentice Language Learning Program," in Hinton and Hale, eds., *The Green Book of Language Revitalization*, 217–26.

16. See Darryl Kipp, *Encouragement, Guidance, Insights, and Lessons Learned for Native Language Activists Developing Their Own Tribal Language Programs* (Browning, Mont.: Piegan Institute, 2000; printed by the Grotto Foundation, St. Paul, Minn.), about his experience getting the Blackfoot Immersion Program up and running.

17. See Janine Pease–Pretty On Top, *Native American Language Immersion: Innovative Native Education for Children and Families* (Denver, Colo., and Battle Creek, Mich.: American Indian College Fund, supported by the W. K. Kellogg Foundation, [2002?]).

18. See Daniel Nettle and Suzanne Romaine, *Vanishing Voices: The Extinction of the World's Languages* (New York: Oxford University Press, 2000), and David Crystal, *Language Death* (Cambridge: Cambridge University Press, 2000).

19. The main federal programs supporting endangered languages are the National Science Foundation (NSF) Linguistics Program (which supports primarily academic research rather than strictly applied work and funds a few million dollars a year of work; an investigation of Recent Awards in Linguistics on NSF's Web site on February 15, 2004, revealed roughly fourteen projects, with a total funding of around $2.4 million); the Documenting Endangered Languages initiative (a partnership among the NSF, the National Endowment for the Humanities, and the Smithsonian, providing around $2 million dollars per year); and the Administration for Native Americans, Language Preservation Grants, which totaled slightly less than $4 million for fiscal year 2004. In contrast, a single program of the U.S. Fish and Wildlife Service, Endangered Species Grants to States, Territories, and Private Landowners, was funded at $6.9 million in 2005 (see http://endangered.fws.gov/grants), nearly equaling the funding for all three language programs. Moreover, private nonprofits such as The Nature Conservancy dwarf equivalent groups such as the Endangered Language Fund.

20. See, for example, N. Dennison, "Language Death or Language Suicide?" *International Journal of the Sociology of Language* 12 (1977): 13–22.

21. House, *Language Shift among the Navajo.*

Chapter 3. "Oh Give Me Land, Lots of Land"

The chapter title comes from the song "Don't Fence Me In" (1934) by Cole Porter and Robert Fletcher.

1. R. Bruegmann, *Sprawl: A Compact History* (Chicago: University of Chicago Press, 2005). Also see S. Stanley, *Smarter Growth: Market-Based Strategies for Land Use Planning in the 21st Century* (Westport, Conn.: Greenwood Press, 2001).

2. D. Hayden, *A Field Guide to Sprawl* (New York: W. W. Norton, 2004).

3. C. Howe, "Balancing Development in the West," *Urban Land* (April 2006), 8.

4. W. Stegner, *Beyond the Hundredth Meridian: John Wesley Powell and the Second Opening of the West* (New York: Houghton Mifflin, 1954).

5. Gilpin's book, *The Central Gold Region: The Grain, Pastoral, and Gold Regions of North America with Some New Views of Its Physical Geography and Observations on the Pacific Railroad,* followed the general thesis of Thomas Benton's Manifest Destiny, which proclaimed that the United States was destined to spread from "sea to shining sea."

6. R. W. Burchell, G. Lowenstein, W. R. Dolphin, C. C. Galley, A. Downs, S. Seskin, K. Gray Still, et al., *Cost of Sprawl 2000* (Washington, D.C.: National Academy Press, 2002), preface.

7. Attempts to document the assumption that sprawl fails to pay its own way date back to 1958 with the first so-called cost-of-sprawl study conducted by the Urban Land Institute.

8. For example, a 1994 study in Loudon County, Virginia, estimated that a new home would have to sell at $400,000 in order to bring in sufficient property taxes to cover the cost of services provided by the county, but the actual selling price of homes at that time was slightly less than $200,000.

9. Burchell et al., *Cost of Sprawl,* 21.

10. Ibid., 66, table 3.2.

11. Ibid., 81, table 3.16.

12. Ibid., 93, table 4.7.

13. Ibid., 95.

14. J. Gelt, "Sharing Colorado River Water: History, Public Policy, and the Colorado River Compact," *Arroyo* 10, no. 1 (August 1997), available at http://cals.arizona.edu/AZWATER/arroyo/101comm.html

15. See D. Porter, *The Practice of Sustainable Development* (Washington, D.C.: Urban Land Institute, 2000).

16. See K. T. Jackson, *Crabgrass Frontier: The Suburbanization of the United States* (New York: Oxford University Press, 1985).

17. H. Gans, *The Levittowners: Ways of Life and Politics in a New Suburban Community* (New York: Pantheon, 1967).

18. M. Mayer, *The Builders: Houses, People, Neighborhoods, Governments, and Money* (New York: W. W. Norton, 1978).

19. For example, Delta County, Colorado, works out development agreements with builders where exaction or development fees are based on what it will cost the county to extend additional infrastructure to the development.

20. Colorado offers something of an exception through its Areas of Critical State Interest statute (typically referred to as the "1041 review" based on the House bill that created it), which allows a local government to challenge the permitting of land use by an adjacent locality if the development will impact that government.

21. A. Best, "How Dense Can We Be?" *High Country News* 37, no. 11 (June 13, 2005), 3.

22. Ibid.

23. A. Berube, A. Snyder, J. H. Wilson, and W. H. Frey, *Finding Exurbia: America's Fast Growing Communities at the Metropolitan Fringe* (Washington, D.C.: Brookings Institution, October 2006), available at http://www.brookings.edu/reports/2006/10metropolitanpolicy_berube.aspx

24. See EcoCity Cleveland, *The Citizens' Bioregional Plan for Northeast Ohio,* in particular "Outmigration of Population," available at http://www.ecocitycleveland.org/smartgrowth/bioplan/outmgrtn.html

25. Comments made during an open-floor panel discussion during the first annual Challenging Suburbia Conference, "The Imperative for Design Quality," April 4 and 5, 2002, sponsored by the Colorado Community Design Network and the University of Colorado at Denver College of Architecture and Planning in cooperation with the Urban Land Institute.

26. Flipping homes often involves buying a home before it is built, then riding up market appreciation so that the home can be sold at a profit once it is ready for occupancy.

27. D. Hayden, *Building Suburbia: Green Fields and Urban Growth, 1820–2000* (New York: Knopf, 2004).

28. C. Fellows, president of Fellows Companies, interviewed by Gene Bressler, March 31, 2006, College of Architecture and Planning, University of Colorado, Denver.

29. Ibid.

30. See the Congress for New Urbanism Web site for a statement of the movement's principles and objectives, at http://www.cnu.org/

31. This quote was taken from the Stapleton Denver Web site at http://www.stapletondenver.com/

32. Gene Myers, "An Occurrence at Belle Creek," keynote address given at the first annual Challenging Suburbia Conference, "The Imperative for Design Quality."

33. See "Village Homes: Design and Philosophy," at http://www.villagehomesdavis.org/

34. For information on energy-efficiency mortgages, see http://www.pueblo
.gsa.gov/cic_text/housing/energy_mort/energy-mortgage.htm For information on
location-efficiency mortgages, see http://www.locationefficiency.com

Chapter 5. Recovering the West

1. The preceding facts come from the U.S. Census Bureau 1997, 2000, 2001, 2007.
The data are subject to sampling variability and other sources of error. Questions or
comments should be directed to the Census Bureau's Public Information Office (tel:
301-457-3030; fax: 301-457-3670; e-mail: pio@census.gov).

2. My discussion of the masking affects of maps benefits from Rogoff 2000.

3. My initial ideas regarding terra incognita began when I read Mary Pat Brady's
work *Extinct Lands, Temporal Geographies: Chicano Literature and the Urgency of
Space* (2002). Brady has also been extremely helpful in the conceptualization of the
chapter, and I thank her for taking the time to read parts of it.

4. Raul Villa (2000) and Mary Pat Brady (2003) make brilliant cases that geog
raphy greatly affects the constitution of Mexican peoples in the United States. This
chapter builds on their ideas by looking at the relationship between landscape, the
body, and the civic constitution of Mexican peoplehood. As such, I am not claiming
to be a geographer, but rather am engaging in the cultural debates concerning geographic and political knowledge.

5. I am well aware that the term *democracy* has become a relative term and that its
meaning is in crisis. My interest is in how the norms and ideals of democracy (rights,
the people, citizenship, and so on) are realized and understood through the imaginative production of cultural forms in the public spheres. Even though the cultural
forms I study do not adhere to one definition or ideology, I suggest that *democracy*
is not a relative term. Rather, the cultural forms I study indicate that democracy is
a political system whose meaning is in flux and is constantly debated. Hence, one
can argue that the logic and meaning of *democracy* reveals itself in a given culture's
rhetorical search for that meaning, a journey mediated by the culture's imaginative
productions. This is what I mean by the term *democratic culture*.

6. The United States also argued in this period that Mexicans were unable to work
the land into a viable capitalist resource and thus that they were unfit for democracy. Hence, Mexicans' relationship to the land became central to how they could be
viewed as political subjects.

7. For an important essay that looks at the function of the "Mexican Problem" in
American public policy, see Gonzalez 1998.

8. I have located more than five hundred essays that specifically use the phrase
"the Mexican Question." All of them have one common theme: they are implicated
in the idea of the U.S. landscape.

9. Antonia Castañeda's (2003) work on Mexican women and the land has been in-
valuable for my understanding of the gendered dimensions of the Mexican Question.
I thank her and all of the Chicana feminists who have done groundbreaking work in

this area, such as Emma Perez (1999), Alicia Gaspar de Alba (1997), Deena González (1998), and Mary Pat Brady (2003). Especially helpful was Casteñeda's "Malinche, Califia y Toypurina: Of Myths, Monsters, and Embodied History" (2003), which is an unpublished working paper. Without her assistance, this chapter would never have been completed.

10. For an excellent examination of John Gast's work and the cultural rise of Manifest Destiny, see Stephanson 1995, 66–67.

Chapter 6. Healing with Howls

1. G. Gerhardt, "I-70 Wolf Was New Arrival to State," *Rocky Mountain News,* June 25, 2004.

2. W. R. Travis, D. M. Theobald, G. W. Mixon, and T. W. Dickinson, *Western Futures Project* (Boulder, Colo.: Center of the American West, 2005), available at http://www.centerwest.org/futures/data_sheet.html; D. S. Wilcove, D. Rothstein, J. Dubow, A. Phillips, and E. Losos, "Quantifying Threats to Imperiled Species in the United States," *BioScience* 48 (1998): 607–15.

3. A. Leopold, "Thinking Like a Mountain," in *A Sand County Almanac* (London: Oxford University Press, 1949), 138–39.

4. J. Terborgh, "The Big Things That Run the World—A Sequel to E. O. Wilson," *Conservation Biology* 2 (1988): 402–3.

5. M. Soulé and R. Noss, "Rewilding and Biodiversity: Complementary Goals for Continental Conservation," *Wild Earth* 8 (1998), 22.

6. U.S. Department of the Interior, National Park Service, *Wolves of Yellowstone* (Washington, D.C.: U.S. Department of the Interior, 2007), available at http://www.nps.gov/yell/naturescience/wolves.htm Accessed October 22, 2007. See also http://www.nps.gov/yell/naturescience/wolfrest.htm

7. R. L. Beschta, "Cottonwood, Elk, and Wolves in the Lamar Valley of Yellowstone National Park," *Ecological Applications* 13 (2003): 1295–309.

8. W. J. Ripple and R. L. Beschta, "Wolves and the Ecology of Fear: Can Predation Risk Structure Ecosystems?" *BioScience* 54, no. 8 (2004): 755–66.

9. Ibid.

10. W. J. Ripple and R. L. Beschta, "Wolf Reintroduction, Predation Risk, and Cottonwood Recovery in Yellowstone National Park," *Forest Ecology and Management* 184 (2003): 299–313; W. J. Ripple and R. L. Beschta, "Wolves, Elk, Willows, and Trophic Cascades in the Upper Gallatin Range of Southwestern Montana, USA," *Forest Ecology and Management* 200 (2004): 161–81.

11. Soulé and Noss, "Rewilding and Biodiversity," 24.

12. R. H. MacArthur and E. O. Wilson, *The Theory of Island Biogeography* (Princeton, N.J.: Princeton University Press, 1967).

13. M. E. Soulé and B. M. Wilcox, eds., *Conservation Biology: An Ecological-Evolutionary Perspective* (Sunderland, Mass.: Sinauer Associates, 1980).

14. W. D. Newmark, "Legal and Biotic Boundaries of Western North American National Parks: A Problem of Congruence," *Biological Conservation* 33 (1985): 197–208.

15. M. L. Shaffer, "Minimum Population Sizes for Species Conservation," *BioScience* 31 (1981): 131–34.

16. R. F. Noss, "A Regional Landscape Approach to Maintain Diversity," *BioScience* 33 (1983): 700–706; L. D. Harris, *The Fragmented Forest: Island Biogeography Theory and the Preservation of Biotic Diversity* (Chicago: University of Chicago Press, 1984).

17. "Spine of the Continent" is a name coined by the Wildlands Project (http://www.wildlandsproject.org/). It includes five conservation-planning areas: Yellowstone to Yukon, two thousand miles of Canadian and American mountains including the Northern Rockies; the Heart of the West, including the sage covered basins of northern Utah and Wyoming; the New Mexico Highlands, where the Rocky Mountains, Great Plains, Chihuahuan Desert, and Great Basin meet; the Sky Islands, comprising forty separate mountain ranges in the midst of southeastern Arizona's deserts and grasslands; and the Northern Sierra Madre of Mexico, home to Thick-billed Parrots and jaguars, among other charismatic species.

18. Soulé and Noss, "Rewilding and Biodiversity," 22.

19. Ibid., 23–24.

20. An *ecoregion* is a large landscape area with relatively consistent patterns of topography, geology, soils, vegetation, natural processes, and climate. These natural patterns help create and influence the myriad smaller ecosystems nested within an ecoregion. The boundaries of the Southern Rockies Ecoregion and adjacent ecoregions are based primarily on scientific criteria developed by the U.S. Forest Service. Although the San Luis Valley and Upper Rio Grande area are technically part of the Central Shortgrass Prairie Ecoregion, and the Gunnison Basin is technically part of the Colorado Plateau, both areas are often included in the Southern Rockies Ecoregion for planning purposes because they are surrounded by the Southern Rockies and are closely tied to the Southern Rockies, especially in terms of animal migration. See D. Shinneman, *The State of the Southern Rockies Ecoregion* (Golden: Colorado Mountain Club Press, 2000).

21. Ibid.

22. See, for example, J. R. Strittholt and D. A. Dellasala, "Importance of Roadless Areas in Biodiversity Conservation in Forested Ecosystems: Case Study of the Klamath Siskiyou Ecoregion of the United States," *Conservation Biology* 15, no. 6 (2001): 1742–54; R. L. DeVelice and J. R. Martin, "Assessing the Extent to Which Roadless Areas Complement the Conservation of Biological Diversity," *Ecological Applications* 11, no. 4 (2001): 1008–18; C. Loucks, N. Brown, A. Loucks, and K. Cesareo, "USDA Forest Service Roadless Areas: Potential Biodiversity Conservation Reserves," *Conservation Ecology* 7, no. 2 (2003), available at http://www.consecol.org/vol7/iss2/art5/; M. R. Crist, B. Wilmer, and G. H. Aplet, "Assessing the Value of Roadless Areas in a Conservation Reserve Strategy: Biodiversity and Landscape Connectivity in the Northern Rockies," *Journal of Applied Ecology* 42, no. 1 (2005): 181–91.

23. See, for example, R. F. Noss, H. B. Quigley, M. G. Hornocker, T. Merrill, and P. C. Paquet, "Conservation Biology and Carnivore Conservation in the Rocky Mountains," *Conservation Biology* 10, no. 4 (1996): 949–63; J. Whittington, C. C. St. Clair, and G. Mercer, "Spatial Responses of Wolves to Roads and Trails in Mountain

Valleys," *Ecological Applications* 15, no. 2 (2005): 543–53; J. A. G. Jaeger, J. Bowman, J. Brennan, L. Fahrig, D. Bert, J. Bouchard, N. Charbonneau, K. Frank, B. Gruber, and K. T. Von Toschanowitz, "Predicting When Animal Populations Are at Risk from Roads: An Interactive Model of Road Avoidance Behavior," *Ecological Modelling* 185, no. 204 (2005): 329–48.

24. A. Treves, L. Naughton-Treves, E. K. Harper, D. J. Mladenoff, R. A. Rose, T. A. Sickley, and A. P. Wydeven, "Predicting Human-Carnivore Conflict: A Spatial Model Derived from 25 Years of Data on Wolf Predation on Livestock," *Conservation Biology* 18, no. 1 (2004): 114–25.

25. Shinneman, *State of the Southern Rockies Ecoregion,* 57.

26. Tom Kenworthy, "Bush Removes Logging Barrier," *USA Today,* May 6, 2005; Mike Anderson for the Wilderness Society, "Final Rule on Roadless Areas and State Petitions," May 5, 2005, available at http://www.lpfw.org/docs/RoadlessAnalysis.pdf

27. Brian Schweitzer, letter to President George W. Bush, June 7, 2005, available at http://www.newwest.net/pdfs/President_Roadless_Letter.pdf

28. Mark Clayton, "States Take on Feds over Environment," *Christian Science Monitor* 97, no. 220 (October 6, 2005): 1–4.

29. U.S. Fish and Wildlife Service, *National Survey of Fishing, Hunting, and Wildlife-Associated Recreation* (Washington, D.C.: U.S. Fish and Wildlife Service, 2002).

30. Outdoor Industry Association, at http://www.outdoorindustry.org/search .php?wm=sub&q=Colorado

31. G. S. Alward, J. R. Arnold, M. J. Niccolucci, and S. A. Winter, *Evaluating the Economic Significance of the USDA Forest Service Strategic Plan (2000 Revision): Methods and Results for Programmatic Evaluations,* U.S. Department of Agriculture Forest Service Inventory and Monitoring Report no. 6 (Fort Collins, Colo.: U.S. Department of Agriculture, 2003).

32. Wilderness Society, *An Economic Boon: Protecting National Forest Roadless Areas in Colorado* (Washington, D.C.: Wilderness Society, 2000). Also see Colorado Department of Labor and Employment, Division of Employment and Training, Labor Market Information Sector, *Colorado Employment and Wages, ES202, Annual Averages 2002,* available at http://www.coworkforce.com/lmi/es202/2002PDF/ 2002_All.pdf

33. See, for example, Thomas M. Power, *Lost Landscapes and Failed Economies: The Search for a Value of Place* (Covelo, Calif.: Island Press, 1996); and Thomas M. Power and Richard Barrett, *Post-cowboy Economics: Pay and Prosperity in the New West* (Covelo, Calif.: Island Press, 2001).

34. Southern Rockies Ecosystem Project (SREP), *Linking Colorado's Landscapes: Phase I Report* (Denver: SREP, 2005).

35. Southern Rockies Ecosystem Project (SREP), *Linkage Assessment Methodology and Recommendations Development, Linking Colorado's Landscapes: Phase II Report* (Denver: SREP, 2006).

36. SREP, http://www.restoretherockies.org/ (accessed October 22, 2007).

37. For example, SREP was recently funded by the Seattle-based Brainerd Foundation to develop and host a wildlife crossings course along the I-90 corridor in the North Cascades. See http://www.brainerd.org or http://www.brainerd.org/grantees/grantee_ search.php?ID=00238

38. Sinapu, "Wolves Welcome in Western Colorado and North Central New Mexico: Survey Finds 66% Bi-partisan Support for Wolf Restoration," 2007.

39. Colorado Division of Wildlife, "Gray Wolf: Overview," updated June 12, 2008, available at http://wildlife.state.co.us/WildlifeSpecies/SpeciesOfConcern/Mammals/GrayWolf.htm

40. Colorado Division of Wildlife, "Probable Wolf Sighting along Colorado Wyoming Border," March 3, 2006, available at http://wildlife.state.co.us/newsapp/press.asp?pressid=3780

41. Rocky Mountain National Park, *Elk and Vegetation Management Plan* (Estes Park, Colo.: Rocky Mountain National Park, 2006), available at http://www.nps.gov/romo/parkmgmt/elkvegetation.htm (accessed October 22, 2007).

42. U.S. National Park Service and Rocky Mountain National Park, *Elk and Vegetation Management Plan/EIS* (Washington, D.C., and Estes Park, Colo.: U.S. National Park Service and Rocky Mountain National Park, 2006), available at http://www.nps.gov/romo/planning/elkvegetation/index.htm

43. Rocky Mountain National Park, at http://www.nps.gov/romo

44. Quoted in Elizabeth Royte, "Wilding America," *Discover Magazine,* September 1, 2002, available at http://discovermagazine.com/2002/sep/featwild

45. Rob Edward, "Proverbial Lone Wolf Spotted in Northern Colorado," *Wolves in the American West* (March 3, 2006), available at http://wolves-in-the-american-west.blogspot.com/

46. Ibid.

Chapter 7. A Scholar Intervenes

1. The book I carried was Susan Guyette's *Community-Based Research: A Handbook for Native Americans* (Los Angeles: Regents of the University of California, 1983).

2. Norma E. Cantú, personal communications with the author, July 2007.

3. I use the term *Hispano,* the Spanish for "Hispanic," in reference to the population of descendants of the original Spanish colonists who settled in New Mexico in 1598, led by Juan de Oñate. The term *Indo-Hispano* (used largely by local academics) refers to the particular mix of Spanish and local Indian heritage, but is in essence the same as the term *mestizo* or *Chicano. Chicano* is also another term for "Mexican American"; however, it is also a politicized term coined during the civil rights movement of the 1960s to signify pride in the land and in those whose sweat built the Southwest. Hispanos, who tend to self-identify in English as "Spanish," do not always identify as Mexican Americans or Chicanos, although they often self-identify in Spanish as "Mexicanos," Mexicans. This latter identification reflects Mexican rule of the region

following independence from Spain in 1820 and a general self-identification with the Spanish language and Mexican culture versus English and U.S. mainstream, white (Euro-American) culture. For further details on the evolution of the danza, see my essay "The *Matachines Danza* as Inter-Cultural Discourse," in *Dancing across Borders: Danzas y bailes mexicanos,* edited by Olga Nájera-Ramírez, Norma E. Cantú, and Brenda M. Romero (Chicago: University of Illinois Press, forthcoming), and other articles I have written on this subject (see notes 5 and 14).

4. Gertrude P. Kurath, with Antonio Garcia, "Matachines: A Midwinter Drama from Iberia," in *Music and Dance of the Tewa Pueblos,* by Gertrude P. Kurath, 257–78 (Santa Fe: Museum of New Mexico, 1970).

5. Brenda M. Romero, "The Matachines Music and Dance in San Juan Pueblo and Alcalde, New Mexico: Contexts and Meanings," PhD diss., University of California, Los Angeles, 1993, 44.

6. *Collins Online Dictionary,* available at http://www.delpiano.com/carnival/html/mattaccino.html

7. Ibid.

8. Such relationships include the primarily Pueblo groups, who predate Hispanos in the region by as much as forty thousand years, as well as Navajos and Apaches, Athabaskan speakers who migrated from the north and predate Hispanos in the region by three to five hundred years.

9. See Tomás Lozano, *Cantemos al alba: Origins of Songs, Sounds, and Liturgical Drama of Hispanic New Mexico* (Albuquerque: University of New Mexico Press, 2007).

10. Protestant denominations, in contrast, teach that traditional religions are demonic and thus prohibit their Native members from participating in traditional religions.

11. Ramón A. Gutiérrez, *When Jesus Came, the Corn Mothers Went Away* (Stanford, Calif.: Stanford University Press, 1991), 159–60.

12. Ibid., 139.

13. According to Américo Paredes, "Greater Mexico" refers to "all the areas inhabited by people of Mexican culture—not only within the present limits of the Republic of Mexico but in the United States as well—in a cultural rather than a political sense." See Américo Paredes, *The Texas-Mexican Cancionero: Folksongs of the Lower Border* (Urbana: University of Illinois Press, 1976), xiv.

14. See the following articles by Brenda M. Romero: "Matachines Music and Dance" (diss.); "Cultural Interaction in New Mexico as Illustrated in the Matachines Dance," including performance on accompanying compact disc, in *Musics of Multicultural America: A Study of Twelve Musical Communities* (no editors), 155–85 (New York: Schirmer, 1997); "The New Mexico, Texas, and Mexico Borderlands and the Concept of *Indio* in the *Matachines* Dance," in *Musical Cultures of Latin America: Global Effects, Past and Present,* edited by Steven Loza, 81–87, Selected Reports in Ethnomusicology, vol. 11 (Los Angeles: Regents of the University of California, 2003); "*La Danza Matachines* as New Mexican Heritage," in *Expressing New Mexico:*

Nuevomexicano Creativity, Ritual, and Memory, edited by Phillip B. Gonzalez, 61–83 (Tucson: University of Arizona Press, 2007); and "The *Matachines Danza* as Inter-Cultural Discourse."

15. By popular vote, the Pueblo reinstated its pre-Hispanic name "Ohkay Owinge," which means "Place of the Strong People," in November 2005. I retain "San Juan Pueblo" in this chapter because that was its name at the time I conducted fieldwork there.

16. My dissertation came on the heels of another dissertation published that year by a priest who had lived in the Pueblo and whose work translated biblical texts into Towa without the Pueblo's permission. My work also cited Elsie Clews Parsons, a 1920s ethnographer said to have stolen Jemez artifacts that later appeared in museums. I was told that the Pueblo had ensured that none of her works on Jemez would ever be reprinted because they were "misinformed."

17. See Romero, "Matachines Music and Dance" (diss.).

18. See Lucinda Coleman, "Worship God in Dance," *Renewal Journal* (Brisbane, Australia) 6, no. 2 (1995): 35–44.

19. See Robert Ricard, *The Spiritual Conquest of Mexico: An Essay on the Apostolate and the Evangelizing Methods of the Mendicant Orders of New Spain, 1523–1572,* translated by Leslie Byrd Simpson (Berkeley and Los Angeles: University of California Press, 1966).

20. See Enrique Lamadrid, Jack Loeffler, and Miguel Gandert, *Tesoros del espíritu: A Portrait in Sound of Hispanic New Mexico, with 3 CDs.* (Embudo, N.M.: El Norte, Academia Press, 1994), 28–29.

21. Francisco de Paula Valladar, *Fiestas del Corpus en Granada: Escrito por acuerdo del municipio para conmemorar las que se celebraron en 1886* (Granada, Spain: Imprenta de la Lealtad á Carge de J. G. Garrido, 1886), 34.

22. Randolph Padilla, personal communications with the author, Pueblo of Jemez, 1990.

23. Victor Turner, "Liminality and the Performative Genres," in *Studies in Symbolism and Cultural Communication,* edited by F. Allan Hanson, University of Kansas Publications in Anthropology no. 14 (Lawrence: University of Kansas, 1982), 28.

24. Victor Turner, "Comments and Conclusions," in *The Reversible World: Symbolic Inversion in Art and Society,* edited by Barbara Babcock (Ithaca, N.Y.: Cornell University Press, 1978), 287–88.

25. Randolph Padilla, personal communications with the author, Pueblo of Jemez, 1989.

26. Frank Fragua, personal communication with the author, Pueblo of Jemez, 1989.

27. See Francisco A. Lomelí, Victor A. Sorell, and Genaro M. Padilla, eds., *Nuevomexicano Cultural Legacy, Forms, Agencies, and Discourse* (Albuquerque: University of New Mexico Press, 2002).

28. For a discussion on the devastating effects that the processes of renaming had during colonization of the Americas, see Malena Kuss, "Prologue," in *Music in Latin America and the Caribbean, an Encyclopedic History,* vol. 1: *Performing Beliefs:*

Indigenous Peoples of South America, Central America, and Mexico, edited by Malena Kuss, ix–xxvi (Austin: University of Texas Press, 2004).

29. Enrique Lamadrid, personal communications with the author, 2000–2007.

30. "Las Matachines de Alcalde," available at http://www.webspawner.com/users/elainegarcia/ (accessed July 15, 2007).

31. Gutiérrez, *When Jesus Came,* 139.

Chapter 8. Cleaning Up Abandoned Hard-Rock Mines in the Western United States

1. Quoted in S. Pettem, *Red Rocks to Riches: Gold Mining in Boulder County, Then and Now* (Boulder, Colo.: Stonehenge Press, 1980), 3.

2. J. K. Aldrich, *Ghosts of Boulder County: A Guide to the Ghost Towns and Mining Camps of Boulder County, Colorado* (Lakewood, Colo.: Centennial Graphics, 1986).

3. M. W. Davis and R. K. Streufert, *Gold Occurrences of Colorado,* Resources Series no. 28 (Denver: Colorado Geological Survey, Department of Natural Resources, 1990), 44–50.

4. P. Smith, *A Look at Boulder from Settlement to City* (Boulder, Colo.: Pruett, 1981), 243.

5. Inscription on the plaque describing the statue memorializing Boulder County miners, Boulder County Courthouse, Boulder, Colorado.

6. Smith, *A Look at Boulder,* 68–69.

7. A. R. Wood, R. Cholas, L. Harrington, L. Isenhart, N. Turner, and J. N. Ryan, *Characterization and Prioritization of Mining-Related Metal Sources in the Streams and Streambed Sediments of the Lefthand Creek Watershed, Northwestern Boulder County, Colorado, during 2002 and 2003,* Report no. 04-01 (Boulder: Department of Civil, Environmental, and Architectural Engineering, University of Colorado, 2004).

8. Colorado Water Quality Control Commission, *Little James Creek and James Creek Nonpoint Source Study* (Denver: Colorado Water Quality Control Division, 1991); S. Bautts, I. Lheritier, and J. N. Ryan, *Assessment of Metal Contamination of Benthic Macroinvertebrates in the Lefthand Creek Watershed, Northwestern Boulder County, Colorado, 2005,* Report no. 06-01 (Boulder: Department of Civil, Environmental, and Architectural Engineering, University of Colorado, 2006).

9. U.S. Environmental Protection Agency (EPA), *Lefthand Creek Watershed Case Study: Use of NPL as Catalyst for Abandoned Mine Cleanup* (Washington, D.C.: U.S. EPA, November 3, 2003).

10. U.S. Environmental Protection Agency (EPA), *HRS Documentation Record, Captain Jack Mill,* Report no. SFUND-2003-0009-0074 (Washington, D.C.: U.S. EPA, 2002).

11. G. Klucas, *Leadville: The Struggle to Revive an American Town* (Washington, D.C.: Shearwater Books, 2004).

12. C. Hogue, "Counting Down to Zero: Debate Is Heating Up in Congress over Whether to Reinstate Superfund Taxes as Reserve Runs out of Money," *Chemical and Engineering News* 80 (2002): 31–34.

13. Lefthand Watershed Task Force, *Final Report to the Boulder County Board of Health* (Boulder, Colo.: Boulder County Board of Health, 2002).

14. H. S. Cobb, *Prospecting Our Past: Gold, Silver, and Tungsten Mills of Boulder County* (Boulder, Colo.: Book Lode, 1988), 23–29.

15. U.S. EPA, *Lefthand Creek Watershed Case Study*.

16. Wood et al., *Characterization and Prioritization*.

17. Quoted in M. Whaley, "Tiny Ward Defies Convention: EPA Met Its Match in Quirky Town," *Denver Post*, July 17, 2001.

18. Quoted in C. Barge, "Superfund Suggested for Some Old Mines," *Boulder Daily Camera*, March 12, 2002.

19. Quoted in ibid.

20. C. Barge, "Superfund Picks Up County Mine," *Boulder Daily Camera*, April 29, 2003.

21. Walsh Environmental Scientists and Engineers, *Final Remedial Investigation—Feasibility Study Work Plan, Captain Jack Mill Superfund Site, Boulder County, Colorado*, Project no. 5681–010 (Boulder, Colo.: Walsh Environmental Scientists and Engineers, 2004).

22. Quoted in Barge, "Superfund Picks Up County Mine."

23. B. A. Kimball, *Use of Tracer Injections and Synoptic Sampling to Measure Metal Loading from Acid Mine Drainage*, Fact Sheet no. FS-245-96 (Washington, D.C.: U.S. Geological Survey, 1997).

24. Wood et al., *Characterization and Prioritization*.

25. Colorado Mining Water Quality Task Force, *Report and Recommendations Regarding Water Quality Impacts from Abandoned or Inactive Mined Lands* (Denver: Colorado Department of Public Health and Environment, and Department of Natural Resources, 1997).

26. K. Custer, *Cleaning Up Western Watersheds* (Washington, D.C.: Mineral Policy Center, 2003).

27. G. Broetzman, *Barriers and Incentives to Voluntary Cleanup of Abandoned Hardrock Mine Sites* (Washington, D.C.: Colorado Center for Environmental Management for the U.S. Department of Energy, 1998).

28. Western Governors' Association and the National Mining Association (WGA-NMA), *Cleaning Up Abandoned Mines: A Western Partnership* (Denver: WGA-NMA, 1998), available at http://www.westgov.org/wga/publicat/miningre.pdf

29. Mark Udall, *Abandoned Hardrock Mines Reclamation Act*, H.R. 504, 108th Cong., 1st sess., 2003, available at http://frwebgate.access.gpo.gov/cgi-bin/getdoc.cgi?dbname=108_cong_bills&docid=f:h504ih.txt.pdf

30. General Assembly of the Commonwealth of Pennsylvania, *Environmental Good Samaritan Act*, House Bill 868, No. 1999–68 (1999).

31. AMD&ART, *Transforming Environmental Liabilities into Community Assets: An Interdisciplinary Initiative Re-creating Place* (Johnson, Pa.: AMD&ART, Inc., 1999), available at http://www.amdandart.org/

32. Ibid.

33. P. Kemp and J. Griffiths, *Quaking Houses: Art, Science, and the Community, a Collaborative Approach to Water Pollution* (Charlbury, United Kingdom: Jon Carpenter Press, 1999).

34. J. A. Kodish, "Restoring Inactive and Abandoned Mine Sites: A Guide to Managing Environmental Liabilities," *Journal of Environmental Law and Litigation* 16 (2001): 101–39.

35. S. T. McAllister, "Unnecessarily Hesitant Good Samaritans: Conducting Voluntary Cleanup of Inactive and Abandoned Mines without Incurring Liability," *Environmental Law Reporter* 33 (2003): 10245–64.

36. P. L. Younger, S. A. Banward, and R. S. Hedin, *Mine Water: Hydrology, Pollution, Remediation* (Dordrecht, Germany: Kluwer Academic, 2002).

37. J. S. Lyon, T. J. Hillard, and T. N. Bethell, *Burden of Gilt* (Washington, D.C.: Mineral Policy Center, 1993).

38. Rock Creek Alliance, *Investments in the Clark Fork River* (Sandpoint, Idaho: Rock Creek Alliance, March 23, 2004), available at http://www.earthworksaction.org

39. U.S. Environmental Protection Agency (EPA), *Meeting Community Needs, Protecting Human Health and the Environment: Active and Passive Recreational Opportunities on Abandoned Mine Lands* (Washington, D.C.: U.S. EPA, Superfund Redevelopment Initiative, 2002).

Chapter 11. Open Wound from a Tough Nuclear History

1. Todd Neff, "Uranium Part of New, 'Natural' Rocky Flats," *Boulder Daily Camera*, May 8, 2007.

2. The Office of Legacy Management was established on December 15, 2003. U.S. Department of Energy (DOE), "Legacy Management," available at http://www.doe.gov

3. "Flats Wildlife Transfer Sooner Than Expected," *Denver Post*, June 15, 2007. The "DOE-retained land" is designated on a site map on the Rocky Flats Web site, http://www.rfets.gov

4. Joe Legare, DOE Rocky Flats Project Office, comments at a public forum sponsored by the League of Women Voters, City Council Chamber, Boulder, Colo., January 26, 2005.

5. LeRoy Moore, "Rocky Flats: The Bait-and-Switch Cleanup," *Bulletin of the Atomic Scientists* (January–February 2005): 50–57.

6. DOE, "Legacy Management."

7. Katy Human, "Blast from the Past," *Boulder Daily Camera*, January 17, 1998.

8. Robert S. Norris and Hans M. Kristensen, "Nuclear Notebook," *Bulletin of the Atomic Scientists* (January–February 2005): 73–75. The authors estimate that

5,300 of the nuclear warheads are operational and another 5,000 are in reserve or inactive.

9. Len Ackland, *Making a Real Killing: Rocky Flats and the Nuclear West*, 2d ed. (Albuquerque: University of New Mexico Press, 2002).

10. Robert S. Norris, "Nuclear Notebook," *Bulletin of the Atomic Scientists* (November–December 2002): 103–4.

11. Len Ackland, "Rocky Flats II in the Works," *Denver Post*, September 14, 2003.

12. Dorothy Ciarlo, interviewed by the author, Boulder, Colo., January 16, 2004. Recent figures on oral histories are in Emily Tienken, "Project Reveals Long-Hidden Stories," *Boulder Daily Camera*, May 12, 2007.

13. Laura Frank, "Lawmakers to Appeal Vote on Nuke Workers," *Rocky Mountain News*, June 14, 2007.

14. George Orwell, *1984* (New York: Harcourt Brace Jovanovich, 1949; Signet Classic, 1969), 32.

15. Donald Worster, *Nature's Economy* (Cambridge: Cambridge University Press, 1982), 339.

16. Quoted in Ackland, *Making a Real Killing*, 158.

17. Ibid.

18. Ibid., 32.

19. Robert J. Lifton and Greg Mitchell, *Hiroshima in America: Fifty Years of Denial* (New York: G. P. Putnam's Sons, 1995), 308.

20. Tom Engelhardt and Edward T. Linenthal, "Introduction: History under Siege," in *History Wars*, edited by Tom Engelhardt and Edward T. Linenthal (New York: Metropolitan Books, 1996), 2.

21. Paul Boyer, "Whose History Is It Anyway? Memory, Politics, and Historical Scholarship," in Engelhardt and Linenthal, eds., *History Wars*, 118.

22. Marilyn B. Young, "Dangerous History: Vietnam and the 'Good War,'" in Engelhardt and Linenthal, eds., *History Wars*, 208 9.

23. Ackland, *Making a Real Killing*, 55.

24. Ibid., 44–50, 59–62.

25. Lifton and Mitchell, *Hiroshima in America*, 305.

26. Dow Chemical Company, the plant operator for the AEC, completed an official investigation report in October 1957 (which was classified "secret" until 1993), stating that 18.3 pounds of plutonium were unaccounted for after the fire. Independent scientists now estimate that a small amount of that, as much as 1.1 pounds, actually went up the smokestack and contaminated the surrounding area. Paul Voilleque, "Rocky Flats Plutonium Releases," presentation to the Colorado Department of Health and Public Environment, March 3, 1997. Mr. Voilleque confirmed this range of releases in a telephone interview by the author on August 5, 1998.

27. Quoted in Ackland, *Making a Real Killing*, 135.

28. Quoted in ibid., 137.

29. Wes McKinley and Caron Balkany, *The Ambushed Grand Jury* (New York: Apex Press, 2004).

30. Quoted in Ackland, *Making a Real Killing,* 238.

31. Ciarlo, interview, January 16, 2004.

32. A statement made by Greta Thomsen, communications specialist for Kaiser-Hill Co., LLC, at a meeting of the Rocky Flats History Project, Rocky Flats Plant, Arvada, Colorado, July 20, 2000 (author's notes).

33. U.S. Department of Energy (DOE), Office of Legacy Management, *Report to Congress: Rocky Flats Museum Options* (Washington, D.C.: U.S. DOE, December 2004), i. The final version of this report was not yet available at this writing.

34. I have received insight about the triumphal discourse at other museums from Bryan Taylor, an associate professor in the communications department at the University of Colorado at Boulder and former president of the Rocky Flats Cold War Museum.

35. Tienken, "Project Reveals Long-Hidden Stories."

Epilogue

1. William Throop, "Introduction," in *Environmental Restoration: Ethics, Theory, and Practice,* edited by William Throop (Amherst, N.Y.: Humanity Books, Prometheus Press, 2000), 12.

2. Bruce Babbitt, address to the Ecological Society of America, Baltimore, August 4, 1998.

3. Lee Clark Mitchell, *Witnesses to a Vanishing America: The Nineteenth-Century Response* (Princeton, N.J.: Princeton University Press, 1981), 5, 6–7.

4. This discussion focuses on efforts to make things right with the natural environment but neglects topics involving the healing of human communities. Later in the chapter, I give more thorough consideration to the similarities and differences between these two enterprises.

5. James A. MacMahon and Karen D. Holl, "Ecological Restoration: A Key to Conservation Biology's Future," in *Conservation Biology: Research Priorities for the Next Decade,* edited by Michael F. Soulé and Gordon H. Orians (Washington, D.C.: Island Press, 2001), 263.

6. Eric Higgs, *Nature by Design: People, Natural Processes, and Ecological Restoration* (Cambridge, Mass.: MIT Press, 2003), 2.

7. Dave Egan and Evelyn A. Howell, "Introduction," in *The Historical Ecology Handbook: A Restorationist's Guide to Reference Ecosystems,* edited by Dave Egan and Evelyn A. Howell (Washington, D.C.: Island Press, 2005), 2.

8. Peter Friederici, *Nature's Restoration: People and Places on the Front Lines of Conservation* (Washington, D.C.: Island Press, 2006), 42, 41, 37, and 44.

9. Higgs, *Nature by Design,* 2.

10. Throop, "Introduction," 17.

11. Higgs, *Nature by Design,* 2.

12. Robert Elliot, "Faking Nature," in Throop, ed., *Environmental Restoration,* 75. Eric Katz takes the case further, arguing that Elliot's comparison of a work of art to

a natural site distorts the otherness of nature and thus obscures the degree to which any human intervention reduces the quality of naturalness. Restoration, Katz says, is a matter of "putting a piece of furniture over the stain on the carpet, for it provides a better appearance. As a matter of policy, however, it would be much more significant to prevent the cause of the stains." See Eric Katz, "The Big Lie: Human Restoration of Nature," in Throop, ed., *Environmental Restoration*, 92.

13. Higgs, *Nature by Design*, 4.

14. Ibid., 3, 11. Higgs phrases the unwanted assurance this way: "If you destroy it, we can build it again." Or "we will end up destroying ecosystems precisely because we can build them up."

15. Ibid., 2.

16. One area of sensitivity on the preservationist side may arise from some restorationists' hope that restoration will supplant preservation and other soon-to-be archaic forms of environmental conviction. See William R. Jordan III, "'Sunflower Forest': Ecological Restoration as the Basis for a New Environmental Paradigm," in *Beyond Preservation: Restoring and Inventing Landscapes*, edited by A. Dwight Baldwin Jr., Judith DeLuce, and Carl Pletsch, 17–34 (Minneapolis: University of Minnesota Press, 1994). Throop summarizes Jordan's position: "William Jordan has argued that with enhanced public participation in restoration and with its ritualization, the practice can become a new paradigm for environmentalism, replacing wilderness preservation." Throop, "Introduction," 13.

17. McMahon and Holl, "Ecological Restoration," 246, 245, and 241. The Rio Declaration on Environment and Development confidently places preservation, conservation, and restoration on the same collaborative team: "States shall cooperate to conserve, protect, and restore the health and integrity of the Earth's ecosystems." Quoted in D. J. Rapport, R. Costanza, and A. J. McMichael, "Assessing Ecosystem Health," *TREE* 13, no. 10 (October 1998), 39.

18. McMahon and Holl, "Ecological Restoration," 259.

19. H. B. Possingham, S. J. Andelman, B. R. Noon, S. Trombulak, and H. R. Pullian, "Making Smart Conservation Decisions," in Soulé and Orians, eds., *Conservation Biology*, 226–27.

20. Reportedly said by Holmes in a speech in 1904, this statement is alternately phrased as "Taxes are what we pay for civilized society, including the chance to insure" (see *Compania General de Tabacos de Filipinas v. Collector of Internal Revenue*, 275 U.S. 87, 100 [1927], Holmes, J., dissenting, opinion published November 21, 1927). The first variation is given above the entrance to the Internal Revenue Service headquarters at 1111 Constitution Avenue in Washington, D.C.

21. Soulé and Orians, *Conservation Biology*, 6, 7.

22. Throop, "Introduction," 14.

23. Egan and Howell, "Foreword," in Egan and Howell, eds., *Historical Ecology Handbook*, xxiv, 5.

24. Eric Jaffe, "Brave Old World: The Debate over Rewilding North America with Ancient Animals," *Science News* 170, no. 20 (November 11, 2006): 314–16. Often

attributed to the hunting practices of new human arrivals, the cause of the Pleistocene megafauna extinction remains a matter of prickliness and sensitivity between contemporary indigenous people and nonindigenous scientists.

25. "Another, as yet unresolved but important, issue surrounds the use of historic ecosystems as reference models. This is the issue of the role climate plays in the historic model—and whether the contemporary climate is similar enough to make the historic data useful." Egan and Howell, "Introduction," 13. See also McMahon and Holl, "Ecological Restoration," 253.

26. Jaffe, "Brave Old World," 316.

27. Richard J. Hobbs and Linda J. Kristjanson, "Triage: How Do We Prioritize Health Care for Landscapes?" *Ecological Management and Restoration* 4, supplement (February 2003): S39–S45. "This approach builds on the emerging concept of ecosystem health, in which an ecosystem or landscape can be viewed as a patient, whose functions can be evaluated in terms of the system's organization, vigour and resilience" (S39). Of similar interest is the discussion of the degree to which the pursuit of ecosystem health should be a matter of prevention rather than treatment of existing degradation. It is also worth noting the most literal point of intersection between these two fields: in the "new field of conservation medicine," the subject matter is "the ecological aspects of [human] health and disease." See Gary M. Tabor, Richard S. Ostfelt, Mary Poss, Andrew P. Dobson, and A. Alonso Aguirre, "Conservation Biology and the Health Sciences: Defining the Research Priorities of Conservation Medicine," in Soulé and Orians, eds., *Conservation Biology*, 156–57.

28. Benjamin D. Haskell, Bryan G. Norton, and Robert Costanza, "Introduction: What Is Ecosystem Health and Why Should We Worry about It?" in *Ecosystem Health: New Goals for Environmental Management,* edited by Robert Costanza, Bryan G. Norton, and Benjamin D. Haskell (Washington, D.C.: Island Press, 1992), 3.

29. David J. Rapport, Connie L. Gaudet, and Peter Calow, "Preface," in *Evaluating and Monitoring the Health of Large-Scale Ecosystems,* edited by David J. Rapport, Connie L. Gaudet, and Peter Calow (Berlin: Springer, 1995), v.

30. See J. Baird Callicott, "Aldo Leopold's Metaphor," in Costanza, Norton, and Haskell, eds., *Ecosystem Health,* 47–49, from which the Leopold quotes come.

31. Rapport, Gaudet, and Calow, "Preface," v.

32. Rapport, "More Than a Metaphor," in Rapport, Gaudet, and Calow, eds., *Evaluating and Monitoring,* 297, 305.

33. Rapport, Gaudet, and Calow, "Preface," v.

34. Rapport, "Ecosystem Health: An Emerging Integrative Science," in Rapport, Gaudet, and Calow, eds., *Evaluating and Monitoring,* 21.

35. Rapport, "More Than a Metaphor," 304.

36. Valentin Schaefer, "Science, Stewardship, and Spirituality: The Human Body as a Model for Ecological Restoration," *Restoration Ecology* 13, no. 1 (March 2006), 3.

37. J. A. Harris and R. J. Hobbs, "Clinical Practice for Ecosystem Health: The Role of Ecological Restoration," *Ecosystem Health* 7, no. 4 (December 2001), 195.

38. Rapport, "More Than a Metaphor," 305.

39. I use my personal experience here with the recognition that the same point can be made with many other forms of medical treatment that consider the patient as a whole and not as a collection of fragmented symptoms.

40. James Bryce, *American Commonwealth,* vol. 2 (New York: Columbia University Press, 1954; first published 1888), 582–83.

41. Friederici, *Nature's Restoration,* 39.

42. Quoted in Ben Ratliff, "He's Frail, but Still Rocking and Preening," *New York Times,* January 17, 2007.

About the Editors

Sharon K. Collinge is an associate professor of biology and environmental studies in the Environmental Studies Program and the Department of Ecology and Evolutionary Biology at the University of Colorado. She is a conservation biologist and restoration ecologist whose research focuses on understanding the ecological consequences of human-induced changes to natural systems. Her work centers on the impacts of habitat loss, fragmentation, and restoration for the persistence of native species, and her research has included studies of plants, beetles, butterflies, small mammals, and prairie dogs. Current projects emphasize how urbanization affects dynamics of plague outbreaks in prairie dog colonies and the use of ecological theory to guide efforts to restore endangered plant species and communities within vernal-pool ecosystems. She is particularly interested in the interface between environmental science and policy regarding endangered species and habitat protection.

Collinge earned her PhD in landscape ecology from Harvard University in 1995 and joined the faculty at the University of Colorado at Boulder in 1998. She was named a 2004 Aldo Leopold Leadership Fellow in recognition of her outstanding leadership ability and desire to communicate scientific issues beyond academic audiences. In addition to her field research in Colorado and California, Collinge is pursuing new research on how human activities affect rodents and disease ecology in central Tanzania. She has published research articles in the journals *Ecology, Landscape and Urban Planning, Landscape Ecology, EcoHealth, Ecological Applications,* and *Ecological Restoration,* and her book length synthesis of the ecological effects of habitat loss and fragmentation is forthcoming.

Andrew Cowell is an associate professor in the linguistics, French, and Italian departments at the University of Colorado, where he specializes in linguistic anthropology and anthropological approaches to literature and verbal performance. His work in French and Italian focuses on medieval literature and society, and he has just completed a book entitled *The Medieval Warrior Aristocracy: Gifts, Violence, Performance, and the Sacred* (2007). His work in linguistics focuses on Algonquian tribes of Native America, in particular the Arapaho. He recently completed a bilingual anthology of Arapaho narratives in collaboration with an Arapaho consultant, *Hinono'einoo3itoono/Arapaho Historical Traditions* (2005) and a grammar of the Arapaho language, *The Arapaho Language* (forthcoming). Cowell directs the Center for the Study of Indigenous Languages of the West at the University of Colorado and has been active in many documentation and language-preservation projects.

Patricia Nelson Limerick is the faculty director and board chair of the Center of the American West at the University of Colorado, where she is also a professor of history. Limerick was born and raised in Banning, California, and graduated from the University of California at Santa Cruz in 1972. She received her PhD in American studies from Yale University. In 1984, she moved to Boulder to join the history department of the University of Colorado. In 1987, she published her best-known work *The Legacy of Conquest,* an overview and reinterpretation of western American history that stirred up a great deal of both academic and public debate and helped set a new course for the field. Limerick is also a prolific essayist, and many of her most notable articles, including "Dancing with Professors: The Trouble with Academic Prose," were collected in 2000 under the title *Something in the Soil.*

Limerick has received a number of awards and honors recognizing the impact of her scholarship and her commitment to teaching, including the MacArthur Fellowship (1995 to 2000) and the Hazel Barnes Prize (2001), the University of Colorado's highest award for teaching and research. In 1986, Limerick and University of Colorado law professor Charles Wilkinson founded the Center of the American West. Limerick and center staff are currently working on a number of projects, including a book about the role of the U.S. Department of the Interior in the West, an illustrated history of the Denver Water Board, and ongoing initiatives focused on energy and mining in the West. In every project, the center strives to help westerners turn historical understanding into the foresight necessary to confront the challenges facing the region. And in an era of political polarization and contention, Limerick and the center strive to bring out the better angels of our nature by appealing to our common loyalties and hopes as Westerners.

About the Contributors

Len Ackland is an associate professor of journalism at the School of Journalism and Mass Communication at the University of Colorado at Boulder and founding director of the Center for Environmental Journalism. He was previously editor of the *Bulletin of the Atomic Scientists,* which under his direction won the National Magazine Award in 1987. Before the *Bulletin,* he was a reporter at the *Chicago Tribune,* the *Des Moines Register,* and other publications. While at the *Register,* he won the George Polk Award in 1978 for local reporting. Ackland began his journalism career in 1968 as a freelance writer in Vietnam. He is author of *Making a Real Killing: Rocky Flats and the Nuclear West* (1999 and 2002). He holds a master's degree from the Johns Hopkins School of Advanced International Studies and a bachelor's degree in history from the University of Colorado at Boulder.

David M. Armstrong has taught at the University of Colorado at Boulder since 1971. He holds degrees from Colorado State University, Harvard, and the University of Kansas. At the University of Colorado, he has been a member of the Department of Integrated Studies, the Center for Interdisciplinary Studies, and the Department of Environmental, Population, and Organismic Biology (now the Department of Ecology and Evolutionary Biology). He is also a member of the core faculty of the Environmental Studies Program and a museum associate curator (mammals) at the University Museum of Natural History.

Armstrong's research focuses on biogeography, ecology, conservation, and systematics of mammals of the western United States and northern Mexico. He is author of *Distribution of Mammals in Colorado* (1972), *Rocky Mountain Mammals* (1975, 1987, 2007), and *Mammals of the Canyon Country* (1982), as well as coauthor of *Mammals of the Northern Great Plains* (1983), *Guide to Mammals of the Plains States* (1985), and *Mammals of Colorado* (1994).

Gene Bressler is professor and chair of the Department of Landscape Architecture at North Carolina State University. He previously served as chair of landscape architecture at the College of Architecture and Planning at the University of Colorado and as professor of landscape architecture at the University of Oregon. In 2006, Bressler received the Outstanding Administrator of the Year Award from the Council of Educators in Landscape Architecture, and in 2007 he was made a fellow of the

American Society of Landscape Architects. Bressler's research and teaching focus on issues of urban growth, sustainable development, and planning and design strategies for "challenging suburbia." In 2003 at the University of Colorado, Bressler founded the Colorado Center for Sustainable Urbanism, which convened Colorado Tomorrow conferences in 2004 and 2005. Bressler received his bachelor's degree in landscape architecture from the State University of New York College of Environmental Science and Forestry at Syracuse University, and his master's degree in landscape architecture from the Graduate School of Design at Harvard University.

Richard L. Byyny, M.D., is a first-generation college graduate. He received his bachelor of arts degree in history in 1960 and his doctor of medicine degree in 1964, both from the University of Southern California. He completed his internal medicine residency at Columbia-Presbyterian Hospital in New York and an endocrinology fellowship at Vanderbilt University. He was an assistant and associate professor of medicine at the University of Chicago and head of the Division of Internal Medicine. In 1977, he became professor of medicine, vice chairman of medicine, and head of internal medicine at the University of Colorado School of Medicine. He then served as executive vice chancellor of the Health Sciences Center, vice president of academic affairs, and chancellor of the University of Colorado at Boulder. He is currently professor of medicine and director of the Mentored Scholarly Curriculum and is involved in international health and education.

Hannah Gosnell is an assistant professor of geography in the Department of Geosciences at Oregon State University, where she is affiliated with the Sustainable Rural Communities Initiative and the Institute for Water and Watersheds. Her research interests have to do with the interconnections between demographic change, rural land-use change, water-resource-management change in the American West, and the ways in which laws and institutions might evolve to better reflect changing geographies. Gosnell has published her research in *Society and Natural Resources, Journal of the American Water Resources Association, Rangeland Ecology and Management, Natural Resources Journal,* and *Mountain Research and Development.* She holds a bachelor's degree in American civilization from Brown University and earned her master's and PhD degrees in geography from the University of Colorado in 2000. She then served as a professional research associate at the Center of the American West until 2006, comanaging the Ranchland Ownership Dynamics Project.

Sarah Krakoff is an associate professor at the University of Colorado Law School. She specializes in American Indian law and natural-resources law. Recent publications include a book chapter on reparations to American Indians, an article on the Navajo Nation's exercise of tribal sovereignty in the shadow of federal law, and several pieces on the U.S. Supreme Court's conceptions of tribal sovereignty. Krakoff is a contributing author to Felix S. Cohen's *Handbook of Federal Indian Law* (2005), the leading treatise in the field. She has also written about ethics and global warming, wilderness and recreation, and law and literature. She received a B.A. from Yale University and a J.D. from the University of California at Berkeley. Before moving to Colorado, she was the Youth Law Project director for DNA-People's Legal Services on the Navajo Nation from 1993 to 1996 and clerked on the Ninth Circuit Court of Appeals for Judge Warren J. Ferguson from 1992 to 1993.

William M. Lewis Jr. is professor and director of the Center for Limnology at the University of Colorado at Boulder and the associate director of the Cooperative Institute for Research in Environmental Sciences. He obtained his PhD from Indiana University and has been with the University of Colorado since 1974. His research and teaching interests include biogeochemistry, food webs, water quality, biodiversity, and ecosystem functions of inland waters, including lakes, streams, rivers, and wetlands. He is former president of the American Society of Limnology and Oceanography, former member of the National Academy of Sciences' National Research Council Board on Water Science and Technology, and current member of the Board on Environmental Studies and Toxicology. He received the Renewable Natural Resources Foundation for Sustained Achievement Award in 1996 and the Naumann-Thienemann Medal for research in limnology in 1998.

John-Michael Rivera is an associate professor of English at the University of Colorado at Boulder and creative director of El Laboratorio. He is a poet and scholar, and his most recent book is *The Emergence of Mexican America* (2006).

Brenda M. Romero holds bachelor's and master's degrees in music theory and composition from the University of New Mexico and a PhD in ethnomusicology from the University of California at Los Angeles. She has been a member of the musicology faculty at the University of Colorado at Boulder since 1988, originally serving as coordinator of ethnomusicology; she served as chair of musicology from 2004 to 2007. Her long-standing research focus is the *matachines* music and dance and its permutations throughout Latin America, including the U.S. Southwest and Mexico, and she has published numerous articles based on fieldwork as far south as Colombia. Her fieldwork focuses on the processes of culture contact and spirituality and their intersections with music. She most recently coedited, with anthropologist Olga Nájera-Ramírez and literary folklorist Norma E. Cantú, and contributed to *Dancing across Borders: Danzas y bailes mexicanos* (forthcoming).

Joseph N. Ryan is a professor in the Department of Civil, Environmental, and Architectural Engineering at the University of Colorado at Boulder. He is affiliated with the Environmental Studies Program and the Center of the American West. His teaching and research focus on the fate and transport of contaminants in natural waters. He is the author or coauthor of more than fifty peer-reviewed journal publications. He also coauthored the Center of the American West report *Cleaning Up Abandoned Hardrock Mines in the West: Prospecting for a Better Future* (2005). He came to Boulder in 1993 as a National Research Council postdoctoral fellow from the Massachusetts Institute of Technology, where he earned his M.S. and PhD degrees in environmental engineering. He earned a B.S. degree in geological engineering from

Princeton University. He lives with his wife and two Colorado-native children in the mountains northwest of Boulder.

Allan Wallis is an associate professor of public policy at the School of Public Affairs at the University of Colorado at Denver, where he has served as the director of the Wirth Chair in Environmental and Community Development Policy and currently directs the programs on local government. Wallis's principal areas of research are regional governance and growth management. He coauthored the monograph *Ad Hoc Regionalism* (2001) with Doug Porter. He is also author of the book *Wheel Estate: The Rise and Decline of Mobile Homes* (1997). Wallis holds a PhD in environmental psychology from the City University of New York, a master's in public administration from Harvard's Kennedy School of Government, and a bachelor's of architecture from the Cooper Union.

Index